The Actuality of Adorno

SUNY Series in Contemporary Continental Philosophy
Dennis J. Schmidt, Editor

The Actuality of Adorno

*Critical Essays on Adorno
and the Postmodern*

*Edited and with an Introduction
by Max Pensky*

State University of New York Press

Published by
State University of New York Press, Albany

© 1997 State University of New York

For information, address State University of New York
Press, State University Plaza, Albany, N.Y. 12246

Production by E. Moore
Marketing by Bernadette LaManna

Library of Congress Cataloging-in-Publication Data

The actuality of Adorno :   critical essays on Adorno and the postmodern
  /   edited and with an introduction by Max Pensky.
        p.   cm. — (SUNY series in contemporary continental
  philosophy)
      Includes bibliographical references and index.
      ISBN 0-7914-3331-5 (alk. paper). — ISBN 0-7914-3332-3 (pbk.
  alk. paper)
      1. Adorno, Theodor W., 1903–1969.   I. Pensky, Max, 1961–
  II. Series.
  B3199.A34A27   1997
  193—dc20   96-22721
                                                                    CIP

10   9   8   7   6   5   4   3   2   1

Contents

Acknowledgments

It should come as no surprise that a collection examining the work of this most difficult of authors should have encountered difficulties and challenges of its own during the long course of its conception and completion. These challenges could not have been met without help from many sources: the generous support of the Alexander von Humboldt-Stiftung, my graduate students in the Program in Philosophy, Interpretation and Culture at Binghamton University, and Colin Sample deserve particular mention. My chief thanks go to the contributors to this collection for their creativity, generosity and patience. Each of them, in his or her own way, exemplifies in work and person an ongoing cultural-philosophical dialogue between Germany and America, a process of mutual coming-to-understanding that constitutes the best legacy of Critical Theory, and the underlying theme of this book.

Chapter 3, "Adorno: The Discourse of Philosophy and the Problem of Language," is reprinted from *Prismatic Thought: Theodor W. Adorno*, by Peter Hohendahl, by permission of the University of Nebraska Press, © 1995 by the University of Nebraska Press. Chapter 4, "Mass Culture as Hieroglyphic Writing: Adorno, Derrida, Kracauer," appears by permission of the author. An earlier version appeared in *New German Critique* 56 (Spring–Summer 1992). Chapter 5, "Adorno, Modernity, and the Sublime," appears by permission of MIT Press, © 1995 by MIT Press.

Editor's Introduction:
Adorno's Actuality

Max Pensky

What is the actuality of the work of Theodor W. Adorno for contemporary Continental philosophy? Posed in this way, such a question is both suggestive and unsatisfactory. "Actuality" is a meager translation for the German "*Aktualität*." This is the sort of linguistic nonaffinity that any serious reader of Adorno in English has long since learned to deal with, or has at least become resigned to. Even in its original, however, the term *Aktualität* contains within it the sort of dialectical ambiguity that is the hallmark of Adorno's own careful deployment of philosophical terminology. "Actuality" can mean both "relevance for the present and its concerns" or "up-to-date," "still in fashion."

Thus the term actuality encompasses dramatically different alternatives: on the one hand, it expresses the quintessence of the modern ephemeral, in which an eternalized present defines itself against its past by a gesture to the arbitrary rules of production and consumption that determine what is popular and what is forgettable. Even in this sense, Adorno's work is "actual," at least within the confines of professional philosophy in Western Europe and North America, as evidenced by the secondary literature on Adorno, which continues to grow nearly thirty years after his death. Clearly, there is something about Adorno still very much in philosophical fashion.

On the other hand, however, actuality denotes a kind of practical affinity between an element of an intellectual legacy and a self-reflective contemporary situation; an affinity that resists or ignores what is intellectually fashionable and instead wants to capture an aspect of a culture's authentic expression of what it needs. The actuality of Adorno's work for contemporary Continental philosophy in *this* sense entails the claim that the current situation of Continental

philosophy, analyzed appropriately, points toward the *necessity* of reading
Adorno now, toward the *warranted* currency or the persistence, of Adorno's
thought—the need to refashion, out of Adorno's work, the elements of a
critical self-analysis of the contemporary state of philosophical discourse. In
this sense, the essays collected in this volume all address Adorno's work not
as a "legacy" to be selectively appropriated through the concerns of the
present, not as "appreciations,"—as if Adorno's currency has somehow grown
in value simply by its aging—but rather very much in the spirit in which
Adorno described his own critical appropriation of Hegel: the question is
what the present means in the face of Adorno.[1] And this critical face-to-face
between the present and an aspect of its philosophical past means not just a
question of the philosophical "legitimacy" of the present, but also—for Adorno
centrally—the question of the present legitimacy of philosophy.

It is this sense of actuality that Adorno had in mind in his inaugural
lecture of 1931, entitled simply "The Actuality of Philosophy." At the beginning of his professional career Adorno had perceived the situation of contemporary philosophy to coalesce around two equally unsatisfactory options. On
one side, the tradition of philosophical idealism had clearly failed to provide
a general and unified theory of the real, of subjectivity, or of time; its totalizing conception of rationality had betrayed not just its own unsuitability to
comprehend the mediated character of social reality, but its own ideological
bias as well. Already, "totality" appears in Adorno's thought as a critical
category, referring negatively to a futural possibility of just social and material conditions, and thereby opposing itself to the inherently dominative totalizing tendency of philosophical reason: "Only in traces and ruins," Adorno
claimed, "is [reason] prepared to hope that it will ever come across correct
and just reality."[2]

For Adorno in 1931, Heidegger ends the tradition of philosophical idealism by ruining the Husserlian project of a general account of the constitution of subjectivity in time—and also exhibits once again the fundamental
untenability of such large-scale projects. After idealism, then, philosophy
might also find itself bereft of a defining project, and hence ready to liquidate
itself, to collapse into the separate disciplines that it had once aspired to
organize and unify. The question of philosophy's actuality, then, was for the
young Adorno first and foremost the question of whether philosophy's self-
appointed task of providing a unified account of human reality—a "grand and
total philosophy"—now appeared untenable in the new landscape of postmetaphysical theory; and whether, in light of this, philosophy now found its
last task in its own self-liquidation:

> By "actuality" is understood not [philosophy's] vague "maturity" or
> immaturity on the basis of nonbinding conceptions regarding the gen-

eral intellectual situation, but much more: whether, after the failure of these last great efforts, there exists an adequacy between the philosophic questions and the possibility of their being answered at all; whether the authentic results of the recent history of these problems is the essential unanswerability of the cardinal philosophic questions. [. . .] Every philosophy which today does not depend on the security of current intellectual and social conditions, but instead upon truth, sees itself facing the problem of a liquidation of philosophy.[3]

In 1931, the "security of current intellectual and social conditions" would be short-lived indeed. Yet Adorno still saw the liquidation of philosophy to be in essence a *philosophical* question, and the tone here—the truth over current intellectual fashion—refers naturally to the other broad current in contemporary philosophy, the logical positivism of the Vienna School and the origins of post-metaphysical analytical philosophy, a current for which, in Adorno's view, the "liquidation" of traditional philosophy had become a self-defining task.

And yet logical positivism's goal to disburden philosophy of its traditional self-understanding and vocabulary—and thereby to dissolve its "grand and total" projects into the special projects of disparate scientific disciplines—ran into properly philosophical problems that formed the counterweight of those encountered by Heidegger's post-idealism. Neither of its two cardinal assumptions, the unproblematically "given" of empirical observation, and the static, ahistorical subject, were philosophically tenable in light of the fundamentally dynamic and historically and socially mediated character of subject-object relations. And the question of the Other, of the "alien ego," received an explanation according to analogy to the self-transparent ego that proved just as unsatisfactory as it had in late phenomenology. Thus properly philosophical problems frustrated logical positivism's efforts to liquidate philosophy from within.

Adorno's assertion at this point is crucial, for he will argue that philosophy's actuality rests in its status as a process of continuous interpretation, whereas the sciences subsist on research. But this is no mere appeal to a well-established debate concerning the epistemological underpinnings of the *Geisteswissenschaften*; the "interpretation" that Adorno has in mind here differs dramatically from traditional hermeneutics. The latter proceeds on the presumption of the meaningful character of the social and historical totality; philosophical interpretation in Adorno's new sense specifically breaks with just this assumption, which for Adorno must always have the immediate political effect of justifying a riven, contradictory and desperately unjust social reality by attributing an overarching meaningful structure to it.

On the contrary, interpretation,—the only justifiable task left to post-idealist philosophy—was for the early Adorno the task of the revelation of historical truth, and this was to be had by the philosophical construction of historical images from out of the material of an inherently unstable, contradictory, and self-fragmenting text of the social world. To the interpreting gaze the social world appears not just as text but as riddle, as visual puzzle or *Vexierbild*. The *recognition* of the puzzle-like character of a supposedly seamless social whole is the first dialectical talent required of philosophy. The *solution* to textual puzzles, however, must consist not in the evocation of some higher-level meta-social meaning beyond appearance, but rather the inherently practical interpretation whereby the puzzle-like character of the real flashes into images which point indirectly toward the dissolution of the puzzle-like character of the real. Interpretation is thus the construction of historical constellations out of the waste products of social reality, and the images that spring forth from it are nonarbitrary and historically precise images of redeemed social reality:

> Authentic philosophical interpretation does not meet up with a fixed meaning which already lies behind the question, but lights it up suddenly and momentarily, and consumes it at the same time. Just as riddle-solving is constituted, in that the singular and dispersed elements of the question are brought into various groupings long enough for them to close together in a figure out of which the solution springs forth, while the question disappears—so philosophy has to bring its elements, which it receives from the sciences, into changing constellations, or, to say it with less astrological and scientifically more current expression, into changing trial combinations, until they fall into a figure which can be read as an answer, while at the same time the question disappears.[4]

This deeply Benjaminian conception of the redemptive power of constellations (or "dialectical images," as Benjamin had it), would, as Susan Buck-Morss has demonstrated, endure throughout Adorno's theoretical development, although not without significant changes.[5] And it is true in some important sense that the "constellation," even if only a metaphor for a method, remains somehow Adorno's most influential and enduring intellectual legacy, one that captures metaphorically a number of different aspects of Adorno's thinking: the overarching sensibility that the collapse of idealism nevertheless leaves at least part of the underlying normative part of idealism's motivation intact; the insight that the drive to unify the world through concepts is in a tense and in the end irresolvable conflict with the desire to redeem the particular, the nonidentical. The form of interpretation through "constellative thinking" that Adorno sees as philosophy's only home for its actuality in 1931 expresses simultaneous and perhaps contradictory ambitions which go on to structure Adorno's philosophical trajectory. The ambition to make good on Benjamin's project of a philosophy that can still think the marginalized particular without violence—a true materialist philosophy—and the ambition to redeem the utopian, reconciliatory dimension of idealist texts subsist uneasily alongside one another. The project of redeeming dominated nature by concentrating attention on the material margins of rational discourses has to accommodate itself to Adorno's characteristic project of rescuing the nonidentical from the center of the concept. Moreover, Adorno was to the end Hegelian in his belief that such an enterprise—thinking the particular without simply submitting it sacrificially to the imperatives of universalization—was in the end a possibility that had rather rigorously logical and methodological parameters; it was in short still philosophy, and not poetry, that was especially charged with the production of truth.[6]

Of course, this range of ambitions places Adorno in a proximity with the later development of poststructuralist theory, and the question of the actuality of Adorno's philosophy—its relation to its own present possibility, or the possibility of a philosophical present in relation to it—is, more concretely, the question of the relation of Adorno's modernist philosophy to the philosophical spirit of the postmodern.

The constellation of "poststructuralist," "postmodern" or "postmetaphysical" philosophy has changed from the one Adorno analyzed sixty years ago. On the one side, analytic philosophy has developed its own institutionalized traditions, and has in large measure exhausted its original intentions through a philosophy of language. On the other side, the influence of Heidegger's destruction of onto-theology, of linguistic analysis, of the French recoveries of Nietzsche and Freud, all led out of existentialism and into philosophical poststructuralism, which in many ways replicates the sorts of interpretive strategies that Adorno had in mind in the essay on the "Actuality of Philosophy," and points beyond traditional philosophical discourse in similar ways as well.

Adorno and contemporary poststructuralist theory certainly bear some intuitively clear affinities: both are efforts to work out the philosophical import of the collapse of philosophical idealism. Both seek to interpret this collapse not in terms of a simple liquidation of philosophy but rather attempt to perform a self-liquidation of the contents and intents of idealist philosophy toward some radically new conception of philosophical practice. Both interpret a crisis of meaning and representation as an indisputable event, for the social reality of Western civilization no less than for the internal development of Western philosophy. Both respond to this crisis of meaning and representation by inaugurating radical projects of methodological and formal innovation. And both find their most characteristic voice in the critical dismantling or deconstruction of established texts of the tradition of Western modernity.

Rejecting the totalizing reason of traditional Continental philosophy, they both appeal to critiques of the dominative aspect of rationality as guides toward a radically new form of philosophical practice, one that will undermine the dominant paradigm of subject-centered philosophy of consciousness, of pristine sources of truth and representation, univocal metanarratives of historical progress or a transparent social world. In both, the liquidation of the philosophical heritage is still, however, a philosophical question.

More significant still, both Adorno's negative dialectic and deconstruction regard the interpretive task of philosophy to consist in the legibility of a fragmented social reality that appears as text. Both dedicate themselves to the gleaning of unintentional moments of interruption, resistance, deferral, or negation that are cryptically encoded within the material that dominant totalizing discourses marginalize or repress. In this sense both Adorno and poststructuralism still understand philosophy as containing the promise, however fragile, of preserving the possibility of thinking differently or thinking difference; Adorno's negative dialectics was in large measure intended as a conceptual practice dedicated to allowing the nonidentical to emerge free of the violence done to it through the application of concepts.[7] Both Adorno and deconstruction frequently draw themselves toward the "trash of history," as Benjamin once put it, in order to address a crisis of meaning and representation, but also as the response to an ethical intuition, according to which the repressed other—the nonidentical—can reappear within the ruins of a dominant discourse.[8] In this overarching sense, poststructuralist philosophy finds in Adorno an essential precursor in terms of its underlying and often murky ethical dimension—and a continuing irritant as well, since Adorno's frequent insistence on the corporeality of the other, on the heritage of physical suffering and deprivation that is the unavoidable horizon of virtually all of Adorno's ethical reflections, challenges the linguistification of human relations that is the hallmark of poststructuralism.[9]

The closest affinity between Adorno and poststructuralism can thus be described as their parallel efforts to recover an ethics of alterity by way of an imminent overcoming of the tradition of philosophical idealism. This affinity extends, in some cases, to the logical level.[10]

In this sense, Adorno and poststructuralist theory generally are united in the essentially ethical-political motivation behind their complex rejection of the model of Enlightenment rationality. For Jürgen Habermas, this point in common, in a rather unexpected way, also determines an aspect of Adorno's actuality—though perhaps in the sense of "fashion" more than "relevance for the present." For Habermas, Adorno's rejection of the tradition of Enlightenment is characterized by his inability to articulate a coherent foundation for the powerful ethical insights and intuitions that structure his work, and this failing also links Adorno with major trends in contemporary poststructuralist theory, in particular Foucault. Habermas's decision to include Horkheimer and Adorno in his analysis of the irrationalist dimension of postmodern theory in the *Philosophical Discourse of Modernity* was a landmark in the debate on the actuality of Adorno, and in more than one sense. Habermas's status as Adorno's heir and chief critic allowed him to focus on an aspect of Adorno's work that has always been strangely troubling: for Habermas there is something dreadfully wrong with the *Dialectic of Enlightenment*. Tracing the oppressive aspect of the achievements of conscious subjectivity all the way back to the early hominids could be persuasive only by virtue of a massively distorted and reductive view of the character and social deployment of reason.

By grouping Adorno's bleak prognoses together with the celebratory departure from traditional philosophical guarantees on truth and coherence typical of French postmodern theory, Habermas argued that both illustrate the *philosophically* unacceptable alternative of a *false* liquidation of the promise of rational modernity. For Habermas, the hypercomplex, claustrophobic, fretful atmosphere of Adorno's late work was the unavoidable consequence of a total rejection of the rational and normative grounds of criticism, and led to a form of performative self-contradiction just as pronounced as the exhilarating gestures of French theory. In both cases, for Habermas, a misguided appropriation of Nietzsche lies behind the doomed attempt to generate texts that criticize the irreducibly dominative character of reason while simultaneously eschewing all rational criteria according to which critique could reach any coherence concerning its own procedure.[11] In the *Theory of Communicative Action*, Habermas also rejects Adorno's scattered references, mostly in the *Aesthetic Theory*, to mimesis as a form of cognition resistant to the violence of conceptual thought, objecting that, on Adorno's terms, mimesis can appear only as a "placeholder" for a primordial, domination-free form of rationality, only as the abstract and vacuous other of reason, hence an impulse both demanding, and immune from, any theoretical elaboration.[12]

Habermas thus grants Adorno a strange actuality by saying that he and the postmoderns are performing the same unwarranted liquidation of the philosophical tradition; he thus highlights a point of commonality—irrationalism—that in fact will prove to be very contentious, for it is clear that the question of reason and the deconstruction of philosophy is just as easily a point on which Adorno and poststructuralism differ *the most sharply*.

Habermas, Adorno's chief philosophical heir in the Frankfurt School seemed eager to range Adorno along with Derrida, Foucault, and Bataille. Ten years earlier, however, Jean-Francois Lyotard had already made a sharply different point: in his essay "Adorno como diobolo," Lyotard had described the insurmountable gap separating Adorno from the Nietzschean enthusiasm of postmodern theory.[13] Dialectics, which Habermas had regarded as decaying into the impotent wishes for a vacuous other of reason, is for Lyotard still hopelessly imbricated in a master narrative of historical progress. In "Adorno como diobolo," Lyotard took Adorno to task for clinging to the logical structure of the dialectic beyond the point where social conditions and the self-liquidation of philosophy allowed the dialectic to be a plausible theoretical alternative. For Lyotard, Adorno is among the last representatives of a commitment to emphatic theorizing that a postmodern spirit would liquidate; Adorno is the quintessentially out-of-fashion, irrelevant modernist thinker, whose tragic mask subverts to its own self-parody. Turning to the *Philosophy of Modern Music*, Lyotard argued that Adorno was unable to keep separate the mournful modernist and the parodistic/pastiche voice of postmodernism; thus modernism a lá Adorno *generates* the sort of postmodern reinvestments that Lyotard wished to champion.

More recently, Fredric Jameson has argued at length that it is precisely Adorno's dialectic—what for Lyotard makes Adorno *permanently* nonactual—that constitutes Adorno's contemporary relevance for a postmodern age. Jameson's controversial attempt to redeem Adorno's negative dialectics as the truly Marxist theory of postmodernity as late capitalism is complex and cannot be summarized here. For Jameson, however, virtually all comparisons of Adorno and postmodern theory are at best misleading. Jameson insists instead on reading Adorno as a modernist, and seeing Adorno's modernism itself as the surest theoretical lens for picturing the postmodern situation.

There is, for Jameson, a sort of historical symmetry between the older Marxist objections to Adorno's abandonment of praxis—his "irrelevance"—and contemporary (Lyotardian) critiques of Adorno's marxism as out-of-date. If, for Jameson, Adorno is on the contrary "consistent with and appropriate for the current postmodern age,"[14] it is because of, and not despite, Adorno's status as a Marxist theoretician; one who is able to deploy startlingly orthodox Marxist concepts (totality, ideology, dialectical development, crisis) in order to grasp the essentially mendacious character of the "perpetual present" of postmodernity as the "cultural dominant" of late capitalism.

Much of Jameson's argument thus rests upon the insistence that Adorno's actuality consists in his *dissimilarity* from contemporary poststructuralism; it is his very out-of-date Marxism that allows him to rewin a relevance for the contemporary situation that currently fashionable Continental philosophy simply does not have. In this sense, Adorno's every anachronism becomes a component of his relevance: his failure to make the linguistic turn, for example, like his clinging to concepts of totality, experience, and historical truth, preserve an aspect of thinking, and constitute a range of negative conceptual possibilities, which imply a critical perspective entirely distinct from that of poststructuralism: "However tortured the Archimedean problems of the negative dialectics as such," Jameson writes, they are only analogous to and not at all identical with the even more elaborate Archimedean dilemmas of deconstruction; both need something outside the system in order to criticize it, but in Adorno's case this something would remain an idea, while in Derrida's thought it ought ideally to be a linguistic possibility: the similarity comes from the fact that in neither case can this urgent need be met, except by an elaborate formal subterfuge.[15]

For Jameson, then, it is precisely Adorno's unparalleled modernism that establishes his relevance for the present, his actuality. But this complicates the question of Adorno's timeliness, rather than resolving it, since it is above all the problematic of time and temporality, of diachrony and its disturbances, that constitutes the standpoint of modernism. Insofar as actuality is itself a concept that, both in Adorno's work, and for our own reception of it, essentially serves to *complicate* temporality, this incipient paradox—the sense that Adorno's antiquated modernism makes him up-to-date for the postmodern present—is worth considering more closely.

In one sense, Adorno's modernism consists for Jameson precisely of a characteristic sense of temporality, and throughout his analysis Jameson is drawn to Adorno's "attention to temporality as a mode of grasping history, the use of existential time protentions and retentions as an instrument for grasping the dynamics of an external collective history otherwise available only in the "facts" and "faites diverses." "[16] And indeed Adorno's work is structured throughout by a distinctive sensibility, inherited in part from Benjamin, in part from Hegel, for the unruly process in which objects, concepts, and persons, in capitalism, age. The "idea of natural history" that was so powerfully formative for Adorno's early work provides a consistent paradigm still evident in his last theoretical projects. Natural history evoked more than just the graphic spectacle of historical processes displayed as fields of dead, abandoned, and forgotten things. It also contained the strategic insight that, conceived as ruin, historical objects were not just dead but also liberated from a totalizing historical reason, and, as liberated, presented themselves to the attention of the critic as material for the construction of constellations. Resistance to the homogenizing imperatives of instrumental reason is to be sought in the temporal slippings, gaps, discontinuities, and paradoxical returns and reanimations of the material, resisting the modern imperative for temporal continuity and historical progress, as much as in the preservation of a supposedly pristine faculty of mimesis. Earlier, I referred to Adorno's first theoretical program, the "Actuality of Philosophy," to show that interpretation, the activity in which philosophy's actuality in a postphilosophical world was to be found, consisted in the construction of constellations from the flotsam of a society that cannot help but designate things—objects, bodies, texts—as losers. Adorno did not always follow up on the promise to transform the impulses of idealism into a historiography of things: whatever we make of the familiar accusations of his *"Beruhrungsangst,"* it is true that, unlike Benjamin, he was always more comfortable as an observer before the stage of the concept than he was wading into the thicket of the historical material. (The most significant exception to this fear of touch seems to me to be Adorno's unsurpassed and uncanny ability to transpose the experience of musical hearing into figurative language.) But what Adorno did excel at was the recognition that the same temporality that hastened the demise of the object, the abstract time that capitalism formalized, accelerated, and commodified, also generated discontinuities. In this Adorno is related to, but distinct from, contemporary theory. From Foucault's genealogy and counter-memory to Derrida's "hauntology," virtually all poststructuralist theory bears, in one way or another, traces of the affirmative temporal vocabularies of Nietzsche ("not yet," "until now," "eternal return") or Heidegger (the invigorating recollection and rescue of what the tradition consigns to a fixed past). Adorno, on the other hand, discovers the seismic critical power contained in an entirely different, negative temporality: "too late," "already over," "almost gone," "never came," "still here."

In the 1930s, Adorno defined actuality as the question of whether philosophy ought to liquidate itself in the face of the more urgent task of materialist cultural criticism. In the 1960s, Adorno famously begins the *Negative Dialectics* with the idea that philosophy can still be practiced at all—is still, in this mournful sense, actual—only insofar as the historical window of opportunity for its "realization" was missed; that only insofar as it missed its appointment with historical reality can philosophy "live on."[17] This attitude is not, of course, a simple act of resignation. It is the willed residence in a form of temporal acuity in which every anachronism is also the site of a transgression. It mandates philosophy's actuality as the fading resonance of its own "practical" failure; having broken its promise with the world, philosophy is now in a state of permanent debt to its past which it can discharge only through continuous self-criticism. It is also, as Eva Geulen points out in this volume, a temporality which already in itself raises the question of the postmodern *within* the trajectory of Adorno's philosophy: "Since philosophy survived its own apocalypse," Geulen points out, "it has become untimely— it comes, from now on, always too late, it will always be a philosophy *post festum*, a post-modern philosophy, as it were. However, only because philosophy paradoxically survived the experience of outliving itself, is there yet a faint chance of one day arriving in time. The 'no longer,' so to speak, holds open the possiblity of the 'not yet'; the negative telos sustains the positive."

There is, however, another side to this sort of time-consciousness. Temporality for Adorno includes an objective component that encompasses a spectrum of strategic deployments (natural history, constellation) but also a subjective, personal component, which is less obvious and hence often mistaken as an eccentricity or an untheorizable affect. Discussing Adorno's characteristic sensitivity to temporality, Jameson refers, correctly, to the "coordination between a personal and idiosyncratic sense of missed occasions and unseasonable survivals and a now more than merely nonsynchronous historical paradigm, in which the 'stages' of social and productive development pile up, fall out, keep us waiting, or turn out to have happened already and to have been forgotten."[18]

This "personal and idiosyncratic" feeling for the losses and survivals of time in capitalism is Adorno's sadness. Throughout his work, Adorno constructs a functional affinity between a sensitivity to the unfolding of the fate of objects under capitalism, on the one hand, and, on the other, a deep sadness that serves as the counterpart of this fate, an affect that forms an inseparable part of the subject's critical vision. In this sense, what might have initially appeared as a caricature of Adorno's relation to the postmodern—Adorno's mask of tragedy, his "damaged life" or "a priori pain," as Sloterdijk calls it—now appears, in fact, to represent something crucial. For Adorno was not insensitive to Benjamin's earlier claim, from the *Origin of German Tragic Drama*, that subjective emotions ought not to be considered as arbitrary productions of individuals, but "respond like a motorial reaction to a concretely structured world." In the world of unreason that Adorno confronted, critique consisted in thoroughgoing negativity, extending from the negative deployment of concepts "straight down" to the construction of a negative persona. In this sense, the a priori pain that Sloterdijk finds so objectionable in Adorno is in fact inseparable from Adorno's critical legacy.

What poststructuralism celebrates as play, critical theory mourns as failure. The crisis of meaning and representation that opens into the exhilarating space of play and contingency for poststructuralism is, for Adorno, yet another sign that meaning is not a fixed quantum but decays in the measure that its effects are rationalized. The constellation, the centerpiece of Adorno's historiography, was to have been *nonarbitrary*; its point was the representation of historical truth from within the shattered material of used-up textualities, and not the spectacle of the free play of liberated textual elements. The constellation—the dialectic—is a construction out of losses, a lading list of all that it is too late to save; critical subjectivity is one generated from loss, and learning from it.

Disappointment seems to me to capture the distinctive Adornian comportment at the crossroads of subject and object, since it refers both to the time of the object (the appointment with the nonidentical is always missed, just as philosophy is still arriving too late), as well as the subjective disposition (to feel disappointed) whose vaguely childish wisdom contains something of the mature power that Adorno was able to bring to bear in his better critical work. This work is powered, throughout, by a disappointment so massive that it remains itself virtually undetectable according to all the familiar theoretical devices, by all the instruments that conceptual thought has hitherto contrived and, like some astronomical singularity, like some impossibly great mass, makes itself felt only by its invisible distortion of each and every formulation that circles ceaselessly around it, unable either to escape its gravity or illuminate it. This testifies to how powerfully, if covertly, Adorno's negative thinking is allied to the utterly "positive" wish for happiness; in this sense, Adorno's distorting effect is similar to that of Proust. If Proust mastered the peculiar productive power of disappointment for the work of memory in literature, then Adorno surely has to count as the most disappointed philosopher we have yet seen. And like Proust, Adorno's disappointment was able occasionally to irradiate his field of critical objects with a care that seems, from this perspective, startlingly different from that of poststructuralism. The project of thinking the singular nonviolently *is* the ethical kernel of what used to be metaphysics. The wreckage of metaphysics, however, does not open up the prospect for the celebration of the nonidentical, the singular, as pure alterity. Ending the *Negative Dialectics* with reflection on the possibility of a metaphysics after Auschwitz, Adorno concludes that,

> [a]ccording to its own concept, metaphysics cannot be a deductive context of judgments about things in being, and neither can it be conceived after the model of an absolute otherness terribly defying thought. It would be possible only as a legible constellation of things in being. From these it would get the material without which it would not be; it would not transfigure the existence of its elements, however, but would bring them into a configuration in which the elements unite to form a script. To that end, metaphysics must know how to wish.[19]

For all the forcefulness with which this last methodological plea reenacts the programmatic ambition of a project of philosophical interpretation from the essay on the "Actuality of Philosophy," what was claimed earlier as a concrete intellectual and political project, is now expressible only in the conditional, and is made contingent upon hope. Hope, in fact, is the subjective element alone that could render this script of dead and dying historical-cultural artifacts legible. It is the impulse that insists upon an advocacy for things because they are small, or thrown away, or tend to get lost; it is the closest one can approach to an axiom of the methodical "micrology," the historiographical account of tiny things that Adorno holds out as the only "place where metaphysics can find a haven from totality."[20] There is certainly an "ethics of alterity" in Adorno's work. It is an ethics that often seems to situate itself between Benjamin's ethical talent (a love of things, of the abandoned souvenir, the shopworn, the gimcrack, slightly sad, dingy, shabby stuff, all of which is now excused from representation and commodification, and can with patience be made to say terrifying and true things about modernity) and that of Derrida (with his ability to find the fissures and gaps in otherwise seamless texts that render the text stuttering and haunted by the voices of those who are silenced; whom the text silences even if it did not know it.) As I mentioned at the outset, Adorno did not consistently focus on either of these poles of matter or text. This makes his early project of the construction of the constellation in a sense unfulfillable; for *that*, he would have had to do what he did not, in the end, see himself capable of doing: liquidating philosophy in the name of the material world, in the name of a truly materialist historiography unleavened with conceptual labor, or conversely, liquidating philosophy into an originless and ungrounded work of textual analysis, music or literary criticism. Adorno's distinctive talent lay neither in the things nor the text, notwithstanding the brilliant work he did with both. His ethics derived from an even stranger crucible: from within the motion of conceptual thinking itself. It is entirely characteristic of Adorno, and very significant for his ethics of alterity, that, if such an ethics exists, it is to be "bodied forth" from the very *last* place that one would have looked for it: within the very maw of the work of the dominating concept. In this sense, Adorno's "disappointment" consists in the ability to read philosophical texts with an eye toward the gaps and inconsistencies within the totalizing work of the concept; gaps which indicate the negative spaces where the nonidentical, in whose service philosophy ought to have been from the beginning, can find a safe place for expression. This is the kind of self-criticism of postmetaphysical philosophy that remains actual after the last philosophical ambitions have been disappointed.

Hope becomes indistinguishable from disappointment in Adorno's late theory, and I would suggest that it is this very disappointment, complete with its distorting effects, that constitutes Adorno's actuality for contemporary philosophy. In this sense too, the present state of philosophy finds in Adorno a continuous contestation of its own legitimacy; Adorno's disappointment is more than a memory or a guilty conscience of how one philosophical path out of metaphysics ended in a critical cul de sac.[21] The "relevance" of Adorno's disappointment for the current ethical reappropriations of poststructuralist theory consists in the *inability* of poststructuralist theory to liquidate philosophical ethics in light of the massive disappointment emanating from Adorno's conceptual work; it consists in the debt that poststructuralist theory owes to the philosophical terminology—subject and object, reflection, identity, concept, totality, particular, reason—that it thought to have banished from the philosophical present.

———————

Adorno's work provides a strong corrective to the unreflective rejection of Enlightenment reason. Even at his darkest, Adorno remained convinced that the same reason that dominates as *Zweckrationalität*, as pure calculation, also remains permanently linked with any possibility for an emancipatory and utopian, a different reason. In the quest for a new, nondominating form of cognition, a total break with rationality in all its forms is not possible. Although Adorno remained convinced that a "theory" of the reconciliatory dimensions of reason could not be responsibly written in an irrational society, he also never abandoned the hope for a loosening of the appropriative motion of rationality, just as he never abandoned the basic conviction that, in its inability to acknowledge true human needs, capitalism is irrational. Reason remains the play of the concept, which encompasses both the aspect of domination and of reconciliation. Irrationalism, for this reason, is merely an abstract possibility for Adorno, whose position toward reason in all its guises remains far more complex than Habermas's despairing claims of irrationalism would suggest. A different reason, embodied, careful, or solicitous of an Other, could only be a reason that sustained itself against, yet still in relation to the unifying work of the concept, just as the negative dialectics of postidealist philosophy continues to uncover traces of a nonsacrificial or reconciled thinking only through its immersions in the core texts of philosophical idealism. In her contribution to this volume, Ute Guzzoni reflects on the possibilities for an "other" reason between the negative dialectics of Adorno and some of the basic themes of postmodern thought. Through readings of critiques of rationality in Adorno, Lyotard, and Sloterdijk, Guzzoni sketches out the possibility of an Adornian "Different Reason" which, beyond domination, acquires "the character of a kind of companionship with the happening of 'nature,' which owns its own coming into the world as itself a natural event."

There are the seeds of a new, naturalist and unantagonistic variety of rational thought in Adorno, even if they are always developed by gesturing toward the negative spaces that such a form of thought would have occupied in a fantasized, reasonable social order. So too Adorno's difficult and often frankly contradictory impulses toward an account of subjectivity do not point to a "disappearance," or an "overcoming" of the subject as much they do to the dismantling of a cumbersome and outdated metanarrative of the centered and autonomous ego. Adorno complains often enough that mass culture dismantles the possibilities for authentic selfhood far more effectively than philosophy ever could. Again, the absence of a grounded subject in Adorno's work responds negatively to the social facts: in a rationalized world, the only permissible discourse of authentic subjectivity indicates the possibilities for a self free of violence, or a subject beyond the subject-object dialectic—but only by depicting an integrity that appears only in the process of its own dismantling. Adorno's dialectical overcoming of subjectivity have less to do with the expulsion of a dominant discourse than with the critical exposure of the price that individuals must pay in a rationalized world. Philosophy stands in the debt of a vision of a nonsacrificial, porous, and fulfilled self;

one which philosophy consistently betrays in its attempts to dedicate concepts of "subjectivity" to it. What emerges in Adorno is not the erasure of subjectivity but rather the search for the moments of possible transgression within the concept itself.

As Rainer Naegele has put it, Adorno thus "does not cancel the subject; he reclaims it through a postulate of transgressions."[22] In his contribution to this anthology, Hauke Brunkhorst takes up this idea in the context of Adorno's aesthetics, demonstrating how deeply Adorno's aesthetic conception of modernism is imbricated with his notion of the transgressive possibilities of modernist art. Linking Adorno's accounts of the aesthetic and the critical experience, Brunkhorst argues that both—against theory—offer powerful transgressive possibilities for a rethinking of the concept of the subject.

The complaint is frequently made that Adorno fails to make the linguistic turn: in the Habermasian sense, this means that he remains stuck in the out-of-date paradigm of consciousness and fails to understand the dynamic sense in which *intersubjective communication* bears a rationality of its own. In the poststructuralist sense, this means that Adorno's unwavering fixation on the category of thought and the work of the concept makes him unable to recognize that, despite his impressively large body of writing on the subject of philosophical style and form, textuality bears a lability and creativity that is far more elusive and interesting than Adorno's paradigmatic commitments allowed him to see. In "The Discourse of Philosophy and the Problem of Language," Peter Hohendahl seeks to correct the simplifying view that Adorno neglects a philosophy of language in favor of a philosophy of the concept. On the contrary, Adorno set out to fashion a distinctive philosophical language for the peculiar historical position of a philosophy whose actuality and critical task consist in its very lateness: philosophical language must be language and anti-language at once. Like postmodern theory, Adorno saw a rethinking of the problem of language as a key element in the deconstruction of philosophical idealism. In total opposition to deconstruction, however, Adorno argues for the *historically* nonarbitrary aspect of the linguistic sign. For him, the word is the meeting point between language and material history. Combined with Adorno's diagnosis of the decay of philosophical language, this insight grounds his search for an alternative linguistic model: a "configurative" language that would move beyond the linguistic models of positivist explanation or Heideggerian disclosure of truth, and adequately reflect the convergence between aesthetic and philosophical linguistic modes.

One of the strongest supports to any argument that Adorno is out of date is the relative lack of success in appropriating Adorno's work for the growth of contemporary cultural studies; a failure normally ascribed to Adorno's condemnation of rationalized culture as a *totaler Verblendungszusammenhang* apparently devoid of redeeming features, and the resulting elitist insistence on an essential distinction between avant garde art and the manipulations of the culture industry. Postmodern theory, on the other hand, has been credited with a pivotal role in effacing just this distinction, and thereby opening up to critical thought an entire spectrum of cultural activities that had previously been dismissed. Miriam Hansen's essay, "Mass Culture as Hieroglyph: Adorno, Derrida, Kracauer," problematizes this distinction. By moving the focus to varying accounts of *writing*, Hansen brings out the dialectics of the hieroglyph that structure Adorno's sense of the legibility of cultural phenomena. The hieroglyphic character of mass culture, that mass culture is structured like a hieroglyphic text, can be taken in two radically different senses: as the masked return of the ur-old function of secret written signs, cultural hieroglyphs can be read as allegories of domination. Yet, as *legible*, these same hieroglyphs open themselves up to a *critical* as well as a duplicitous kind of reading. Contrasting Adorno's account of the legibility of mass culture with that of Derrida and Sigfried Kracauer, Hansen works toward an understanding of the mimetic aspect of hieroglyphic writing, and suggests that, notwithstanding its many limitations, Adorno's account of the cultural hieroglyph provides a powerful corrective to Derridean accounts of cultural texts.

Few aspects of Adorno's work resonate more powerfully in the "modernity versus postmodernity" debate than his aesthetic theory, and, accordingly, it has received more critical attention than any other aspect for those interested in Adorno's relation to the postmodern. It seems trivially true to say that there is no easy sense to map Adorno's aesthetic theory against any simplified binary modern versus postmodern; the theory is far too complex, far too fragmented in its articulation and its ambitions, to allow such a description. Adorno employs thoroughly postmodern means to develop a theory in defense of aesthetic modernism, a constellation of aesthetic positions already out of date by the time Adorno wrote his *Aesthetic Theory*. With all its problems, then, Adorno's late aesthetic theory emerges as the key site for working out the question of modernism and postmodernism.

The contributions by Albrecht Wellmer and Wilhelm Wurzer address the implications of Adorno's aesthetic theory for the question of modernity and postmodernity. Taking up Adorno's relation to the key elements of Kantian aesthetics, both essays call for a radical transformation of the reading of modernity in the *Aesthetic Theory*—and there the similarity ends.

For more than a decade, the third-generation Critical Theorist Albrecht Wellmer has worked to establish a space for theoretical *rapprochement* between Adorno and Habermas, the first and second generations of the Frankfurt School. In the essays collected in *The Persistence of Modernity*, Wellmer develops the argument that Adorno's theories of mimesis and of the critical-utopian dimensions preserved in avant garde art can be shown to share a common ground with the forms of intersubjective interaction developed in Habermas's *Theory of Communicative Action*.[23] To summarize a complex argument, Wellmer believes that the critical aspect of Adorno's aesthetic theory is deeply compromised by Adorno's fixation on the inherently metaphysical, even theological categories of reconciliation and negative utopia; that Adorno allows the ethical force of his notion of aesthetic mimesis to deplete itself in the vision of a relationship with a redeemed nature. With the crucial shift in perspectives from a production to a reception-based aesthetics, Wellmer argues, the irredeemably metaphysical dimensions of Adorno's account of the emancipatory dimension of avant garde artworks can be shown to supplement and expand, rather than undialectically contradict, Habermas's account of the dynamic and open processes of self-constitution and self-transgression that are essential features of communicatively structured intersubjective interaction.

In his contribution to this volume, Wellmer continues and radicalizes this project. He shows how even the most rigorously metaphysical categories of Adorno's aesthetics, such as the sublime, can be separated from Adorno's metaphysics of reconciliation and read through a discourse-theoretical paradigm. Beginning with a discussion of Adorno's complex appropriation of the Kantian idea of the aesthetic sublime, Wellmer demonstrates how Adorno's development of this concept decisively breaks with the Kantian noumenal, developing instead a "noumenality" based on the aesthetic movement between the unrepresentable Absolute and the abyssal as radical absence of meaning. Wellmer argues that this dialectic need not be articulated according to the Adornian model of alienated and redeemed nature; that is, according to the paradigm of reconciliation. The sublime, he argues, can be recovered from Adorno's late aesthetics as a powerful reconstruction of the aesthetic dimension of the overwhelming and liberating force of the world of linguistic meaning in the context of *inter*subjective life. As a part of his broader project to demonstrate "the persistence of modernity," Wellmer's intervention here demonstrates how a creative reappropriation of Adorno's late theory—a "stereoscopic" reading of Adorno against Adorno—can decisively overcome the metaphysical residues that make Adorno's work other than actual, and can point the way toward a critical social aesthetics that bears decisive advantages over any available poststructuralist aesthetic theories.

Wilhelm Wurzer's essay, "Kantian Snapshot of Adorno: Modernity Standing Still," will also take up the complex relations to Kant in the *Aesthetic Theory*, but with radically different aims. Rather than recovering the tools for the *persistence* of modernity in Adorno, or reading the *Aesthetic Theory* as yet another theoretical *resistance* to the displacements of traditional metaphysical concepts through postmodern thought, Wurzer instead finds the traces of a *desistance* of modernity in Adorno's aesthetics.

Agreeing with Wellmer on Adorno's crucial transformation of the Kantian relation between natural beauty and the aesthetic sublime, Wurzer will not follow Wellmer in the implications of this transformation. Desistance gestures toward the work of the *Aesthetic Theory* beyond the categories of traditional aesthetics; desistance which "marks a standing away from, a standing down of, a ceasing to proceed in the manner of, a letting go of, even, finally, a fictioning of a certain textual metaphysics of nature" thus constitutes the motion of Adorno's text. Introducing the concept of the inhuman, Wurzer illustrates how a "desistance of the inhuman" is the sublime moment of Adorno's account of the beautiful-in-nature; a desistance of subjectivity or a letting-go of subjectivity which points toward a postmodern appropriation of the *Aesthetic Theory* radically different from that of Wellmer.

An impossible subjectivity once again evokes the possibility of an Adornian ethics; the topic of the last two essays of this anthology. J. M. Bernstein's "Fragment, Fascination, Damaged Life: The Truth about Hedda Gabler" begins, like Wurzer, with an analysis of the play of fascination, reflective judgment, embodiment, and a post-Kantian conception of the aesthetic sublime, this time played out in the work of Maurice Blanchot. Bernstein argues that the opening onto exteriority, the sublime *within* the sphere of experience which violates the possibility of that same experience, is in Blanchot ultimately both the possibility of the ethical relation and also ineffable; the fascination of bodily suffering which can only mark the site of an impossible empathy. By contrast, Adorno's tangled efforts to delineate an openness to the nonidentical are inherently relational and empirical, materially engaged: the nonidentical indicates what is effaced and excluded in this world, not by some aporias at the heart of language.

Bernstein enacts this contrast through an extended reading of the fragment from the *Minima Moralia*, "The Truth about Hedda Gabler," Adorno's interpretation of Ibsen's character. In a subtle and powerful exegesis, Bernstein shows how an Adornian ethics—one that is politically committed, material, sensitive to the other *in* the other's concrete situation—emerges from, and subsists in, the fragmentary form. The fragment allows Bernstein to pose the question of the ethics of sublimity in Blanchot and Adorno at a higher level, or, better, at a lower one: against postmodern ethical orientations, Bernstein's reading of the "Hedda Gabler" fragment allows him to argue, against poststructuralism, that it is to this empirical world, with its victims, losses, and chances for transformation, and not to any aporias at the heart of language, that ethics must ultimately concern itself.

Closing the anthology, Eva Geulen's "Theodor Adorno on Tradition" undertakes to read another short text, Adorno's "On Tradition," as a way of describing how Adorno's ethical motivations inhabit the intellectual landscape of the modern/postmodern. After an illuminating discussion of the manner in which the postmodernity debate has played itself out in Germany, Geulen turns to Adorno's text, showing how the motion of the text itself demonstrates Adorno's dialectics of tradition. Focussing particular attention on Adorno's readings of the ethical import of the bodily gesture—the handkiss, the handshake, the farewell—Geulen moves to a discussion of the gesture of farewell, taking leave or *Abschied*, which at once crystallizes some distinctive aspect of Adorno's ethical sensibility, and allows us to see Adorno's position in the modernity/postmodernity question with a new clarity: "If the postmodern is the continuing 'Abschied' from the modern tradition," Geulen writes, "then its relation to that tradition cannot be one of overcoming or preserving, liquidating or reinterpreting. All of these depend upon a stable distinction between old and new, and that is the first thing that 'Abschied'—and tradition—take leave of."

NOTES

1. See Theodor W. Adorno, "Aspects of Hegel's Philosophy," in *Hegel: Three Studies* (Cambridge: MIT Press, 1993), 1.

2. Theodor W. Adorno, "The Actuality of Philosophy," *Telos* 31, Spring 1977, 120.

3. See n. 2 above, p. 124.

4. See n. 2 above, p. 127.

5. Susan Buck-Morss, *The Origin of Negative Dialectics. Theodor W. Adorno, Walter Benjamin, and the Frankfurt Institute.* (New York: The Free Press, 1977), 102–104.

6. For a detailed discussion of this question, see Peter Uwe Hohendahl's contribution to this volume.

7. See Rainer Naegele, "The Scene of the Other: Theodor W. Adorno's Negative Dialectic in the Context of Poststructuralism," in Jonathan Arac, editor, *Postmodernism and Politics. Theory and History of Literature*, vol. 28 (Manchester: Manchester University Press, 1986), 106.

8. Adorno expressed this intuition most clearly in *Minima Moralia*: "If Benjamin said that history had hitherto been written from the standpoint of the victor, and needed to be written from that of the vanquished, we might add that knowledge must indeed present the fatally rectilinear succession of victory and defeat, but should also address itself to those things which were not embraced by this dynamic, which fell by the wayside—what might be called the waste products and blind spots that have escaped the dialectic. . . . Theory must needs deal with cross-grained, opaque, unassimilated material, which as such admittedly has from the start an anachronistic

quality, but is not wholly obsolete since it has outwitted the historical dynamic." *Minima Moralia*, 151.

9. An excellent discussion of this opposition is J. M. Bernstein, "Whistling in the Dark: Affirmation and Despair in Postmodernism," in Francis Barker, Peter Hulme and Margaret Iverson, eds., *Postmodernism and the Re-reading of Modernity* (Manchester and New York: Manchester University Press, 1992).

10. Peter Dews, for example, has pointed to the analogous revelations of the logic of the "supplement" that structure both the *Dialectic of Enlightenment* and Derrida's early work; in both cases, a deconstruction of the narrative of subjective self-creation and self-maintenance, inspired by critical appropriations of Nietzsche and Freud, gestures toward the moment of domination and self-delusion indwelling in subjectivity itself. See Peter Dews, "Adorno, Post-Structuralism, and the Critique of Identity," in Andrew Benjamin, ed., *The Problems of Modernity. Adorno and Benjamin* (London: Routledge, 1989), 1.

11. See Habermas, "The Entwinement of Myth and Enlightenment: Horkheimer and Adorno," in *The Philosophical Discourse of Modernity* (Cambridge: MIT Press, 1985), especially 126–130.

12. See Habermas, *The Theory of Communicative Action, Volume I: Reason and the Rationalization of Society* (Boston: Beacon Press, 1981), 380–383.

13. Translated as "Adorno as the Devil," in *Telos* 19 (1974), 127–137.

14. Fredric Jameson, *Late Marxism: Adorno, or, The Persistence of the Dialectic* (London: Verso, 1990), 229.

15. See n. 14 above, 235.

16. See n. 14 above, 243.

17. T. W. Adorno, *Negative Dialectics* (New York: Continuum, 1973), 3.

18. See n. 14 above, 243.

19. See n. 17 above, 399–408.

20. See n. 17 above, 407.

21. Jameson refers to this sense of Adorno, half-ironically, when he writes that "[t]his, then, is indeed some first service that [Adorno's writings] might do for us: to restore the sense of something grim and impending within the polluted sunshine of the shopping mall—some older classical European-style sense of doom and crisis, which even the Common Market countries have cast off in their own chrysalid transmogrification, but which the USA can now use better than they can, being an older and a now ramshackle society by contrast . . ." Jameson, 248.

22. Rainer Naegele, "The Scene of the Other: Theodor W. Adorno's Negative Dialectic in the Context of Poststructuralism," in Jonathan Arac, ed., *Postmodernism*

and Politics. Theory and History of Literature vol 28 (Manchester and New York: Manchester University Press, 1986), 102.

23. See Albrecht Wellmer, *The Persistence of Modernity. Essays on Aesthetics, Ethics, and Postmodernity* (Cambridge: MIT Press, 1991).

Chapter 1

Reason—A Different Reason—Something Different Than Reason? Wondering about the Concept of a Different Reason in Adorno, Lyotard, and Sloterdijk

Ute Guzzoni

To think within a domain that opens after modernity means, not least, to think against a reason that for two thousand years has understood itself as dominating and unifying its objects. The following is a consideration of the meaning and significance of the contemporary critique of reason and, in consequence, the concept of a different or an alternative reason. I am interested neither in the systematic and historical aspects of the critique of reason in traditional philosophy nor in an exact and complete reading of the respective texts of Adorno and some postmodern thinkers. Rather, I want to discuss a specific aspect, namely the relationship of an alternative reason to the concept of rationality, with reference to the connection between human beings and nature. This latter specification means that I want to lay aside the relationship of humans to humans and their moving and behaving within a human and linguistic world; I do so not because I believe these to be unimportant and negligible, but because in these days an adequate reflection on our naturalness and on nature itself seems to be nearly nonexistent.

I thus want to have a sort of dialogue with various positions of Adorno, Lyotard, and Sloterdijk, concerning reason and the critique of reason. In the first two of them, at least, we find very different and occasionally even contradictory thoughts about the problematic that concerns me; accordingly, I will be somewhat selective in the moments of the arguments of each that I will focus upon. It is not my first intention to do justice to the manifolds and the variability of their thoughts. Rather, I want to bring forth the very question about the properties and possibilities of an other, a different reason.

I.

In general, one can distinguish between two different kinds of critique, according to the attitude each has toward its object. Critique is concerned with either the criticized matter as such, or with only some distinct feature of it, with one of its ways of appearing. When we undertake a critique of a certain matter, we either want it to exist in another way, or not to exist at all. Capitalism, for example, may be criticized because it is thought of as a form of economy and society that perverts human community and therefore has to be overcome. But the critique of capitalism may also be understood as the attempt to bring it into a new and "more social" form or organization. In this case critique does not attack the criticized matter as such; it does not aim at its devastation or overcoming. It merely points at its actual historical form or to the fact that its significance is overestimated. As with Kant, critique in this sense means putting a limit to something.

The contemporary critique of reason seems to belong to this second kind of criticism. It does not question the very existence of reason, nor does it wonder about the fact that reason has become the most important means in the interaction of humans with reality and the key to their effort toward self-definition. Instead, reason is criticized because of the way it exists and is employed today. Philosophy's primary concern, even today, is still reason, knowledge, rationality. (Even where the main interest seems to have passed to language and to "the philosophy of language's decentration of the subject,"[1] language still remains something wholly rational and therefore, in Wellmer's words—although against his intentions—"*within* discursive rationality.") The nearly exclusive concentration on the problematic of reason and rationality has prevailed at least since the beginning of modern times, with Descartes, with Leibniz, with Kant, and Hegel. Reason has determined the era of enlightenment that changed into the era of modernity in the strict sense of the term. It is true that there were countertrends—in the last two centuries the early Marx, for example, or in part Nietzsche and Heidegger. Adorno's critique of the priority of the subject, however, is still to a vast extent animated by his persistent interest in rationality, although understood in a new way.

Nevertheless we may, with a certain degree of simplification, say that it is the specifically modern concept of reason and rationality that has challenged the postmodern thinkers, as it had earlier challenged Wittgenstein, Heidegger, and Adorno, to attempt a more or less fundamental revision of the concepts of thought and reason in traditional philosophy.[2] The "outlines . . . of a post-rationalistic concept of reason" and the "experience . . . of the death of reason" may well go together (ibid., 48). In his essay on the postmodern condition of knowledge, Lyotard, who has studied Adorno intensively, has written the leading text of the philosophical branch of postmodern thought;

Welsch tries to show a transversal reason as the internal aim of this line of thought; Vattimo speaks of a "weak thinking," his thoughts developing, as is well known, from Heidegger; Sloterdijk, who earlier wrote a "Critique of Cynical Reason," wants to move towards a form of thinking that in a certain sense combines Heideggerian *Gelassenheit* with Adorno's Critical Theory. The postmodern thinkers try to escape the dominance of modernity with the aid of the concept of a different, alternative reason.

However, what we are to understand by this critique of the modern concept of reason, and consequently the term "alternative reason," differs widely from case to case. We might distinguish three main directions:

In the first, the starting point for critique is reason's tendency to overpower the object; that is, its drive to force that toward which reason is directed into a position of generalized objectivity, so that the latter can appear only in the form of the concept, cut off from its individuality and particularity, its own nature. The form of rationality that Heidegger analyzed as "representational," and Adorno as "identifying," and which one can generally describe as dominating thought, proceeds according to the presupposition of an absolute priority of the subject over the object. Here, then, what has grown suspect in critical philosophy is modern reason's objectifying, classifying, quantifying grip of its objects. Against this, an alternative reason would be one that would think from out of that space of communication with the Other, whose otherness is accepted in communication itself. An alternative reason would let its objects be, letting them come to speak by themselves.

In a second direction, critique emphasizes that reason in Western thought has from its beginnings always been regarded as comprehensive and uniform. In contemporary postmodern thought, this critical point has moved to the foreground. Wellmer very clearly refers to a "cancellation [*Aufhebung*] of a unitary reason in an interplay of pluralistic rationalities" (ibid., 109, 164). This statement evidently lays bare a critical intention different than the one that led Adorno to refer to the "spell" of identity, since with Adorno it is the empirical individual, with all its qualities and particularities, who is submitted to the oppression of identification, whether it be a rabbit that, "mistaken as a mere example," undergoes the passion of the laboratory,[3] or the self-aware individual compelled into the "mimicry of the amorphous" (ibid., 75).

Postmodern thought, in contrast, concentrates less on the suffering that injustice inflicts upon the individual than on the fact that modernity has led to the development of differentiated forms of discourse, implying different forms of rationality. "It has become conceivable," as Welsch says in reference to Derrida, "that truth lies in multiplicity—which is discredited as 'confusion' only from the perspective of the drive toward unification."[4] The counterconcept to unity or identity is no longer to be thought of as nonidentity, but rather as multiplicity [*Vielheit*]. Accordingly, an other reason would now be

one that is in itself multivalent, or, to use the French term, *différend*; whereas Adorno moves toward a state that is characterized above all by the absence of domination, where different objects share in each other, that is, towards a "state of reconciliation."[5]

Finally the third form of the critique of reason: this also criticizes the unifying and dominating tendencies of Western rationality but above all stresses the fact that such a rationality sets itself in opposition to sensuousness and sensuality, and against nature in general. In this sense, the *Dialectic of Enlightenment* tells us that "the separation of these two realms leaves both of them damaged" (ibid., 42). Rather than blindly persisting in that separation, an alternative reason would tend—in Derrida's words—toward "a structure in which the traditional opposition of mind and matter no longer has a place" ("*une structure absolument autre de l'opposition traditionelle esprit matière*").[6]

None of these three critical directions goes so far as to negate rationality as such. Thus the accusation of "irrationality" is one of the "defamations" against which contemporary thinkers usually defend themselves most forcefully. The confirmation of the rational and enlightened character of one's own thinking seems still to be a self-evident and undeniable presupposition in today's thinking, even as reason is thought to transform itself into a kind of reason that has to change, or that is changed.

But why does thinking cling so stubbornly and with such certainty to rationality—in spite of, even *within* the critique of reason itself? I want at least to cast some doubt on the self-evidence of this persistent grasping of the predominantly rational character of the human comportment toward nature and reality. I think that the attempt to conceive of a reason that would be truly alternative must fail as long as critique does not dare to undertake a radical question of rationality as such. And I doubt whether the emphasis on multiplicity, that is, the negation of the unitary character of reason, is sufficient to get to a radically different reason, and to successfully think it through.

In saying this, I deliberately make use of a fundamental difference that exists between "reason" (*Vernunft*) and "rationality," (*Rationalität*), a difference that until now I have almost completely neglected. The equation of these two terms is common in the relevant literature. But it is acceptable only insofar as we are dealing with a rather general critique. As soon as we address ourselves to reason in a stricter and more thematic way, however, we must differentiate between them.

II.

A precise and historically differentiating demarcation between rationality and reason cannot be drawn in this context, especially since both of these

terms are here used as mere representatives for a broader spectrum of concepts, which could also include such terms as mind, intellect, sense, consciousness, subject and subjectivity, the "I," reflection, and so forth. I will confine myself to some basic features that seem to be relevant for our question.

The demarcation may proceed from the Greek differentiation between *nous* and *dianoia. Nous* and *noein* are names for the simple perceiving of something in its essence. Already in Parmenides, and later in Plato and Aristotle, the element of pure perceiving and touching was connected with an active catching-sight of something and with an active perceiving (and re-membering), at least in the sense of an explicit letting-be. *Noein* certainly is no production of essence, but it is a sort of letting-arrive in the open realm of *Noein* itself: only the seeing and insightful eye is able to perceive the visible.

Dianoia develops in Plato's thinking and in the disputes of the Sophists, and becomes the vital organ of Aristotle's Organon. It is what later on was contrasted to reason as rationality and intellect, as the faculty of concepts, judgments and conclusions, of differentiation and negation. As reason is marked by simplicity, unity, and immediacy, so rationality is characterized by order and analysis, as well as by connection and relation. Like Hegel two thousand years later, Aristotle showed an ambivalent attitude towards this distinction: he surely valued reason as the most supreme and blissful human comportment, but he nonetheless actualized his own scientific interests in an elaborate dianoetic and rational activity. The *ti en einai*, for example, the pure essence of a thing, is to be touched in and by the nous, whereas it is dianoia that recognizes the definition, the scientific knowledge of that essence by genus and specific differences.

It is not reason but rationality that opposes sensory perception. Adorno and Horkheimer evoke the "autocratic intellect that separates itself from sensory experience in order to overcome it" and the "intellectual function by means of which the domination over the senses takes place" (*DoE*, 44). The models for the relation between sensory perception and rationality are the relations between servant and master and those between material and form. In Kant's transcendental system, the hierarchical character of the relation between sensuality and rationality is essential for the constitution of the object of experience. More exactly, these two faculties differ from one another as receptivity and spontaneity, and thus as passivity and activity.

To summarize and clarify the distinction between reason and rationality, we may emphasize the following features: reason essentially perceives the unitary and the united, while rationality articulates and analyzes its objects into their constituent parts and elements. Truth for reason, aiming at the individual, is unconcealedness; for rationality it is the truth of judgment. Reason perceives what is original and originating; rationality deduces from

principles through arguments—"rational" is synonymous with "justified" and "well-founded." Reason, analogously to sensuality, is determined and impressed by its object and thus lets it be and happen as it likes to be and happen; reason is passive and receptive. On the contrary, rationality defines and determines, processes and masters its object; it controls and dominates, rules and orders sensuality.

The contemporary critique of reason and the search for a different reason in many cases hold on to these distinctions without making them explicit. The critique of reason often deliberately criticizes not rationality but reason. Starting from the premise that the concept of an all-embracing, absolute unity is no longer plausible for our present state of consciousness, one arrives very quickly—indeed perhaps far too quickly—to the conclusion that we must "cancel a unitary reason in an interplay of pluralistic rationalities." Thus rationality itself not only remains uncriticized, but it shows up as the very result, even the intrinsic aim of all critiques of reason. To put it succinctly, more formally and even polemically: I think that the "novelty" of the postmodern conception of reason consists primarily in the fact that, in it, reason is now *explicitly* understood as—or better, changed into—ratio and rationality. Cancelling the one unitary reason also abolishes any reason that would insist on its difference from rationality. And in this process rationality is in essence understood very traditionally, rather than as something new or alternative. At the most, its sphere of activity and its significance is expanded even farther, and the rationalization of the world and of thought itself becomes totalized.

III.

I would like first to look at Lyotard, whose position in the problematic of reason seems to me an ambiguous one. At least in the past few years, Lyotard has been primarily interested in questioning the autonomous and autocratic subject and the rationality belonging to it. It is not mind but nature that tends toward language. As I said earlier, I will at a later point in my argumentation introduce some statements by Lyotard that in part contradict what I am dealing with now. I doubt that the decisive conclusions that Lyotard draws from the refusal of the dominating subject—passing over to the concept of permeating and overwhelming forces and powers, on the one hand, and testifying on behalf "of the nonrepresentable" on the other[7]—really imply an affirmation of the entwinement of humans in an already given rationality; in many places it is nearly impossible to make out whether his statements are meant as descriptive or as critical.

I question whether the alternative to the self-understanding of the subject, as it has been generated in the Western tradition and especially since the

beginning of modern times, has to lead to the conclusion that individual humans, and consequently individual things, are to be postponed in favor of super-individual beings such as language, law, history and tradition, or occurrence and event. Isn't the single and unique person (and not the subject), aren't we ourselves, in our being-in-the-world, the first and most relevant reality that is given to us and constitutes our point of departure?

And two further comments: if mind and rationality are no longer what is decisive, then is it still certain that we must cling to the contrast of mind and material (and nature)? Is it sufficient to think their relationship differently? Is it still possible, for instance, to look to Kant for leadership for the task of posing the mind-nature duality radically enough? And doesn't a philosophical approach that is no longer determined by subjectivity suggest a kind of philosophizing that relies more on the sensual experiences of our being-in-the-world than on the highly abstract and artificial domain and language of concepts? Lyotard's processes of thought and representation in *"Le Differend"* are without doubt highly rational.

I only want to make brief mention of these fundamental doubts concerning Lyotard's position; within the context of this essay I cannot treat them in more detail. I would also prefer that the view that I will suggest at the close of the essay speak for itself.

If we now turn to Lyotard's relation to rationality, we must say that, although he decisively opposes himself to a merely argumentative (and in this sense rationalistic) form of philosophical thought, he nevertheless seems to move in a purely rational world of concepts. An example is his concept of a fundamental difference between different forms of discourse. As early as *The Postmodern Condition*, he emphasized that one of the main features of language games is their rule-governed regularity. These rules are of course not conceived of aprioristically; on the contrary they are determined anew, case by case, by the language game-players, or, more exactly, by the very game as it occurs. Nevertheless, regularity signifies some sort of rationality or form. In addition, the competitive character of language games—an essential feature for Lyotard[8]—refers to rationality, at least insofar as it constitutes a commitment to some standard of comparability. For rationality is, as Sloterdijk defines it, "the principle that tells us to apprehend the things that encounter us from the vantage point of their relativity, measurability, and calculability."[9]

The differences that exist between differing connections of sentences or phrases are strengthened by the fact that each of these connections appears as a system of rules on its own. There is no balancing mediation between them, because this would require still another system of rules that could overrule them. This is why Lyotard, by contrast, works toward the activation of manifest differences; that is, he tries to show the inevitable differentiation and the legitimacy of each individual in itself. It is thus a matter of what

Hegel called the "activity of differentiation"; that is, what for Hegel is "the power and the work of the *understanding* [Rationality, *Verstand*], the most wondrous and the greatest, or better the absolute power."[10]

Further: the problem that Lyotard poses, and answers through the activation of difference, is a problem of legal action. In fact, the question of the legitimation or the justification of the particular sentence arises in part because there is no longer any unitary or higher authority of reason that could offer any help in questions of truth. Moreover, in moving into the realm of the juridical, Lyotard returns to an old topos that has accompanied the thought of reason from the very beginning of the history of metaphysics. For example, already in the poem of Parmenides and even earlier in the fragments of Anaximander, law and justice played a central role. And Plato's *logon didonai*, adopted from legal language and practice—to account for and to justify something—was decisive for the understanding of thought throughout the history of philosophy. Finally, since Kant the concept of "judgment" has become so familiar to us that we usually no longer remember its origin in the realm of law and jurisdiction.

Regularity, as well as the legal character of the rationality of the differend, go together with its claim to truth. Evidently this no longer consists in the claim to truth in judgments alone. Rather, the latter is joined by certain correspondences belonging to the differing complexes of sentences, and by their legitimation. Truth has become the legitimation of a speech-act or a move in a game; it guarantees the conformity to a rule. Moving beyond the truth of judgments, its "logical logic," rationality consists of showing that the components of a game fit into it in the right way.

In yet another major current of postmodern thinking—and not only of Lyotard—we can recognize the continuation of something that has always belonged to rationality, even if not in the same way as in traditional thought: generality in the sense of a fundamental superindividuality. Rational relations are structures in which the individuals find their place, perhaps a varying place. But precisely in this way they are necessarily transcended by rational structures which do not directly relate individuals to one another, but stand over them, or through them. The earlier Lyotard radicalized this overpowering aspect of rationality, which in our tradition has become a rationality of purposes and aims, by dissolving the connected things into rationality itself, into powers, deployments, "an economy without purposes or laws."[11] Moves in the playing of the game of "powers" are rational insofar as they are systems of rules and orders. Concerning these moves, Lyotard arrives at the recommendation that "instead of curing the subject, we should try to cure ourselves of it, by making it still more fluid, and diving into the anonymity, the orphanization, the innocence and the incidental plurality of 'the' desire with its little desiring machines" (ibid., 125).

"The incidental plurality of desire" does not oppose itself to rationality. On the contrary, I think that only the cool and rationalistic vision of an objective and neutral observer may come to such a terrible[12] and totally abstract view of human life as the one evident in the talk of "little desiring machines." If a desiring machine is reasoning at all, does it do so in an essentially different way than that of rationality, as it has always been represented in the tradition of Western science and technology? Will it not continue to be a sort of atomized rationality, capable of calculation and quantification but not, for example, of having the simple experiences of distance and proximity of humans and things? Can we really be satisfied with a concept of a different reason or a different thinking that in the end can only stress the rationality of reason? Does this critique in fact succeed in approaching a truly different reason? Or are there, on the contrary, still too many old presuppositions that are uncritically adopted in it?

IV.

To move toward an answer to these questions, let us return to the notion that the concept of an all-embracing, absolute unity is no longer plausible for our present consciousness. What were—or are—the causes of this loss of plausibility? I will confine myself to mentioning four of these, of differing relevance.

A first cause might be found in the fact that enlightenment itself, that is, the confidence in one's own reason, has weakened the faith in the existence of a unique and transcendent reason. A second and more important factor can be seen in the fact that the different realms and forms of life have differentiated themselves to such a degree that conceiving of them as embraced by a single horizon of meaning seems unrealistic wishful thinking.

A third element consists in the simple fact that the Western paradigm of a universal, founding Being, and of the identity of Being and thought, has exhausted itself after its Hegelian apotheosis. Finally, unitary reason has lost its plausibility through its own self-prolongation within the systems of the diverse rationalities mentioned above, such as the realms of science and technology, and modern social life. In this line of argument, the plurality of individual rationalities, far from meaning the opposite of reason, is perceived as the last consequence of a reason that understands itself—and misunderstands itself—as dominating, even constituting the real world.

If we consider this last line of argument—that of Heidegger as well as Adorno—we can evidently no longer accept those consequences of postmodern thought that I described earlier. According to these, it is not only a matter of the obsolescence of a unitary reason, leading to a differentiation of a cognitive,

a moral-political and an aesthetic rationality, so that the latter comes to be criticized along with the former. Rather, the accidental, undetermined, and essentially open plurality of language games, discursivities or forms of life is described as the given structure of reality itself, which as such is beyond good and evil. But isn't this only a description of the historical state or condition of today's science, technology, and social organization? Doesn't it simply reflect the consequences of a unitary reason that itself has been transformed into rationality—without criticizing it or looking for another comportment of reason towards reality or world, as in fact both Heidegger and Adorno try to do?

What about the critique of reason in Adorno? In Heidegger, the demand for a new and different kind of thinking seems simple and clear. Critique directs itself toward rationality and its calculative propositions, while the different form of thinking maintains and radicalizes certain traits of reason that in part have already been conceived by traditional philosophy. Different thinking listens to and opens itself to what it perceives and experiences, it is a "thinking with one's heart,"[13] an attentive and receptive, a calm thinking, one that has taken leave from the principle of sufficient reason, leaping out of the realm of principles and reasons.

But what about Adorno? His relationship to reason and rationality is far from simple. In clear and explicit contradiction to Heidegger, Adorno maintains the necessity of a thinking that he powerfully criticizes at the same moment: thinking is as such conceptual thinking, and concepts are as such identifying. Thus the concept can only be overcome through the concept itself; the spell of identification, which leaves the particular no chance for ownness and otherness, must be contradicted and avoided through its own means. This supposedly unavoidable dialectic of thought is perhaps most unequivocally—and contestably—expressed in the following moment of the essay on "Progress":[14] "The concept of progress is dialectical . . . in that its organon, reason, is unified: a level of reconciliation and a level of the domination of nature do not lie separated within it, but rather both share all its determinations. The one moment transforms itself into its other only insofar as it literally reflects itself, that reason applies reason to itself and, in its self-limitation, emancipates itself from the demon of identity."[15]

We can understand what is referred to here as the "level of the domination of nature" as what I have called, in this context, rationality. It is this characteristic of thought by which thought distances itself from things, and subsumes them under itself—in which, as we read in the *Dialectic of Enlightenment*, "the creating God and the ordering Mind" come to resemble one another (ibid., 12). The dialectic of enlightenment—understood now no longer merely as a book title but as an actual state of affairs—is based on the fact that human existence as such, together with the development of consciousness

and self-consciousness (or mind) would not have been thinkable without the domination of nature, so that this represents something like an anthropological necessity. "Humanity had to choose between their domination by nature— or that of nature by the self," (*DoE*, 32) since "Only presence of mind [*Geistesgegenwart*] wrests existence from nature" (ibid., 33).[16]

Horkheimer and Adorno remained convinced that mind never exists apart from the domination of nature, which in turn reverts back to captivity by nature. Precisely for this reason, they were also able to maintain that "if mind confesses itself as domination and withdraws back into nature, it is dissolved from the dominative claim that enslaves it to nature." This is the "mindfulness of nature in the subject" in whose enactment lies hidden the "unseen truth of all civilization" (DoE, 39). This mindfulness is not something "salvific" that bursts into the ruined present from beyond it; rather, it is in itself the other, "reasonable" side of reason, that is constituted by the fact that reason turns back to itself, reflects itself and thus takes a step out of the force of the imperative of domination. That such a stepping out, "emancipation," has domination over nature as its own presupposition, lies in the very logic of this conception of "mindfulness." This is not a merely historically given fact: were it not the case, a reason capable of reflecting itself would never have been able to emerge, would have remained in the mute captivity of nature.

I think that it will be immediately clear that here as well, the question of the possibility of a different reason, a fundamentally different behavior toward and interaction with nature has remained stranded within a rationalistic conception of reason; one which not only preserves the differentiating and discursively ordering access to things, but establishes it as law.

Nevertheless, Adorno also has a concept of an entirely different thinking, an experiential thinking that gives itself over to its objects and lets itself be determined by them, and this concept is nowhere clearer than when Adorno characterizes his own thinking. In the context of the following reflections, it is this thinking that I would like to address.

V.

How, then, can we think of a truly different reason; one that, on the one hand, no longer bears the stamp of the "old" rationality, but on the other hand no longer simply persists as the old reason, bound up, as it has always been, with an everlasting, foundational, and general Being? A reason capable of evading the modern tendency toward calculation and mastery would neither stand over its object, nor try to embody and manifest itself through it. It would instead move with its object, listening to it and remaining open to the

object's speaking and asking. The essential comportment of this perceiving and experiencing reason would no longer be the pathos of functional planning and purposeful activity, but the receptive attitude of a patient attention and an acceptance of the other's attitude and action.

In current philosophical discussions one can find traces of this different reason, which regards itself as passive rather than active. In his book *Eurotaoismus*, Peter Sloterdijk distinguishes between a postmodern passive and a modern active reason (for instance, on p. 43). And Lyotard evokes— initially in the context of the attitude required by the analysand in the course of psychoanalysis—the "*passibilité*," the "receptibility" of mind as well as its obligation to "be patient in a new sense of the word."[17] To be patient, to listen, to feel and to sense, to let the other speak—all of these attitudes are alien to rationality as such, although the latter may take them under control; it may even need them for experimental purposes.

In the essay just cited, Lyotard talks neither about reason nor thinking, but only about the relation of philosophy to modernity; a relation he describes as "*réécrire*," "rewriting." However, I think that the explanation that he gives for this rewriting has a significance that goes beyond this relationship. To rewrite modernity is an attitude that can be explained and advanced by means of what Freud called *Ausarbeitung*, "working through." In this comportment Lyotard particularly stresses a "free and floating attention" (ibid., 211). It is the letting-come and the opening-toward what approaches the mind from "a 'something' that it does not know" (ibid., 210). The mind does not choose what it accepts as its object, leaving itself without reservation to what "may come into mind and over its body." The mind no longer selects the approaching things and events with its prejudices and categories as nets and security systems of coordinates. In this sense, Kant's model of a sensuality providing the material on the one hand, and the pure forms of sensuality and rationality on the other, has been left behind.

But the concept of "material" leads to absurdity when Lyotard names the "thing" that concerns thinking as "what afflicts 'language,' tradition, material, with which, against which, and within which we write" (ibid., 213).[18] That to which thinking is attentive, what it listens to, what it opens itself to, is not mere material nor a mere element to be worked upon and formed; it has a voice of its own because it is itself that which "occurs." Adorno says that "the tasks, whose fruitfulness determines the fruitfulness of thinking itself, are themselves autonomous,"[19] that they are not set, but rather set themselves. A similar kind of autonomy is meant in the following passage from *The Differend*: "Reflection demands attention to the occurrence; it demands that you do not already know what is occurring. It leaves the question open: *does it occur?*[20]

Here the traditional activity of rational reason, which "already knows what is occurring," is left behind. "When an event is occurring then it is

always already anticipated by an interpretation that exactly blocks the possibility of its showing up."[21] We find a similar thought in the following remark: "It is not the "recognition" of the given (as Kant said) that is at stake, but the ability to let things arrive, as they present themselves. According to this attitude, each moment, each 'now' is something like a 'self-opening.'"[22] Not the representation of the subject but the self-representation of things is important and decisive, is "at stake." Of a game with given rules and regularities, not a trace.

When things are free to arrive or not to arrive, to arrive incidentally and on their own, then what happens to the regularity and the truth-claim of each language game? Are they not all called into question by this ability of letting-arrive? If reason truly, decisively adopts a character of passivity and receptivity, then the claims of legitimacy and truth must lose at least some of their former importance. In this context, I think, a frontier within the postmodern critique of reason emerges; one that weakens and calls into question critique itself unless and until it is identified for what it is, and crossed.

Crossing this frontier would mean moving away from rational reason and its rules, and toward an attentively listening interaction with the object. Lyotard, however, would probably point out that what he had in mind was more a "passability" than a "passivity" of rationality; that is, a permeability whereby rationality tries "to make itself permeable for the events that move against it from a 'something' that it does not know."[23] This emphasis on the powers and forces that pass through the subject stands in stark opposition to a receptivity that—as shows up in Adorno—involves itself in its object by means of an active passivity or an "enlarging concentration" which must "nestle against its object."[24]

It is difficult to see the clear differences between one passivity and the other (in this specific context we might even say, between Lyotard and Adorno). But I think it is a "difference in the whole." Lyotard's receptivity does not lead to a communication between different things as different, because he leaves no place open for *both sides* of such a communication; accordingly, things tend to dissolve into the effects or impressions of powers, forces, and moves in a game, so that human perceiving and speaking become a mere field which they traverse.

This last conception undoubtedly constitutes a radical threat of insecurity for the modern subject and its will to efficiency and expansion, for its activistic drive toward mobilization. Nevertheless, I think that this conception is still not radical enough. The sense of passivity developed in it is not radical enough for decisively putting into question the deployment of rational reason—quite apart from my insistence that a concern for the individual and the particular must be maintained; an insistence which I share with Adorno. Can Sloterdijk's "postmodern passive," which he contrasts with the "modern active" take us further?

VI.

The modern active: the meaning of this formulation is clear. Active means dynamic, efficient, mobile, progressive, rational. The list expresses the active will of the efficient subject, forming and changing the world according to its own ideas, energetically and decisively solving problems as they emerge. We can easily imagine this subject—whose characterization could have been taken from the help-wanted section of the newspaper—as a successful manager, an industrialist, an engineer, or star athlete. Yet such a positive image is also no doubt a ridiculous cliché, somehow ideological. "The horrible" that according to Horkheimer and Adorno "humanity had to inflict on itself, until the self, the identical, purposive and male character of man had been created," (*DoE*, 40) glimmers through this modern active the moment we look at it closely.

And the postmodern passive? Sloterdijk's understanding of what he terms the postmodern passive has a critical, therapeutic component. The active, against which the passive comports itself passively, is modernity itself; its will toward overcoming and triumphing, its urge toward continuous acceleration. Sloterdijk therefore describes an attitude that on the one hand has renounced the production of an identity in which subjects appropriate and assimilate the otherness of the other through conceptuality—by the "undistanced self-release from the process of acceleration"[25]—and on the other hand has begun to conceive of itself self-critically as a "thinking avalanche" and a "self-reflexive natural disaster," (ibid., 26); an attitude that is prepared to suffer the resulting situation in a "passionate consciousness of human finitude" (ibid., 28) virtually as a form of *Trauerarbeit*.

Passivity is thus understood initially in a purely literal sense as suffering—a suffering from sheer human ability that leads Sloterdijk to ask if "the ego, capable of destroying nature, is not also something that happens to 'itself' as if an anonymous fatality? And doesn't the potency of Acting and Doing of modernity in turn also stand in relation to itself as a suffering and a helplessness?" (ibid., 120). But it is also, at the same time, a self-aware act of bearing and tolerating; one that, in its suffering distanciation from what makes suffering, directs itself against it, thus becoming itself critical.

If it is to avoid regressing into a state of "blind mobilization" itself, (ibid., 110), the critique of the activist subject and its "active care for the correct" (ibid., 110) obviously cannot be carried out in the form of an activity in the immediate sense or in the form of "praxis." This is why critique's "bizarre" and "absurd" results appear initially as a kind of "hesitation," as a "withdrawing into a more exact perception," a "finishing with business as usual" in favor of an "imperceptible liberation for right motion" (ibid., 73, 76).

What Adorno called the enlarging concentration and the "patience for its matter," the "long and unforced gaze upon the object,"[26] is in fact related to what Sloterdijk, carrying on a form of ancient Asian thought, grasps as "the ascendance to silence in force" (ibid., 94), and particularly as *Gelassenheit*, the radical "alternative to mobilization" (ibid., 144). This passivity is a letting-be and letting-happen, more exactly a letting-come-forth, a giving-birth and a "transgression from a mode of being prepared to do anything to one that is calm and collected, that is *gelassen*" (ibid., 203).

These formulations show that this letting-happen in passivity is—in a way analogous to Adorno—active at the same time. Human thinking and behavior are not merely acting for action's sake, just as they are not a mere passing stage for powers, events, and moves in a game. On the contrary, they themselves form the sphere or the field within which an event can develop and decide itself. Adorno says that "thoughts that are true must constantly renew themselves in the experience of the matter itself; which nevertheless only determines itself within them . . . Truth is emergent constellation."[27] Such a self-determination of experience within thought surely requires the activity of judgment, of analysis, and synthesis, in short, the discursivity of thought, which engages itself actively and spontaneously with whatever it encounters. But when this discursivity no longer constitutes the crucial feature of self-experiencing thought, the clean split between active and passive, between spontaneity and receptivity, begins to decay. Rationality then belongs to a "different" reason; it has ceased dominating it.

A concentrated acceptance of that which approaches; an encounter with what is received that brings one's own experiences into play—only *together* do these two dimensions constitute a real communication with the other *as* other and stranger. Concerning the relationship of humanity to itself, one could say that the affirmation of one's own natality, one's own status as having been born, also means the passive appropriation of one's own life as an active comportment. If we leave out all the theologizing overtones here, this taking or giving of one's self back into the whole field of the natural can be described, as Adorno described it, as the "reconciled" relation between humanity and nature. It is a relation in which reconciliation doesn't close off the possibility of difference, dissent, and communication that is a form of being-with-others.

VII.

When we now speak of a different reason, it is thus no longer a reason situated in opposition to natural and sensual things. It no longer appears as something strange or sublime, nor is it the all-penetrating roar of power. It now has the character of a kind of companionship with the happening of

"nature," which owns its own coming into the world as itself a natural event. Sloterdijk asks, "Might we think of an alternative to the scheme of the incarnation of logos? . . . In post-metaphysical culture, a consciousness is gradually emerging that it is not the case that the word must become flesh, . . . but rather that it's enough to make a place for the spontaneous tendencies of flesh to become word . . . The illumination of the inspired contexts of life belongs properly to the dynamic of life processes itself. This [. . .] must be taken in an ever more literal sense."[28]

Nothing remains here of a nature thought as mere material for the process of conceptual formation, of the "elements delivered through sensibility." Nature is neither the material nor the medium for the self-realization of the mental and of reason, but is rather something that stands within, or gives itself into the said and the understood, insofar as reason itself "comes to word" or "flashes" in the context of life. Reason rejects the dominating and disciplinary dimensions of discursive rationality (*diskursiven Vernunft*); by virtue of its "origin from nature"—as the *Dialectic of Enlightenment* puts it, insofar as it "withdraws back into nature" (ibid., 46)—reason is the perception, conception, reception of that which gives itself to reason. That the object gives *itself* implies that it has something to say—itself—and that it itself makes demands on perception and conception.

These remarks may well sound "romantic" or "mystic"—as we often say when we encounter something that deviates from the normal paths of identity. However, what is meant here can be clarified without imbuing nature or the world with a mystical voice, as if it were to be taken as another form of subjectivity. What is required is nothing more than to oppose oneself decisively to traditional philosophy's understanding of the relation between thought and its object. In this philosophical history, thinking has understood itself increasingly as the Other of Being, of nature. Developing a consciousness of itself as *Geist*, it placed itself in opposition to nature. Still Horkheimer and Adorno remark, presumably without any critical undertone, that "[i]n thinking, human beings distance themselves from nature, in order for them to set it up in front of them as an object of possible domination. Like the thing, the material implement . . . that fits into the place of all things where one can grasp them. In consequence thinking becomes illusionary wherever it denies its function of separating, distancing, and objectifying" (ibid., 46).

But it was exactly this rationalistic distancing that increasingly forced thinking to make the other into its own, to submit it to its own laws and categories, to identify it as something that can be grasped in its rational structure, through justification and legitimation. The forms that this appropriation have taken and continue to take are divergent, whether we think of cognition, science and technology, or production. The common character of these and other modes of comportment toward the "outer world"—and

towards inner nature as well—is that the other is meant to cease to be fundamentally other and different, strange and astonishing. Stood before the theorizing and acting subject, it becomes caught, integrated, adapted. The discursive concept has its object ready, laid-out.

To move in the opposite direction from this traditional attitude means to deny—against Horkheimer and Adorno—the inescapability and ahistoricality of a merely distancing and objectifying function of thinking, or, put simply, to let the Other be Other in the interaction with it. Sloterdijk says, "After the historical production [*Inszenierung*]of the Own and the Proper, the discovery of the forgotten real Other is once again possible, and it is now time for this discovery" (ibid., 306). In this context, "other" means other than reason; that is, coming from another place, from itself, anarchic and in constant change, brightly colored and multiple, in self-transforming constellations, situations, atmospheres. Traditional reason, having unfolded into rationality, is driven by the fundamental otherness of the world into the will toward appropriation of objectivities; conversely, the acknowledgment of the astonishing otherness bears witness to a new experience of human belonging to their world and their things.

As I have already implied, this belonging is held together (not uniquely, but in particular) by human sensibility and sensuousness. Sensibility and sensuousness seem, on the one hand, to be the means by which the other and the natural reaches and enters us. They deliver the message of the other to us; its appearance and taste, its sounds, the way it smells and feels. It enters us by coloring our moods and feelings, our sensual and physical being-in-the-world. On the other hand, however, sensibility is also the way that we reach and enter the world. This is why the historically fundamental, fatal process of appropriation is only capable of being carried out with the aid of the senses, or, more generally, of human physical being.

This is also why the attempt to attain a new relationship to our own sensual nature might be an occasion to relate ourselves differently to the sensual world, which essentially means to develop—or better, to let emerge—a different reason. The two sides of a reason open to sensuousness can be shown in the already discussed model or example of touching: is touching active or passive? Does touching move in one direction or the other, from what is touched to that which touches, or the reverse? Or do both directions touch upon each other in their touching—as happens when we make contact by looking at each other, where contact is distinguished by just this ambiguity?

A different reason worthy of the name stands, I think, somewhere between reason and the other of reason, nature or sensibility. More exactly, it can act as a connecting link that could release both "sides," rationality as well as sensibility and physicality, from the burden of their own self-reliance. A different reason would be something like the "organ" that bears our

exchanges with the world; yet at the same time it appears as a field on which, or in which, our perception in its broadest sense interacts with the world. A different reason preserves elements of the old reason, as well as elements of sensual-physical perception. Only in this way can it free itself of the heritage of a legitimating and verificational, dominating mode of rationalistic knowledge on the one hand,[29] and the abstract "purity" of reason on the other.

A different reason is something truly different. It is something different from rationalistically determined reason, which is (as Adorno says) purely discursive and dominates nature. It is at the same time a reason that is different in itself, because it listens to different things without trying to identify them. And it surely remains different from nature. But insofar as it is ready to renounce its former domination over nature, it might become a participant in and a part of nature as well. So—in a certain sense—a different reason might also become something different than reason.

ABBREVIATIONS

DoE: Max Horkheimer and Theodor W. Adorno, *Dialectic of Enlightenment*, translated by John Cumming (New York: Continuum, 1994).

NOTES

1. Albrecht Wellmer, *Zur Dialektik der Moderne und Postmoderne. Vernunftkritik nach Adorno*, in id., (Frankfurt: Suhrkamp, 1985), 97.

2. In this way the critique of reason is very often paired with a critique of language. I cannot present here a justification for not going more carefully into the philosophy of language in this presentation. The concept of a different reason, as I am attempting to develop it, also makes it necessaray to rethink language, as well as "being-in-language." An exhaustive treatment of the conception of language in Lyotard is not possible within the limited frame of the project that I am pursuing here.

3. Max Horkheimer and Theodor W. Adorno, *Dialektik der Aufklärung* (Frankfurt: Suhrkamp, 1969), 16.

4. Wolfgang Welsch, *Unsere postmoderne Moderne* (Weinheim: VCH, 1987), 114.

5. Theodor W. Adorno, "Zu Subjekt und Objekt," in *Stichworte* (Frankfurt: Suhrkamp, 1970), 153.

6. "Philosophie in der Diaspora. J. F. Lyotard im Gespräch mit Jacques Derrida, in *Jean-Francois Lyotard mit anderen. Immaterialität und Postmoderne* (Berlin, 1985), 23.

7. Jean-Francois Lyotard, "Beantwortung der Frage: Was ist postmodern?" in Wolfgang Welsch, ed., *Wege aus der Moderne. Schlüsseltexte der Postmoderne-Diskussion* (Weinheim, VCH 1988), 203. The nonrepresentable is that which by virtue of its sensuous and eventful qualities cannot be represented in an argumentative, rational language: it may in some sense break into such a language, becoming audible in it, if at all, solely through its absence. It is thus a matter of "discovering the allusive occurrences of something thinkable which nevertheless cannot be represented" (ibid.). On the other hand, Lyotard is convinced that "the yearning for . . . the rconciliation of concept and sensuality, for transparent and communicable experience " (ibid.) leads necessarily to terror. I regard this as an abstractive, *super*humanly thesis, and not one that is grounded in our factual and physical being-with-one-another in the world. Moreover, Lyotard's essentially skeptical-resignative comportment towards the present realigns Lyotard with Adorno, who for the most part consigns the experience of a genuine Other to a utopian future. I think that both Lyotard and Adorno—in different ways and to different degrees—have developed their respective "anxiety for the individual, for the particular, the deviant, the individual, which is threatened with extinction in a general communicative system" (Lyotard, "Wie vernunftig ist die Vernunft?" Interview in the newspaper *taz*, 4.11.87) without paying sufficient attention to this particular itself, and its own unique forms of behavior and representation.

8. But just as there is a reflective-sensuous kind of thinking, [*das besinnlich-sinnliche Denken*], there is also the submerged play of the particular with itself or with the Other; a play which is precisely not a matter of what is comparable, what is measurable, and so forth.

9. Peter Sloterdijk, *Eurotaoismus. Zur Kritik der politischen Kinetik* (Frankfurt: Suhrkamp, 1989), 243.

10. G. W. F. Hegel, *Phaenomenologies des Geistes* (Hamburg: Meiner, 1948), 29.

11. Jean-Francois Lyotard, "Energieteufel Kapitalismus," in *Intensitäten* (Berlin: 1978), 127.

12. The concept of the "desiring machine"—which is not Lyotard's responsibility—seems to me to really be one of the most gruesome and the most revealing formations in all of philosophical terminology.

13. Martin Heidegger, *Gelassenheit* (Pfullingen: Neske 1959), 27.

14. Theodor W. Adorno, "Fortschritt," in *Kulturkritik und Gesellschaft* (Frankfurt: Suhrkamp, 1977).

15. This passage, however, makes it particularly clear that reconciliatory reason is in no way an essentially messianic or ultimately theological reason for Adorno, as Wellmer maintains.

16. Even if this were the case, however, does the domination of nature necessarily lead to hierarchical social relationships and the autonomy of the apparatus of domination? Or would one be possible without the other? There is virtually no examination of other, precivilized socieites in the *Dialectic of Enlightenment*; pre-Western

of non-Western peoples, when seen at all, are seen only as "wild" or "primitive." But mustn't one ask how the domination of nature and the domination of the same over the other is for *them*? From the perspective of their experiences of the world, couldn't we think of a relationship of self-conscious human being to its natural and nonnatural environment; a relation that takes seriously the differences between the human and the nonhuman, and be able to realize such differences without conceiving of them in terms of domination?

17. See note 7 above, 210.

18. Thus his references to the "elements delivered from sensuality" seem to me to be at the very least prone to misinterpretation (211).

19. Theodor W. Adorno, "Anmerkungen zum philosophischen Denken," in *Stichworte*, 19.

20. See Jean-Francois Lyotard, *Le Differend* (Paris: Editions de minuit, 1983), 14.

21. Lyotard in the already cited conversation with Jacques Derrida, 23.

22. See n. 17 above, 212.

23. See n. 17 above, 210.

24. See n. 19 above, 14–15.

25. Sloterdijk, *Eurotaoismus* 70.

26. See n. 19 above, 14

27. Ibid., 16.

28. See n. 25 above, 234ff.

29. Naturally this does not mean a ban on rationality. As I said before, I want only to reject the dominating claim of rationality to be reason, and thus implicitly to integrate rationality into reason. In this context we should differentiate between what we may call the discursive part of a sensual reason and a rationality that is nothing but the appropriation and the processing of reality. In the latter's case, we need not integrate it but delimit it. At the end of the essay "Die Moderne redigieren," Lyotard asks "how might the working-through still evade the law of the concept, knowledge and predictability?" (214), and calls on us to oppose what is determined by them. Science and technology, and particularly the new technologies, seem at present to be thinkable only as organs of mere rationality. They are thus based on "the law of the concept, knowledge, and predictability." But could they continue to pose a threat to the "free forms that are given here and now to sensibility and imagination" if the dimensions of reason and rationality are treated separately, that is, if rational technology or technological rationality is regarded and used as what it in fact is or might be— as a useful instrument in a limited domain?

Chapter 2

Irreconcilable Modernity: Adorno's Aesthetic Experimentalism and the Transgression Theorem*

Hauke Brunkhorst

According to Adorno, art that is modern—that is, experimental, fragmented, shattered—irreconcilably opposes false social conditions, false consciousness, false or "extorted" reconciliation. "That consciousness kills," he writes in *Aesthetic Theory*, "is an old wives' tale. False consciousness alone is deadly."[1] Irreconcilable and "without model figure,"[2] a rapidly aging yet persistently new art stands opposed to life and its reification. Yet the irreconcilability of modern art is not only directed outward. It is also turned against itself, driving its own contradictions to the fore so that the works "crumble with necessity and rigor" until—as Adorno says of Beckett's *Endgame*—they conduct a "game with elements of reality, free from all representationality."[3]

Modernity brings the destruction of sense, unity, fixed meaning, and "conclusive" orientation to unreconciled expression "without taking a position."[4] Things are not as the realist Lukacs had hoped from socialism, nor as the all-too-realistic literary critic of the *Frankfurter Allgemeine Zeitung* expects from the end of socialism.[5] Were society to master its catastrophic constitution and to emancipate itself from superfluous domination, the great bourgeois novel would not return, nor would the narrative bursting with life or the classical symphony, as though nothing had happpened and all were well now. To the contrary. The shattered form of open works, the incessant struggle never recognizably rounded off into totality, into which the countless endgames of modernity have incurably disintegrated, *is* as such *also* a moment of successful emancipation from the constraints of totality and from the triumphal gesture of affirmative art and culture, which—in Adorno's words—had always already participated in "all injustice." For Beckett's "game with elements of reality, free from all representationality, that takes no position," finds "in such freedom

from the prescribed business" "its happiness."[6] It is real freedom, "the mate-
rialization of the most advanced consciousness."[7] Art emancipated from the
spell of "blackmailed reconciliation" and "disreputable affirmation," from the
constraints, the "lies" and the "ideology" of traditional art, *has need* of a
place in an emancipated society. Indeed, it is possible only in a society in
which the relations of reaching understanding [*Verständigungsverhältnisse*]
are at least somewhat accomodating to it.[8] "One is not to believe," suggested
Adorno "unconstructively" ["*zur Ungüte*"] at the 1959 Baden-Baden art sym-
posium, "that modern art is the way it is because the world is so bad, and that
in a better world it would be better. That is a hotel-art perspective."[9] Adorno
recognized in Lukacs' opinion of Beckett's work—that it is merely the mirror
of late-capitalist pathology and "worldlessness" enlarged into anthropological
dimensions—nothing but the "philistine cliché that modern art is as ugly as
the world in which it arose."[10] It is no mere accident that the *Aesthetic Theory*
closes with lines which show how much Adorno held to the letter and spirit
of aesthetic modernity, even contrary to his own construction of history: "It
is possible that the art of the past, that has become today an ideological
moment of the unfulfilled society, would devolve upon a fulfilled society; but
that the newly emerging art would thereby return to rest and order, to affirmative representationality and harmony, would be the sacrifice of its freedom. Were the art of the future to become positive, then the suspicion of the
real endurance of negativity would be acute; so is it always, relapse threatens
incessantly, and freedom, which would be freedom from the principle of
possession, cannot be possessed."[11]

Adorno remarks in such passages the internal relation between aesthetic modernism and an extra-aesthetic, experimental conception of freedom, a relation which belongs in the dynamic center of a democratic culture.
To be sure, this relationship is concealed by another, negative-theological or
abstract utopian layer of meaning in the text that points to the image of a fully
"satisfied society" and claims to recognize reification as total. But there is no
necessary connection between these two layers of meaning, which consistently overlap and penetrate one another in Adorno's works.[12]

I.

Modernity, which Adorno, in avant-garde fashion, always identifies with
modernism, is thus also irreconcilably opposed to its own—and Adorno's—
tendency to utopia and to the cognition of totality, to final reconciliation and
ultimate grounds: whether *ex negativo* in an "ontology of the false condition"
or as the overwhelming insight that the whole is the false. Precisely *as* consistent modernism, it comports itself irreconcilably toward its own historical

self-understanding: that it is the already completed end of history, or a culmination of history imminently to be brought forth.[13] Thus the consistent consciousness of aesthetic modernity already becomes in Adorno himself the falsifier of a construction of history turned negative. Just as *Negative Dialectics* allows itself the thought of universal solidarity only in the moment of the *collapse* of metaphysics and in the face of its remaining ruins, so art participates in the utopian gleam of reconciliation only in *departure* from the metaphysical thought of its final *sublation* (*Aufhebung*) in life. The triumphalism of sublation and the confidence in a universal reconciliation of "violated nature" dissolve in the sorrow of departure and the pain of collapse. Adorno recognized already in the romantic outburst of unmastered sorrow, that makes an Impromptu of Schubert's sound "so incomparably more sorrowful than even the darkest pieces of Beethoven," an essential motif of modernity, indeed its first breakthrough.[14] Schubert is more sorrowful than Beethoven to the degree that he is more modern. The reason, for Adorno, is that sorrow follows immediately out of the "release of the particular" from the compulsion to dialectical reconciliation of the whole with the parts. The "persistence of the particular"—embodied by Beethoven in music and by Hegel in philosophy—is freed from the compulsion to a higher, superimposed unity. The *loss of reconciliation* is inseparably bound to this *emancipation* from the compulsion to totality. Hence the sorrow: "The Schubertian sorrow depends, accordingly, not merely upon the expression (which is itself a *function* of the musical complexion), but upon the release of the particular." Yet the "emancipated detail is also abandoned and suffering, negative."[15] Music, like philosophy, overcomes on the threshold to modernity the idealistic and early-romantic *expressive model of the spirit*, which condenses everything singular and particular into an organic form of life.[16] Schubert's music is so sorrowful because it does not find its way back to the integral expression of the musical complexion and loses itself in the freedom of the particular and the detail. It is not the still metaphysical "sorrow over the death of the bourgeois subject," an idea attributed to Adorno in the 1960s. Schubert's sadness is rather a consequence of the emancipation from the spell of such subjectivity; it is only through its destruction that the sadness first becomes possible and aesthetically experiencable. Further, a passage such as that quoted here from the sketches for the Beethoven book clearly emphasizes how distant Adorno's radical individualism lies from all forms of communal or collective identity. Whereas, for instance, the "communitarianism" fashionable today in the West consists in a renewal of the expressive model of collective life developed from Herder to Hegel, for Adorno *all* freedom of modernity begins with criticism of that model's metaphysical character of compulsion, which the inner logic of Beethoven's composition still follows. The "dual character" of "totality" is proper to the organic expression of the particular in the universal:

"the totality has the character of the *persistence* of the particular (which is missing from Schubert and from the entire Romantic, including Wagner); and something ideological, transfiguring, that corresponds to the Hegelian doctrine of the positivity of the whole as the epitome of all particular negativities; thus the moment of untruth."[17]

Adorno has a strong predilection for romantic metaphors of fluidity and amorphousness, of the diffuse and the impulse which overwhelms the ego: "Only he who were able to determine utopia in the blind somatic desire that knows no intention, and stills the last, would be capable of an idea of freedom that endured."[18] But at the same time Adorno warns of the "horror of the amorphous" and against false immediacy. With regard to the dialectic of modernity, which in the history of music initiates in the transition from Beethoven to Schubert, Adorno follows the impulse of Schubertian sorrow, which *releases* the particular; yet he wishes to preserve in this release the moment of *persistence*, which endures and holds open the contradictions that rend art and life equally. The "nonidentical" is *not* simply the "unidentical": "Dissociation is possible only against identity, falling under its concept; otherwise it would be pure, unpolemic, innocent manifold."[19]

Adorno's conception of freedom, however, is entirely directed toward the experimental play of such manifold, which does not let itself be understood, mastered, interpreted. The metaphors of streaming and flowing that dissolve the rigidity of self-identical subjectivity are aimed at this play: "released and flowing nature"[20] breaks its path through Hölderlin's parataxes just as it does in Mahler's music, which, as Adorno repeatedly says, "desires to go out into the open." Adorno gives the name "transgression" (*Verfranzung*) to the *internal* dissolution of the boundaries between the individual art forms and between art and life, which was long ago anticipated by surrealism and has become ubiquitous since the 1960s. The explosive dynamic between classical modernity, neo- and post-avantgardism forces art *of its own accord* to transgress the particular boundaries of its forms. Music, the classical temporal art, spatializes itself by consciously renouncing its expressive force, and painting temporalizes itself by becoming expressive and nonrepresentational. Adorno was always already interested in the transgressions and overlapping moments on the boundaries of poetry and music, music and writing (the silent reading of the score as the ideal of reception!), of philosophical essay and art, notes and literature. It is a process to which he contributed: "Words without Songs," "Notes to Literature." Adorno's sensibility for the violation of borders and for transgressions shows that by no means everything falling under the rubric "postmodern" falls outside the horizon of his late aesthetic. It is of decisive importance for the concept of transgression that no *Gesamtkunstwerk* arises out of it, and that life does not become an artwork, as in fascistic and Stalinistic mythology. The tendency toward overlapping and infringement is

partial, subversive, spontaneous, punctual, but it is never total nor in a totalitarian manner aimed at the whole. Trangression is an alternative to the model of sublation that oversteps the autonomy of art without destroying it.

Modernity emancipates itself from tradition at the point at which it *willingly* "lets itself be carried along by the rushing current of the tones themselves," as Hegel formulated it in a sharp turn of phrase against all romanticism.[21] Adorno uses nearly the same words, but he reverses the evaluation. What Hegel execrates and represents as a loss of freedom, becomes for Adorno the genuine ideal of freedom for modern music, and in his apology for an informal music it is the "desideratum of musical freedom."[22] The unity of melody and the regularity of meter, "the finite recognition of a harmonic position, and above all of the tonic," (Schopenhauer), were for Hegel and Schopenhauer the guarantee that what Adorno once called the "tempting sensual" would not exceed the bounds of the musical. For Hegel, melody guarantees the popular pedagogical contribution of music to "the free being-with-itself of subjectivity"; for Schopenhauer, the harmonic position both reflects and reinforces "man's sober life and striving."[23]

Adorno confronts this tradition first of all with a different conception of freedom, one that is oriented toward an experimental disposition. The subject finds its freedom precisely in the fact that it puts itself into danger, abandoning itself to the force of its own *impulses* just as it exposes itself to a multiplicity of principally uncontrollable *situations*. "Artists do not sublimate," states Adorno apodictically in the article "Exhibitionist" from the *Minima Moralia*: "Instead, they display forceful, neurotically drawn instincts that are at the same time free-flowing and yet collide with reality. Even the philistine phantasy of the actor or violinist as a synthesis of a bundle of nerves and a heartbreaker is more apt than the no less philistine drive economy, according to which the model schoolchildren (*Sonntagskinder*) of renunciation let off steam in symphonies and novels. Their lot is rather a hysterically excessive lack of inhibition with regard to every conceivable anxiety; narcissism driven to the limit. They harbor idiosyncracies against the sublimated."[24]

Adorno's conception of freedom is closely bound to the image of an unfixed identity; hence his penchant for metaphors of free flooding, streaming, flowing. The individual who would "go out into the open" must withstand a situation over which he has lost the power of administration, one to which he has abandoned himself. Modern music culminates for Adorno in late Schoenberg with the expression of weeping, which washes away all intentions and any distanced self-mastery. As already in E. T. A. Hoffmann's Romantic music aesthetics, the sensible human voice is swallowed up by emancipated instrumental music.[25]

The unity that was already broken in Beethoven's work decays along the path from Romanticism into modernity, into the "musical style of free-

dom"—a negative freedom *from* repetition compulsion, from the recognition of the always identical meaning contents, from sensible communication. What aesthetic modernity denounces is the "glorifying" sublation of the individual and particular in a comprehensive other.

Should Adorno in fact be, as Rüdiger Bubner recently remarked, the "most important aesthetician of a century rich in artistic production, but rather impoverished in the theory of art," then his importance rests in my opinion in the fact that Adorno *comported himself aesthetically toward aesthetic theory*—whether idealistic, romantic, materialistic, or like his own, negativistic.[26] In so doing, Adorno traced the *movement* and *dynamic* of modernity, the *temporal core* of its truth and the rapidly transforming "symptoms of a powerful tendency," without smoothing over the contradiction between the actual movement of the arts and their *concept*.[27]

Paradigmatic for Adorno's aesthetic comportment toward his own theory, which neither subsumingly adapts under theory the comportment that opens itself to the the experience of the new, nor allows theory to become aesthetic and to decay into "conceptual poetry," is the *transgression theorem* developed by Adorno in the 1960s: As Christine Eichel has shown in an important recent study of Adorno's music aesthetics, the theorem sets a synthesizing sublation of the arts into art and of art into life in the place of the model of the subject.[28]

From the perspective of the lecture held by Adorno on "art and the arts" in July of 1966 (which has a place of relevance in his work similar to that of the paper "Vers une musique informelle" of ten years before), a new light falls upon the *Aesthetic Theory*, which at least in the first years of its reception stood too much under the spell of the work concept, the emphasis on truth, the rehabilitation of semblance, even of beauty in nature. Adorno, who was hardly free from prejudices against America and the culture industry, and in favor of Austro-German music, had distanced himself noticeably from the avant-garde and the "latest developments."[29] But the subterranean surrealism of *Aesthetic Theory* poses a consistent contrast to that position: the truth-shattering force of semblance; the "fundamental layers" and "invariants" of modernity, which Adorno spun as always between "dissonance," "explosion," and "construction"; the consistent emphasis upon "suddenness" and "subversion"; the talk of an "infiltration of the aesthetic with the moral";[30] finally the postulate of the "normativity of modernity," which grounds itself solely in its "antitraditionalistic energy."[31]

The diagnosis of "anti-avantgardism" is at any rate false and must be corrected and differentiated in light of the transgression theorem.[32] Adorno does reject the avant-garde's *imperial* claims of sovereignty, which encroach upon life and destroy autonomy, on the ground that they still follow the false metaphysical model of *sublation*. Yet Adorno saw in the transgression

process—which was already then clearly perceptible in its initial stage, and has now become overwhelmingly unmistakable—the objective justification of a breakaway movement that merely misundertood itself as an avant-garde.[33]

The insight into the simultaneous necessity and impossibility of a *theory* of the aesthetic is of decisive importance for Adorno's judgment and attitude toward informal and serial music; to the conscious blurring of the boundary between image and tone; to the dissolution of fixed spatiotemporal order and of the classical art forms; to the manifold introduction of the principle of chance and of improvisation; to the return of montage; to happening and film. The insight into the antinomies of aesthetic theory goes back to Kant. Art stimulates thought, sets the concept in motion and lets the murmur of the recipient audience's voices become louder and louder. Yet no thought can grasp the meaning of art, the movement of the concept comes to an end and the many voices contradict one another. Adorno—like Heidegger in his Kant book from 1929—takes this as his point of departure. Whereas Kant speaks of "concept" and "understanding," Adorno gives preference to "rationality" and "construction"; and in place of "intuition" and "sensibility" steps the word "mimesis," which Adorno directs negatively back upon the Aristotelian tradition. Yet it is an antipathy toward "mediation," indebted to Nietzsche, that differentiates Adorno from Kant. In the *Critique of Pure Reason* it is the doctrine of the schematism which so reconciles understanding and sensibility that the latter learns to *see* and the former receives *something to see*. In the *Critique of Judgment* it is the receiving, communicating and reasoning audience that forges public meaning out of the sense-distant "idiocy" of the artworks, that refines taste and lets itself be ethically impressed by the beautiful symbols. Adorno rejects this sort of communicatively rational reconciliation and replaces it with a negative dialectic that has no center; a "dialectic in standstill" (Benjamin) that lets all contradictions stand unreconciled.

In this manner, Adorno deepens the abyss sundering and splitting concept and sensibility, construction, and mimesis. The works stimulate the senses and the understanding, they excite sensual perception and provoke the comprehension of meaning. Yet the more closely one looks, the more distantly they return the gaze, and with each recognized meaning another collapses. Because understanding always falls short, the light that focuses the "explosion" of the works into a "tongue of flame" falls upon an eye going blind.[34] The artworks shove the narratively comprehensible meaning roughly from themselves, or "damage" it through "small acts of sabotage."[35] Adorno sets the "hermetic principle" of "inimitability" against the hermeneutics of the fusion of horizons.[36] "Gestures are counterpoint to the words," in Kafka's work the "traces of experiences that are covered over by meaning."[37] Kafka's first principle is: "Take everything literally, cover nothing from above with concepts. Kafka's authority is that of texts." Adorno construes texts here

literally as their dense materiality, from letter to letter, and not as the meanings that are always and everywhere identical, as the spirit (Geist): "Only
faithfulness to the letter, not the *oriented understanding*, will one day be of
aid."[38] Admittedly, the anticipation of that which will one day be of aid does
point toward the quasi-theological construction of history made by theory.
Yet *criticism* makes visible merely the contradiction in the work through
which Kafka's faithfulness to the letter sabotages and damages the hermeneutic
orientation-knowledge, indeed letting it "crumble" with "necessity and rigor"
in the "unhindered progress of the aesthetic domination of the material."[39]
Therein lies for Adorno a socio- and ideology-critical moment of successful
works. The aesthetic quality of literary texts and musical composition is
always also measured by the extent to which, as dense and dark "material,"
they stubbornly frustrate the need for "relief" (Gehlen) from quotidian cares,
for "innerworldly salvation" (Weber) or "compensation for the damages of
modernity" (Lübbe). They comport themselves ascetically toward all forms of
sociological and social functionalization.

II.

Adorno utilizes consistently, in the construction of history belonging to
his aesthetic theory, the language of German Idealism ("subject," "object,"
"consciousness," "reflection," "identity," "nonidentity," etc.), only to let it
break down each time in the aporetic dialectic of subjectivity and reification.[40]
In so doing, he follows still the metaphysical paths of idealistic dialectic.
Roughly, the *objective truth* of art consists in the recognition of the hopeless
condition of the world. Adorno speaks in this sense of art as a *"fait social."*
Yet art is nonetheless, despite such realism, no faithful mirror of the world's
false condition. For its other, *aesthetic truth* lies alone in the semblance that
falls upon the things and lets them appear, arranges them, as the game pleases:
a "game with elements of reality" that remains sealed off, neutralized, coldly
distanced from reality; that, as Adorno explicitly says, "takes no position."[41]
Aesthetic semblance comports itself ascetically toward reality: "The citizen
would have art be sumptuous and life ascetic; the opposite would be better."[42]

In what then does the *aesthetic* truth consist? *One* answer that Adorno
gives—which I would like to name the answer of theory—reads: The aesthetic semblance is true as the coming to light of a missing reconciliation, and
it contradicts as such the *objective* truth of art, which, because it "does not
lie,"[43] is "the impress, the negative of the administered world."[44] The dissolution of the contradiction between appearance and reality, between aesthetic
and objective truth would be found then in a utopia of reconciliation become
indistinguishable from negative theology. In semblance, the *higher* truth of

art would appear. On this view, the metaphysical figure of a sublation of art into a higher, substantial ethical life (*Sittlichkeit*) stands once again at the end of the aesthetic antinomy. Understood in this way, the theory of art would remain platonically contemplative. And there are formulations of Adorno's which suggest such an interpretation, all the way up to the distinction of the "bios theoretikos" as the highest form of life: theory is for the Adorno of *Negative Dialectics* the "lingering gaze of thought,"[45] and already in the *Minima Moralia* he defines thought as the "forceless contemplation, from which all happiness of truth stems."[46]

Yet this interpretation is contradicted by the fact that Adorno understands theory through and through as *critique,* and couples it in art with an *aesthetic-practical conception of freedom.* In the *Introduction to the Sociology of Music*, he writes: "The common aether of aesthetics and sociology is critique."[47] And the *Aesthetic Theory* postulates a "critique of culture through art."[48]

It is of decisive importance that criticism follows art and not theory. It lets itself in for and exposes itself to the experience of contradictions and antinomies, complex and uncontrolled situations and impulses. It transgresses itself in them and comports itself ascetically in the *execution* of critique toward the prefabricated *solutions* of theory, which in the end it allows us to see through as illusion and false generalization. For theory is in Adorno an irrevocable premise of the philosophy of consciousness, and cannot but identify, classify, order, impose unity from *outside* and *above*. Theory is inextricably bound to the perspective of the *dominating subject*, and must proceed by subsuming, even where it strains to get beyond the concept through the concept. In this respect, it is evident that Adorno's conception of theory remains still entirely within the horizon of Western metaphysics.

But critique and aesthetic experience follow a *different* paradigm. For critique—in this respect similar to aesthetic comportment—the communicative everyday reality is simultaneously proximate and distant. Yet critique is not withdrawn from reality, has not left *this* world for the forceless gaze upon the thing itself in order to retreat into the shadow realm of pure ideas of reason, or into the dream of a complete satisfaction of drives and the salvation from all evil. In essays like that on "informal music" or on the transgressive tendencies of the arts, Adorno comports himself *onesidedly* as a critic, so that in such texts the tension between a negative-theological construction of theory and the materialism of criticism comes remarkably to the fore.

What Adorno interpreted in 1966 as the process of transgression is a development that initiates *inside the particular works* and crosses over the boundaries with other art forms and with life *from the inside out.* As Adorno sees it, the "latest development" contradicts in this manner the all-too superficial tendency of the avant-garde to align itself with the model of sublation. The sublation model does not speak the language of the works, but rather the

comprehensible, communicative language of propaganda, and it approaches art and the arts from above, with the logic of subsumption. Film, despite all criticism of the culture industry, is paradigmatic for the latest development: "While film would of immanent necessity cast off its artistic aspect—almost as if that aspect contradicted its artistic principle—it remains in this rebellion art and expands it. This contradiction"—which Christoph Menke, drawing on Derrida and Adorno, has defined as a contradiction between *autonomy* and *sovereignty*—"is the vital element of all genuinely modern art."[49] What Adorno observes is related to the inner logic of the aesthetic language, which escapes every extrinsic, comprehending, and instrumentally classifying grip. "What tears down the boundary posts of the art forms is moved by historical forces that awakened inside the boundaries and finally overflowed them."[50] In Adorno's interpretation of the prose of Hans G. Helm, of Calder's mobiles, the "swelling paintings of Bernhardt Schulze," and the compositions of Donatoni, Ligeti, and Varese, the art forms "seem to delight in a sort of promiscuity that violates civilizing taboos."[51]

The transgression process, the liquifaction of boundaries, brings the *proper* language of art and its anarchistic impulses to the fore in the world and opposes the unitary logics of subjectivity, the *Gesamtkunstwerk*, cosmological synaesthesis and communicative reaching of understanding. The concrete shape of the sound of language, its thing-like, dense materiality, does not let itself be transformed into identical meaning: "The Same, which the artworks mean as their What, becomes, through *how* they mean it, an Other."[52] This persistent Other of the arts that *escapes* the intersubjective reaching of an understanding remains nonetheless in its vicinity. For it is not equivalent to the "entirely Other" (*ganz Andere*), on which the solitary *thinker* of an "ontology of the false condition" eavesdrops, but is rather an Other that the arts *place* in the real public space of our everyday world. It is the "second-order thing"[53] which the critic comes across, to which he comports and exposes himself, yet about which he must nonetheless speak in an unavoidably communicative language that strives to reach an understanding. Adorno shares an observation with Gehlen: Because the works of modernity pry loose their thing-like substratum from the horizon of great representative orders, from their connection to an ethics, religion, culture, and nature comprehensible to all; because they finally contradict all ordinary understanding and become abstract, intellectual (*geistig*) and reflective, they become *needy of commentary* to a degree as yet unknown. Yet the more understandable the commentaries become, the less comprehensible the work; they demand "interpretation," yet interpretation only lets their "puzzle character" emerge ever more clearly and metamorphizes in the end all art, even the putatively understandable old art, into consistently new puzzles.[54]

Criticism experiences the "second-order things" *as* things in the world. And in this point Adorno even corrects his previous criticism of Heidegger, whose essay on the origin of the artwork he takes under his wing against Rudolf Borchardt, otherwise estimated highly as a poet by Adorno: "If Borchardt conflates art and religion, suppressing the inevitable moment of secularization in the artwork, then Heidegger's text on the origin of the art-work from the *Holzwege* has the merit of soberly describing the thing-like aspect of the object, which, as Heidegger with good reason ironically notes, even the much-touted aesthetic experience cannot get around."[55] Beyond that, Adorno praises Heidegger for forcefully emphasizing the "linguistic charac-ter of all art."[56] Adorno the *critic* conducts a polemic merely against the hierarchy of being set up by Heidegger, which offends against the democratic equiprimordiality of all the arts in favor of poetry, since Heidegger joins the concept of art once more with that of a higher truth of being. Yet this criti-cism would rebound on Adorno, were one to reduce him to the status of a *theoretician* of the aesthetic.

But Adorno and Heidegger, in their most progressive and metaphysic-antagonistic guises, cross paths in a decisive point: the relation of *thing* and *language*, which sets in motion the transgression of the arts out of the pecu-liar linguisticality common to them. This language is both antitraditional and anti-instrumental, and thus *uncommunicative*: it is neither informative and objectively understandable, nor the expression of an always already compre-hensible event of tradition. We learn with it neither to master the world nor ourselves. It affords us neither knowledge nor vitally necessary orientation meaning. Instead it works disorientingly and confusingly. Heidegger empha-sizes just as decidedly as Adorno the *alienness* of the works and the *rift* that yawns between the mute earth—upon which they contingently stand or are displayed—and the public world—into which they are interpreted and in which they are always already linguistically disclosed.[57] Their productivity, their innovative force and their mysterious alienness depend on the uncalmable and irreconcilable strife that is enflamed upon that rift. Adorno speaks simi-larly of an "objective contradictoriness in the phenomena."[58]

III.

Adorno had proposed in the *Aesthetic Theory* that the alien and alien-ated language of the "second-order things" is dependent upon the medium of criticism for explanation and interpretation; upon criticism that for its part does not elude ordinary language. Thus criticism misses the opaque impenetrability of aesthetic, sensually perceived things to the degree in which it understands them. Adorno left open in his theory the question how the

thing-like language of the works is related to ordinary language. Yet in his role as *critic*, particularly of music and literature, he at least came close to a clarification. That clarification contains the *other*, postmetaphysical answer to the question wherein the aesthetic truth consists. It is the answer of the critic who comports himself aesthetically towards the things. The "critique of culture through art" is also on the trail of an exemplary self-criticism with regard to the absolutizations of Adorno's own theory. Whereas theory—hardly differently from Heidegger's "thought"—banishes the "linguistic character of all art" beyond ordinary language, theory-oblivious criticism shows how the language of the things is "entwined in a single line" with that of ordinary humans.[59]

Criticism rests upon a premise on which Adorno himself, as the author of an unfinished book on Beethoven, shipwrecked. The premise is that the extra-aesthetic, objective-realistic truth content of the works discloses itself alone through an immanent analysis of "technique" and "form," "compositional" or "poetic process" and "procedure."[60] This leads Adorno in his analysis of Beckett's *Endgame* to the central thesis that I mentioned already, and quote in its entirety here: "The game with elements of reality, free from all representationality, which takes no position and finds in such freedom its happiness as freedom from the ordained business, unmasks more than an unmasker who takes a stand."[61] Thus Adorno makes it clear that the objective truth of the works, insofar as they have one, does not consist in the representation of the false condition. The work represents neither a positive nor a negative truth. "Beckett silences out of tenderness the tender no less than the brutal."[62] Reference to reality lies only in the game with its elements. This game has social content, but no cognitive truth. After all, the mass media inform us incessantly of the world's condition. Adorno emphasizes repeatedly that Beckett's *Endgame* would be fundamentally misunderstood as a valid representation of the current horror. This is brought to expression in the metaphysical misunderstanding of the existentialist interpretation current in Adorno's day, which presents the play itself as a "simultaneously stereotypic and erroneous prattle of self-alienation."[63]

If criticism has dissolved the work's objective truth to the point of negating every objective propositional meaning, then in a second, subsequent step it destroys the *aesthetic truth of semblance*.

Along with the objective truth claim, the possibility of any metaphysical foundation of meaning through artworks is revoked. And thereby a reference of aesthetic semblance to reality—which ex negativo would be the glimmer of imminent reconciliation—become questionable, indeed impossible. Thus Adorno posits consistently an internal relation between the destruction of "metaphysical" and that of "aesthetic meaning": "The explosion of metaphysical meaning, which alone guaranteed the unity of the aesthetic

structure of meaning, allows the latter to crumble with a necessity and rigor in no respect lesser than that of the traditional dramaturgic formal canon."[64]

As Christoph Menke has noted with regard to this this passage, the extra-aesthetic, entirely unmetaphorical "explosion of metaphysical meaning" that cuts deeply into life is a social prerequisite for the development of an autonomous aesthetic thing-language "free from all representationality." This language brings the nature-bound and violent process under an entirely rational and forceless control. Only after its transformation into aesthetic meaning can the metaphysical meaning "crumble" with necessity and rigor, thus rationally and under control, without the violence of an explosion. At the same time, the aesthetic destruction of meaning attains cultural stability through its necessity and rigor, and can become an element of the rational self-understanding of a social collective. And it is just this that is not ensured by the mere explosion of metaphysical meaning. After the explosion, there are at first no argumentative and culturally deep-set barriers put up against reconstruction. One absolutism can be replaced by another, as is taking place in the case of nationalism after the destruction of Soviet communism, or as occurred in the case of Leninism after the explosion of czarism.

While the explosion that tears life asunder *annihilates* the truth content of metaphysical meaning, the artful aesthetic crumbling of meaning *rescues* many possibilities for truth, without any longer binding itself together into one truth. The aesthetically controlled destruction of meaning unchains instead a pluralistic, multidimensional "truth potential" of art; not—as Adorno and Heidegger believed—its one truth.[65] The "truth" of the works thus by no means disappears in the aesthetic destruction of appearance; rather it decomposes into multiple, mutually contending dimensions, which can then indeed, in the public criticism and reception of the works, become effective both for ethical self-understanding and for an emancipatory learning process, that loose themselves from tradition and bring an aesthetically experimental conception of freedom to the fore within social reality.

This peculiar achievement of destruction, that criticism makes cognizable in art, is bound up with characteristics of our ordinary language of everyday use. Thus art remains dependent upon ordinary language, even if it has specialized itself in the material, aural, thingly graspable and therefore incomprehensible aspect of ordinary language. To have shown this is, moreover, the genuine achievement of deconstructionist literary theory.[66]

Adorno showed through examples such as Eichendorff's lyric and *Endgame* how *both* dimensions of our ordinary language—the irreducible sound shape and the prosaic literal meaning; the opaque materiality of the words on the one hand; and on the other hand communicative speech, which transforms meanings identically and raises universal truth claims—have intertwined themselves into a collapsing "toppling movement out of the

meaning."[67] In *Endgame,* the social relation of lord and bondsman, an "element of reality," is first of all transformed into a purely linguistic role game
in the dialogue between Hamm's communicative offer of meaning and Clov's
communication-breaking reply: "It sounds as if the law of its progress were
not the reason of speech and counter-speech, not even their psychological
hooking together, but rather listening, related to the law of music that emancipates itself from preordained types. The drama listens to hear what sentence
will follow upon the last."[68] Here too the transgression of the arts shows itself
equiprimordial with their peculiar "linguistic character." The scene with the
alarm clock is exemplary. Just as Clov has in other passages consistently
punctured the overblown poetic cliches of the poet-lord Hamm by taking
them literally in slavish prose, so he plays in this scene an ironic game with
the informative linguistic meaning of the alarm sign, to which he listens as
though it were a piece of music. Thus Clov transforms the earnest communicative reaching of an understanding concerning the informational content of
the communicative medium "alarm clock" into a gourmet [*geschmäcklerisch*]
discourse upon the aesthetic quality of the sound.

> *Clov*:   I'll go and see.
>   (Exit Clov . . . Enter Clov with alarm clock. He holds it against
>   Hamm's ear and releases alarm. They listen to it ringing to the
>   end. Pause.)
>   Fit to wake the dead! Did you hear it?
> *Hamm*: Vaguely.
> *Clov*:   The end is terrific!
> *Hamm*: I prefer the middle.[69]

The artwork sunders the communicative reaching of an understanding
in experimentally arranged, "released self-motion of the linguistic material."[70]
The meaning content is dashed to pieces on the materiality of the sounds and
the hills of ink. It is in this sense of a thing-like language resistant to all
understanding that "great music" is "eloquent beyond all words."[71] But it is
nonetheless not language that here—as Heidegger says—"thinks," or—as
Adorno says—"speaks." We can only know that something is "eloquent beyond all words" because we have already experienced and practiced it in the
ordinary discursive use of the words and sentences of our everyday language.
It is not language itself but rather we who speak through the works. But we
abandon ourselves spontaneously in aesthetic comportment, whether as producer or as consumer or recipient, to the flow of language and its conflicting
games. It is in this manner that we make language speak, as though it spoke
to us itself through second-order things, through hills of ink, sound shapes
and their literality (*Buchstäblichkeit*).

In every ordinary reaching of an understanding, however banal and cliched, these two moments—sound and sense—enter into a relation of tension. Normally the understanding of meaning, which refers by means of validity claims to the universal communication community of all those who could object, functions relatively without compulsion or significant disturbances through the opaque materiality of language. Art sets its peculiar linguistic character in motion at those places where the ordinary functioning of language has been penetrated by violence and become indistinguishable from pathological rigidity. It is in this sense that art opposes the "false condition" of society. It objectifies the communication-breaking power of language into "second-order things," in order sustainedly, though without doing violence, to "demolish" and "shatter" the only apparently living meaning of culture. As Adorno said of Mahler: "Jacobinean, the lower music storms into the upper . . . The self-satisfied polish of the mediary form is demolished by the disproportionate sound from the pavilions of military bands and the palm-garden orchestra . . . Symphonic music digs for the treasure that alone the roll of distant drums or the murmer of voices promises ever since music established itself domestically as art. It would seize the masses that flee from culture-music, yet without making itself equivalent to them [*gleichzuschalten*]."[72]

I wish to add nothing more to this "beautiful passage" out of Adorno's ouevre.

NOTES

*Translated by Colin Sample.

1. Theodor W. Adorno, *Ästhetische Theorie* (Frankfurt: Suhrkamp, 1970), 318. ["Daß Bewußtsein töte ist ein Anmenmärchen; tödlich ist einzig falsches Bewußtsein."]

2. [Translator's note]. An allusion to the title of a set of Adorno's essays: *Ohne Leitbild. Parva Aesthetica* (Frankfurt: Suhrkamp, 1967).

3. Adorno, *Noten zur Literatur (Frankfurt: Suhrkamp, 1974)*, 290. ["aller Spiegelbildlichkeit lediges Spiel mit Elementen der Realität."]

4. Adorno, "Versuch, das Endspiel zu verstehen," in *Noten zur Literatur* (Frankfurt, Suhrkamp 1974), 282, 290. ["ohne Stellung zu beziehen."]

5. Cf. the special literature section of the Frankfurter Allgemeine Zeitung for the Frankfurt Book Fair, October 1993, 1.

6. See n. 4 above, 290.

7. See n. 1 above, 285. ("Materialisation fortgeschrittensten Bewußtseins").

8. Cf. Hauke Brunkhorst, *Theodor W. Adorno. Dialektik der Moderne* (Münich, Piper 1990), 15ff., 116ff., 125ff., 181ff; see also Albrecht Wellmer, "Wahrheit, Schein, Versöhnung," in Wellmer, *Zur Dialektik von Moderne und Postmoderne* (Frankfurt: Suhrkamp 1985), 43ff. (English in Albrecht Wellmer, "Truth, Semblance and Reconciliation," *Telos* 62 (1984–85), 89–115.)

9. Adorno, *Ohne Leitbild*, Frankfurt Suhrkamp 1967, 58; cf. also Baden-Badener Kunstgespräche, 1959, *Wird die moderne Kunst "gemanagt?"* (Baden-Baden, 1959).

10. Adorno, *Ästhetische Theorie*, 386. Cf. "Versuch, das Endspiel zu verstehen," in *Noten zur Literatur*, 290.

11. See n. 1 above, 386.

12. The necessity of such a relationship between the distinct layers of meaning in Adorno's texts, which would be accessible to a "stereoscopic reading" (Wellmer) under the unity-grounding a priori of a negative philosophy of history, is now disputed from entirely different points of departure in Adorno scholarship. Cf. for example A. Wellmer, *Zur Dialektik von Moderne und Postmoderne*, 9ff., 48ff., 135ff.; J. Ritsert, *Ästhetische Theorie als Gesellschaftskritik*, Frankfurt o.J.; H. Brunkhorst, *Theodor W. Adorno. Dialektik der Moderne*; H. Brunkhorst, "Die ästhetische Konstruktion der Moderne," in *Leviathan* 1, 1988, 77–96; H. Brunkhorst, "Eine Verteidigung der 'Ästhetischen Theorie' Adornos bei revisionistischer Distanzierung von seiner Geschichtsphilosophie," in H. Münkler and R. Saage, eds., *Kultur und Politik* (Opladen: Westdeutscher Verlag 1990), 89–106.

13. On modernity/modernism in Adorno, cf. H. Brunkhorst, *Theodor W. Adorno. Dialektik der Moderne*, 113ff.

14. Adorno, *Beethoven. Philosophie der Musik* (Frankfurt: Suhrkamp 1993), 48.

15. *Ibid.* I am grateful to Andreas Kuhlmann for references. Cf. his review of the Beethoven book in *Die Zeit*: "Technik und Transzendenz."

16. On the "expressive model," cf. Charles Taylor, *Hegel* (New York: Cambridge University Press, 1975).

17. See n. 14 above, 48ff.

18. Adorno, *Minima Moralia* (Frankfurt: Suhrkamp, 1964), 102.

19. Adorno, *Noten zur Literatur*, 300.

20. See n. 19 above, 471.

21. G. W. F. Hegel, *Vorlesungen über die Ästhetik III*, (Frankfurt: Suhrkamp, 1971), 154. On Hegel and Schopenhauer versus E. T. A. Hoffmann and Adorno, Andreas Kuhlmann, *Romantische Musikästhetik*, Diss. (Bielefeld, 1989), 80ff. (Part 3: "Musiksprache als Sprachnegation.")

22. Adorno, "Vers une musique informelle," in *Gesammelte Schriften* (Frankfurt: Suhrkamp, 1978), vol. 16, 495ff.

23. G. W. F. Hegel, in the work cited in n. 21, p. 190; A. Schopenhauer, *Die Welt als Wille und Vorstellung I*, (Zürich: Haffmans Verlag, 1988), 348ff., cit. in Kuhlmann, *Romantische Musikästhetik*, 102.

24. See n. 18 above, 136.

25. A. Kuhlmann.

26. R. Bubner, "Heiter ist das Leben . . . Anmerkungen zu einem aktuellen Phänomen der Grenzüberschreitung," in Bubner, *Zwischenrufe* (Frankfurt, 1993), 61. On Adorno's aesthetic reaction to his own theory, cf. the informative anecdotal observations in G. R. Koch, "Flaschenpost auf Vermittlungskurs. Gibt es ein Weiterwirken Adornos im Musikbetrieb?" in R. Erd et. al., eds., *Kritische Theorie und Kultur* (Frankfurt: Suhrkamp, 1989), 53–68.

27. W. Adorno, "Die Kunst und die Künste," in Adorno, *Ohne Leitbild. Parva Aesthetica* (Frankfurt: Suhrkamp, 1967), 159.

28. Cf. Christine Eichel, *Vom Ermatten der Avantgarde zur Vernetzung der Künste. Perspektiven einer Interdiszplinären Ästhetik im Spätwerk Adornos* (Frankfurt: Surhkamp, 1993).

29. With particular regard to music, see the differentiated estimation of G. R. Koch, "Flaschenpost auf Vermittlungskurs," in the work cited.

30. Adorno, *Ästhetische Theorie*, 79.

31. See n. 30 above, 416.

32. For the diagnosis, see Peter Bürger, *Zur Kritik der idealistischen Ästhetik* (Frankfurt: Suhrkamp, 1983), 128ff.

33. For empirical confirmation of the unraveling theorem, cf. C. Eichel, in the work cited 251ff.

34. T. W. Adorno, *Prismen* (Frankfurt: Suhrkamp, 1969), 106.

35. T. W. Adorno, "Aufzeichnungen zu Kafka," in *Gesammelte Schriften* 10 (Frankfurt: Suhrkamp, 1977), 275.

36. See n. 35 above, 265.

37. See n. 35 above, 258ff.

38. See n. 35 above, 257; emphasis mine.

39. Adorno, *Noten zur Literatur*, 282, 303.

40. See n. 12 above, 23.

41. See n. 39 above, 290.

42. See n. 30 above, 27.

43. See n. 30 above, 16.

44. See n. 30 above, 53.

45. T. W. Adorno, *Negative Dialektik*, (Frankfurt: Suhrkamp, 1966), 46.

46. See n. 18 above, 157.

47. T. W. Adorno, *Einleitung zur Musiksoziologie* (Frankfurt: Suhrkamp, 1962), 222.

48. See n. 30 above, 143.

49. Adorno, "Die Kunst und die Künste," 181. On the dialectic of autonomy and sovereignty, cf. Christoph Menke, *Die Souveranität der Kunst* (Frankfurt: Suhrkamp, 1991). A sovereignty of art broken by radical, "hermetic" autonomy is for Adorno in 1966 the unraveling of the individual works out of an inner drive. Adorno was long on the trail of such fraying, for example in the 1951 essay "Zum Verhältnis von Musik und Malerei Heute," in R. Tiedemann, ed., *Adorno-Noten*, (Berlin, 1984), 150–163. Cp. also the following passage from the "Aufzeichnungen zu Kafka": "Insofar as his brittle prose spurns all musical effect, it proceeds like music. It breaks off the meanings like monuments in cemeteries of the nineteenth century" (*Gesammelte Schriften* 10: 278). The texts on Eichendorff and Rudolf Borchardt from the *Notes on Literature* are also characteristic for the anticipation of the unraveling theorem; after all, the *critic* offers here notes in the form of essays.

50. Adorno, "Die Kunst und die Künste," 160.

51. See n. 50 above, 161.

52. See n. 50 above, 169.

53. Adorno, *Ästhetische Theorie*, p. 152.

54. Cf. Arnold Gehlen, *Zeit-Bilder* (Frankfurt: Klostermann, 1986), 162ff.

55. See n. 50 above, 174.

56. See n. 50 above.

57. Martin Heidegger, "Der Ursprung des Kunstwerks," in *Holzwege*, (Frankfurt: Klostermann, 1972), 54ff. English as "The Origin of the Work of Art," in Martin Heidegger, *Poetry, Language, Thought*, trans. Douglas Hofstadter (New York: Harper and Row, 1971), 15–89.

58. See n. 50 above, 170.

59. Adorno, *Noten zur Literatur*, 313.

60. Here and in the following I take the lead of Christoph Menke's "Der Stand des Streits. Literatur und Gesellschaft in Samuel Becketts *Endspiel*," unpublished manuscript and his "Literatur und Gesellschaft. Zu einigen methodischen Aspekten von Adornos Beckettinterpretation," MS, (Frankfurt, 1993).

61. See n. 59 above, 290.

62. See n. 59 above, 290.

63. See n. 59 above, 306.

64. See n. 59 above, 282.

65. See n. 40 above.

66. Cf. Paul de Man, *Die Ideologie des Ästhetischen* (Frankfurt, 1993); and Harold Bloom et al., *Deconstruction and Criticism* (New York: Seabury Press, 1979).

67. Christoph Menke, "Der Stand des Streits." I also adopt from Menke the following example from Beckett's *Endgame*.

68. See n. 59 above, 308.

69. Samuel Beckett, *Endgame. A Play in One Act* (New York: Grove Press, 1958), 48.

70. See n. 69 above.

71. Adorno, *Beethoven*, 16. (The quote is taken from Tiedemann's "Vorrede" and stems originally from Adorno's Iphegenie essay.

72. Adorno, *Mahler*, in *Gesammelte Schriften* 13 (Frankfurt, 1971), 184ff.

Chapter 3

Adorno: The Discourse of Philosophy and the Problem of Language

Peter Uwe Hohendahl

More than one commentator has remarked that Adorno approaches truth as something mediated through language. For this reason, it is not uncommon to link his thought to the linguistic turn of cultural theory and propose a special proximity between Adornian theory and poststructuralist attempts to rethink the role of language in contemporary philosophy. As tempting as it may be to interpret Adorno's position as close to and compatible with poststructuralist thought by using the category of negative dialectics as the mediating term, this path could ultimately lead us away from Adorno's conception, since it neglects the specific constellation out of which his concept of truth emerged. Although it is certainly correct that Adorno would not separate truth from linguistic considerations, his approach does not easily fit the more recent description of a general linguistic turn in matters of epistemology and criticism. An indication of the difference is Adorno's continued insistence on the need for conceptual language in the discourse of criticism. We can see that the original introduction to *Aesthetic Theory* underscores the impossibility of a traditional systematic philosophy of art, but Adorno holds on to the requirement of conceptual rigor and epistemological reflection. For him, the question of language (which he certainly took more seriously than did most other members of the Frankfurt School) is embedded in the larger question of the status of philosophy, and, specifically, of logic. His concern with the logical aspect goes back to the 1930s and 1940s, when he discussed problems of logical theory with Horkheimer. In any event, we can locate Adorno's (mostly implicit) theory of language most easily, I believe, by looking first at his critique of traditional philosophy.

We have to keep in mind that the beginnings of Adorno's philosophical writings coincided with a more general change in the perception of language. In a number of crucial areas the conventional understanding of language as a means of communication and a tool for attaining knowledge came under scrutiny. Specifically, the problematization of language imposed itself on literary, philosophical, and religious discourse. In the critical discourse on literature, for instance, Hofmannsthal's letter of Lord Chandos (1902) called into question the signifying power of language. Fifteen years later, from a different viewpoint, the literary experiments of the dadaists radically undermined traditional assumptions about poetic meaning. At the same time, within the discourse of philosophy, Lukács's *History and Class Consciousness* developed a rigorous critique of linguistic reification and from a different perspective Ludwig Wittgenstein's early work implied a complete rejection of the neo-Kantian model of epistemology. Furthermore, and particularly important for Adorno (who was trained in the neo-Kantian tradition), Walter Benjamin reconceived the epistemological parameters of philosophy in his early essays, especially in "On Language as Such and the Language of Man" (1916) and "On the Program of the Coming Philosophy" (1918). Adorno came to follow the path of his older friend and mentor, who set out to reformulate the task of philosophy in the light of the limitation of Kant's theory of knowledge and the reoccurrence of these limits in neo-Kantian attempts to salvage the transcendental epistemology. Against the Kantian insistence on the subject, Benjamin underscored the objective and divine character of truth and therefore characterized Kant's theory of knowledge as modern mythology. For this reason, Benjamin accentuated the linguistic aspect of philosophy and argued that philosophy must be grounded in a theological theory of language.[1]

Particularly instructive are two essays in which Adorno explicitly raises questions about philosophical discourse: the early (1931) essay "Die Aktualität der Philosophie" ("The Actuality of Philosophy") and the lecture "Wozu noch Philosophie?" ("Why Philosophy?"), published in 1962. These can serve as a frame for Adorno's philosophical oeuvre. Though they differ considerably in tone and mood—the later one being obviously more pessimistic than the earlier one—they share a radical critique of systematic philosophy, a critique that draws on the immanent evolution of philosophy after Hegel as well as on the historical context of the philosophical project within advanced Western societies. In the 1962 essay, Adorno underscores objective aspects by offering a critical analysis of existing philosophical schools; only then does he point to the remaining path of philosophical reflection: namely, a dialectical procedure that resists the lure of closure. Clearly, however, he rejects the reduction of philosophy to a methodology of science that is exclusively concerned with formal problems. In this respect, Adorno is prepared to defend the metaphysical tradition against its scientific critique. At the same time, he takes issue with two versions of philosophy that dominated the West German discourse after 1945: the renewal of ontology in Heidegger's philosophy, and the existentialist project of Sartre and his German disciples. What these approaches have in common with positivism, Adorno argues, is their polemical stance against metaphysics.

> In both positivist theory and that of Heidegger—in his later work, at all events—the current is set against speculation. The idea which arises independently from, and indicatively of, the facts, and cannot be separated from them without leaving a residue behind—a remainder, as it were—is stigmatized as vain and idle cerebration: according to Heidegger, however, ways of thinking that follow the typical pattern prescribed by the historical evolution of thought in the West at bottom fall short of the real truth. The latter comes to light of itself, and stands revealed: correct thinking is no more than the ability to perceive it.[2]

Adorno's critique is twofold. First, it stresses the problematic implications of the antimetaphysical attitude: the naive acceptance of that which is given, and the passivity of the subject toward truth—both the result of unmediated thought. Second, it underscores immanent problems, especially in Heidegger's philosophy. For Adorno, Heidegger's understanding of truth misses the mediation of the concept[3] or, more precisely, the moment of mediation in conceptual work. "Thought itself, of which all ideas are a function, cannot be represented in the absence of thinking activity, which the word thought designates."[4]

This is not the place to pursue Adorno's critique of Heidegger in more detail; it may suffice to note the importance of its linguistic aspect. For Adorno, Heidegger's ontology misrepresents the nature and function of human language. At no point can Adorno overlook the involvement of philosophical thought in language, not only as an instrument of theoretical articulation but also—and emphatically so—as a self-conscious reflection of its own historical character. Thus, both positivism and ontology, historically situated, must be recognized as forms of reified thought. Adorno's project can be defined, at least in part, as a relentless self-conscious critique of ossification as it is reflected in the language of positivism or ontology, exposing the jargon of ontological murmuring that mystifies its actual function in the social realm. Clearly, this project extends to the Marxist tradition as well; its orthodox strands, as Adorno stresses, are no less reified than scientific positivism.

This is not the place to pursue Adorno's position in 1962 cannot be summarized as a mere critical continuation of the dialectical tradition. As much as the later Adorno holds on to the Hegelian tradition, he does not see himself as a neo-Hegelian;

rather, his critique includes all forms of idealism, especially of absolute idealism. Under these conditions, philosophical thought, after losing its hegemony, is restricted to negativity, to a refusal of fulfilling a positive function. "Because philosophy is good for nothing, it is not yet outmoded."[5] Adorno hastens to add that even this program is not reliable and safe; it is as much open to criticism as any traditional theoretical position.

Adorno's "Why Philosophy?" isolates certain moments in his thought without, however, fully articulating his reservations against the claims of systematic philosophy. It is in *Aesthetic Theory* that the radical moment of this critique comes into the foreground. In particular, the original introduction, written in the late 1950s, underscores the fundamental impossibility of systematic philosophy with regard to works of art. But as Adorno makes clear at the very beginning, the problems of aesthetic theory are closely related to fundamental epistemological problems, which almost immediately resurface in aesthetic theory, since the material of aesthetic theory depends in principle on the concepts of subject and object provided by epistemology. What Adorno calls the "extreme nominalism" of modern art—that is, its resistance to preconceived genres and forms—seriously undermines the form of traditional aesthetic theory, which stressed systematic categories. Consequently, Adorno has to deal with the fundamental contradiction between the conceptual apparatus (which includes, of course, the concept of the artwork) and the concrete piece of music or literary text. Conceptual language is, Adorno maintains, at the same time inadequate and indispensable: inadequate for the task of rendering the individual artwork; necessary, however, for disclosing its truth content (*Wahrheitsgehalt*). "The truth content of a work of art calls for philosophy. It is only in philosophy that philosophy converges with or expires in art. The way to this point is that of the most immanent reflection of works of art, not the external application of philosophical tenets" (*GS*, 7:507; *AT*, 468). Yet this typical Adornian strategy, stressing the need for immanence, does not solve the dilemma of aesthetic theory, since it does not automatically provide the mediating moment. One could certainly argue that the concrete artwork is not open to philosophical articulation at all, that any transition from one discourse to the other is impossible. This would leave Adorno with a fundamental gap between art and philosophy, the aesthetic and truth. For Adorno, however, it is language after all that makes the mediation possible, since language is not limited to a model of identity (*a* is *b*) but can, through negativity, articulate difference.

In his late writings Adorno stubbornly defends the task of philosophy without giving it a positive program, without even assuming an unquestionable legitimacy. At one level, this strategy proposes an ongoing critique of the philosophical tradition (Kant, Hegel, Marx, Husserl) which balances its claims by emphasizing its internal tensions and contradictions—which cannot simply be taken as proof of errors but must also be seen as aspects of truth. At another level, however, *Aesthetic Theory* introduces an even more radical critique of the philosophical project by calling into question the nature of conceptual language, suggesting not only its inadequacy for the articulation of the meaning of art but also its incompatibility with the expressive quality of art. For Adorno, the advanced work of art is the most radical challenge to the philosophical discourse and its claim to truth: "The truth of discursive knowledge is undisguised, but for that reason it does not have the truth. The knowledge which is art has the truth, but as something with which it is incommensurable" (*GS*, 7:19; *AT*, 19). What distinguishes the truth content of the artwork from the concept of truth in philosophy is, according to Adorno, its nonconceptual logic: "Although works of art are not conceptual and do not judge, they are logical" (*GS*, 7:205; *AT*, 197). Ultimately, as much as he questions the idea of the rounded artwork, Adorno gives greater importance to art than to philosophy as a bearer of (historical) truth. "It can be said of philosophy, and of theoretical thought in general, that it suffers from an idealistic prejudgment insofar as it has only concepts at its disposal. Solely through them can it deal with what it reaches for, but never grasps" (*GS*, 7:382; *AT*, 365). Therefore, the Hegelian subsumption of art under philosophy has to be reworked: philosophy now may help to disclose aesthetic appearance, the "enigmatic quality" (*Rätselcharakter*) of the work of art.

Aesthetic Theory does not explicitly develop a comprehensive theory of language, but it is shot through with reflections and notes on the problem of language and its relationship to knowledge on the one hand, and to expression on the other. In *Aesthetic Theory*, more than in *Negative Dialectics*, Adorno retrieves essential elements of his original philosophical project of the early 1930s. Both "Die Aktualität der Philosophie" and "Thesen über die Sprache des Philosophen" are early but important attempts to respond to Benjamin's language theory and, at the same time, to refute the claims of Heidegger as the legitimate heir and "conqueror" (*Überwinder*) of Husserl.

At this juncture, we can disregard Adorno's map of contemporary philosophy and concentrate on his "program," which stresses the dialectical movement of philosophical discourse. Unlike the late Adorno, the young Adorno—at this point very much under the influence of Walter Benjamin's *Ursprung des deutschen Trauerspiels* (*The Origin of German Tragic Drama*)— was prepared to offer a programmatic statement in his inaugural lecture at Frankfurt University. Quite consciously, already setting himself off against positivism on the one hand and ontology on the other, he harks back to an earlier model of philosophy (for which the name of Leibniz has to stand in): "The organon of this *ars inveniendi* [art of invention] is fantasy. An exact fantasy; fantasy which abides strictly within the material which the sciences present to it, and reaches beyond them only in the smallest aspect of their arrangement."[6] But what Adorno has in mind has little to do with a return to older models; rather, it is his unmistakable distance from axiomatic grounding that propels him toward essayistic models such as those of Francis Bacon and Leibniz.

Although the inaugural lecture focuses on the methodological aspect, it does not spell out the linguistic consequences for the philosophical discourse. In his "Thesen über die Sprache des Philosophen" (*GS*, 1:366ff.), Adorno explores some of the implications of an "essayistic" position. The short essay contains a radical break with the linguistic model that guided the Enlightenment and idealist philosophy—a model in which semiotic and semantic levels are clearly distinguished and in which, furthermore, the sign is defined as arbitrary. As a result, subject philosophy concentrates on consciousness as the unifying principle and leaves objective reality out as a sphere that can be reached only indirectly through linguistic constructs (concepts). "For a way of thinking that conceives of things exclusively as functions of thought, names have become arbitrary: they are freely posited by consciousness" (*GS*, 1:366). The modern linguistic model (as clearly articulated by Ferdinand de Saussure, for instance) is to be replaced with a paradigm in which signs and reality, language and history are thoroughly intertwined. Only through language, Adorno suggests, does history partake of truth. Words are never mere signifiers for what can be conceptualized; rather, words are penetrated by as well as filled with history, and truth is the result of this fusion. "The share of history in the word absolutely determines the choice of the word because history and truth meet in the word" (*GS*, 1:366–67).

Adorno's suggestion appears to be out of touch with modern linguistic theory, and his insistence on the semantic reality of language collides so obviously with contemporary practice that further explanation is needed. His argument takes the latter objection into account by suggesting that linguistic models are historically determined. His own model would pertain only to a premodern society, whereas modern societies are characterized by a reified model that splits signs and referents. For Adorno, under the sign of modernity the retreat to a prehistorical realm of linguistic purity is impossible—a point that he makes against Heidegger's attempts to escape traditional philosophical terminology.

Adorno's proposal remains ambivalent; it follows two strategies that are not easily compatible. On the one hand, he criticizes modern linguistic theory, postulating a semantically grounded understanding of language; on the other hand, he insists on the historicity of language and polemicizes against any attempt to return to an older paradigm. The task of the philosopher is to confront the decay of present-day philosophical language: "[The philosopher's] material is the ruins of the words to which history binds [him]" (*GS*, 1:368). Adorno's later work follows up both sides of the argument but not necessarily by keeping them together. Well known, of course, is his critique of philosophical jargon as a form of reified language and his discussion of the limits of conceptual language. Less known is his attempt to unfold an alternative model.

In "Theses on the Language of the Philosopher," Adorno suggests a "dialectical" solution that makes use of objective configurations. To use his own language: words are supposed to "surround" truth; their configuration is expected to articulate the "new" truth. "The procedure is not to be identified with the intention to 'explain' new truths with conventional words; on the contrary, configurative language will have to avoid entirely the explicit procedure that presupposes the unbroken dignity of words. As against conventional words and the speechless [*sprachlosen*] subjective intention, configuration is a third way." (*GS*, 1:369). It is worth noting that Adorno speaks here of a dialectical procedure but not of mediation. A configuration, in other words, is not the result of a mediation between oppositional concepts. Adorno conceives of the disclosure of truth not as a formal and conceptual process but as an aesthetic event. Thus knowledge and art begin to converge: "The growing significance of the philosophical critique of language can be formulated as the onset of a convergence between art and knowledge" (*GS*, 1:370). Adorno's *Aesthetic Theory* unfolds precisely this program. Some four decades earlier, as Susan Buck-Morss and others have shown,[7] the first attempts of the young Adorno to work out the problem of truth and language owed a great deal to Walter Benjamin's writings of the 1920s, especially to his study of the baroque tragic drama. In the introduction to that study Benjamin had introduced the concept of the configuration in order to redefine the truth content of works of art without falling back on a historicist approach. In the context of my argument, however, Benjamin's influence is less important than Adorno's response, which takes the form of a double-edged critique of language. He takes issue not only with an ontological approach to language but also with a formalist-semiotic approach that underscores the arbitrary nature of signification. This means that he is equally opposed to Heidegger's and Saussure's models of language. For Adorno, the critique of the reified linguistic theory of semiotics is as crucial as the critique of ontology, since both approaches share an inability to take the historical moment seriously. The Marxist theory of reification enables him to pinpoint the element of ossification in modern language theory, just as Lukács had emphasized the moment of ossification in Kant's philosophical discourse. As a result, Adorno's own model of language and truth does not fit easily into conventional linguistic or philosophical discourses. Attempts to integrate his thought into existing models have a tendency, therefore, to pressure his approach one way or the other. This unique position creates certain problems when Adorno carries out his own epistemological project in *Against Epistemology* and *Negative Dialectics*, since his critiques of Husserl and Heidegger are not launched from the perspective of the expected opposition—that is, semiotics.

Already in *Against Epistemology*, partly written in 1937–38 and completed in the early 1950s, Adorno's earlier program has become less visible, replaced to a large extent by a more traditional critique of phenomenology from a Hegelian point of view (albeit a Hegel without idealism). Especially the introduction grounds its critique of "foundational philosophy" (*Ursprungsphilosophie*), from Plato to Husserl, in a historical dialectic that basically follows Hegel's critique of Kant's rationalist formalism but radicalizes this critique to the extent that its own method is equally drawn into the problematic sphere of epistemology.[8] Internal criticism, following up on given premises and implications, remains locked into the system, and can be overcome only through attention to the language of the argument itself, its figures and tropes. For instance, Husserl's preference for juridical and contractual language still links him to "the myth of the first" (*AE*, 26; *GS*, 5:34). Adorno's critique of Husserl's "categorical intuition" (*kategorische Anschauung*), as a crucial element of his epistemology, relies on Hegel's critique of immediacy and his insistence on mediation. For Adorno, Husserl's "doctrine of ideation" (*Lehre von der Ideation*) has fallen behind Hegel: "The equivocal usage steps in for the immanent movement of the concept. In Husserl's antecedent, 'being' is used in the most universal, abstract, and mediated sense. The conclusion substitutes entities for being as the immediately intuitive moment of whatever sort which attains categorization" (*AE*, 207–8; *GS*, 5:210–11).

What Adorno, with the help of Hegelian dialectics, wants to isolate in Husserl's use of language is its static, almost passive understanding of description as a way to grasp "things" (*Dinge*). Husserl's ideal of description undercuts arguments: "Phenomenology gives notice, provisionally and inadequately, of the end of the discussion" (*AE*, 210; *GS*, 5:212). Adorno is not interested simply in maintaining "the discussion," in which language serves in its traditional role as a tool; rather, the point of his criticism is the static character of Husserl's model, in which statements are expected to approximate facts (*Sachverhalte*) and the subject-object relation remains fixed and undialectical. As a result, Husserl's phenomenology is doomed. Despite its desire to get closer to things (*Sachen*), it cannot overcome the gap between the conceptual apparatus and the facts: "One concept is evolved out of another so that contradictions may be corrected in ordered succession, but none would come closer to the 'thing' than the first one. Indeed each falls deeper into the thicket of invention." (*AE*, 211; *GS*, 5:214) In other words, for Adorno the failure of Husserl's project, the failure of renewed idealism, is closely related to the latter's understanding of language and the language-truth relation where the levels of sign and referent are set apart. Husserl's discourse aims at descriptions not unlike those of the scientist who organizes the world according to types and systems of types.

As much as Adorno criticizes the propensity toward a systematic approach, especially in Husserl's later writings, in *Against Epistemology* he more or less refrains from presenting an alternative position. The mode of criticism is mostly immanent, with an emphasis on the late bourgeois character of Husserl's thought, the search for ultimate security in an age in which security is no longer available. Only occasionally does Adorno's interest in the fragmentary, unresolvable nature and the dialectics of language come to the fore—in his preference for Husserl's isolated phenomenological analyses, for instance, which exhibit an antisystematic character. In this context, Adorno points at least in passing to Freud's resistance to the traditional opposition of logic and intuition (shared by Husserl) and underscores the logic of the intuitive as part of the rational (*AE*, 46; *GS*, 5:54). By and large, however, in his struggle with the phenomenological model and especially with its postulate of absolute grounding, Adorno does not unfold his own position.

This is where the later *Negative Dialectics* goes a decisive step beyond *Against Epistemology*; here the scope of the questioning has significantly widened and with it the problematization of traditional philosophical language. The later study, however, also extends the involvement with conceptual language, as Adorno states at the very beginning. In his definition of dialectics he stresses the moment of difference between objects (*Gegenstände*) and concepts and, therefore, the problematic attempt of all philosophy to establish identity through statements. Hence, Adorno's interest in dialectics emphasizes contradictions rather than synthesis as a way of reestablishing identity: "Contradiction is nonidentity from the viewpoint of identity; the primacy of the principle of contradiction in the dialectic measures the heterogenous against identity-thinking" (*ND*, 5; *GS*, 6:17). Thus, dialectics emerges as the radical consciousness of nonidentity. Yet this consciousness has to be expressed in a philosophical—that is, conceptual—language. The introduction insists emphatically on the necessity as well as feasibility of this task, turning against Henri Bergson and Ludwig Wittgenstein, who want to limit the scope of philosophical discourse.

> The plain contradiction of this yearning [for transparent language] is that of philosophy itself: it is qualified as dialectics before it becomes entangled in its particular contradictions. The labor of self-reflection consists in unravelling those paradoxes. Everything else is signification, second-hand construction, and today—as in Hegel's day—pre-philosophical. (*ND*, 9; *GS*, 6:21)

The language of philosophy is predicated on the problematic but inevitable desire to get closer to a prelinguistic realm. This attempt, Adorno points out, does violence to the nonconceptual (*Begriffslose*) by repressing, marginalizing, and eliminating it through its stamp of identity.

Despite his critique of mystical or irrational approaches to epistemology, Adorno does not mean simply to restate the traditional domain of philosophy and its language. Rather, he describes philosophical reflection in *Negative Dialectics*, as consistently confronting its own limits and its own culpability. Far from defining dialectics as a mediated path to truth, Adorno calls it an "ontology of the false state of affairs" (*ND*, 11; *GS*, 6:22), which can be overcome only through reflection on its own state. Knowledge of "reality," in other words, depends entirely on language but cannot place its trust in concepts. For this reason, Adorno rejects both the empirical and the rationalist model of language; that is, he opposes equally a model of reflection and a model of conceptual autonomy (where empirical reality does not really matter). Philosophical discourse, he suggests, strives toward the Other without being allowed to leave its own domain. "Philosophy which realizes that, which annuls the autarchy of the concept, wipes the scales from its eyes" (*ND*, 12; *GS*, 6:23–24). To put it differently, philosophy can survive only by questioning its survival. But in this procedure of questioning it remains tied to its own tradition. For this reason, Adorno is especially critical of programs that seek a completely new beginning or a return to a past state, as does Heidegger's ontology. For Adorno, Heidegger's demand for a reorientation in philosophy misses the present condition of philosophical discourse; it postulates a new language and new categories without reflecting on the need for and the limits of conceptual language.

Ontology, to summarize Adorno's critique in part two of *Negative Dialectics*, is the refusal to accept the paradox of philosophical language: that its task is to do what it cannot do by reconstituting the realm of the absolute under the category of Being (*Sein*). In Heidegger, absolute knowledge is disclosed not through the dialectical process of conceptual work but through "intellectual intuition [*intellektuelle Anschauung*]" (*ND*, 62; *GS*, 6:70), where mediation is no longer necessary. In this framework, ontology presents itself as a solution to modern problems without working through these problems. Adorno treats ontology as a form of ideology that has a specific political and social function in postwar Germany: "In the categories to which fundamental ontology owes its resonance—and which it therefore either disavows or so sublimates that they no longer serve for an unwelcome confrontation—one can read how much they are the imprints of something lacking that is not to be produced, how much they are its complementary ideology" (*ND*, 65; *GS*, 6:73).

Yet for the purposes of my argument, this critique is less central than the immanent critique of Heidegger's categories presented in the second chapter. Here Adorno focuses on the conceptual apparatus of ontology and its (almost desperate) attempt to overcome the boundaries of conceptual language. He demonstrates the very abstractness of the category of Being as the supposed origin: "If one tries to accomplish Heidegger's differentiation of

Being from the concept that logically circumscribes it, one is left—after subtracting entity as well as the categories of abstraction—with an unknown which has only the pathos of its invocation over the Kantian concept of the transcendent thing-in-itself" (*ND*, 98; *GS*, 6:105).

In fact, as Adorno points out, Being derives its significance and power from a strategy of hypostatization applied to the copula "is." "Heidegger, in misplacing it beyond the sole source of its meaning, succumbs to that reified thought to which he took exception" (*ND*, 101; *GS*, 6:108). In this setup, Heidegger—very much against his intention, of course—remains caught in an obsolete model where "subject, copula, and predicate would again—as in obsolete logic—be hermetic, completed details after the model of things [*Sachen*]" (ibid.). Against this model Adorno sets his own, in which the copula has a very different function: namely, that of a "promissory note on particularization" (ibid.) In other words, the copula in a statement is designed not only to identify subject and predicate but also to bring about the characterization of the particular which it can only claim to accomplish.

As we can see, Adorno's critique of Heidegger is very much involved in a critique of Heidegger's language, not only at the level of its jargon but, more centrally, at the level of Heidegger's most basic category, which provides the ground for his ontology. Yet one must not overlook the fact that Adorno does share with Heidegger certain concerns and presuppositions that neither analytic philosophy nor contemporary semiotics would necessarily grant. He shares with Heidegger the belief that language is more than signification (*ND*, 101; *GS*, 6:109) and that facts (reality) and language (signs) are not independent of each other. Still, he refuses to follow Heidegger's elevation of the copula "is" to a first principle of origin in the argument that the judgment "*A* is *X*" contains an irreducible element that can be abstracted as Being. The following passage presents the crucial point in Adorno's critique:

> Heidegger gets as far as the borderline of dialectical insight into the nonidentity in identity. But he does not carry through the contradiction in the concept of Being. He suppresses it. What can somehow be conceived as Being mocks the notion of an identity between the concept and that which it means, but Heidegger treats it as identity, as pure Being itself, devoid of its otherness. (*ND*, 104; *GS*, 6:110)

Whereas Heidegger tries to transcend the dualism of the judgment in his striving for Being, Adorno resolutely reminds his reader that the moment of nonidentity in the judgment must not be repressed; in fact, it must be foregrounded so that the subject-object dialectic becomes visible. In other words, he rigorously holds on to the process of conceptual procedures (work) that he himself had described as problematic.

For Adorno, the problematic side of the philosophical discourse is at the same time its strength, the relentless attempt "to express what cannot be articulated [*das Unausdrückbare auszudrücken*]" (*ND*, 106; *GS*, 6:114). Of course, this task must not be confused with a search for the irrational; rather, Adorno's postulate must be understood as a way of distinguishing philosophy from the sciences (including the historical sciences). Philosophy shares with the sciences, of course, the methodological use of language, but it proceeds in a mode that Adorno refers to as a "suspended state" (*Schwebende*), and "the determinant of its suspended state is that even while keeping its distance from the verifying type of cognition it is not noncommittal—that the life it leads has a stringency of its own" (*ND*, 109; *GS*, 6:115). Where Heidegger went wrong, Adorno suggests, was in his attempt to articulate *das Schwebende*, to bring it into the form of a definitively worked out terminology, and thus to claim for it a "quasi-superior rank" (*ND*, 109; *GS*, 6:116).

It is, of course, not accidental that Adorno compares *das Schwebende* of the philosophical discourse to music: that is, to a medium without concepts, one in which truth cannot be achieved through the method of judgment. Likewise, the language of philosophy cannot be satisfied with a positive doctrine or a deduction of such a doctrine (*Lehre*) from first principles. Even the category of reflection, which carries a great deal of weight in *Negative Dialectics*, does not quite suffice to express the inexpressible. For this reason, Adorno's relentless critique of Heidegger can never quite come to grips with the nature of philosophical discourse, since it is limited by its own object: that is, the ontological model of Being. The legitimacy of philosophy, which Adorno treats as questionable but not hopeless, depends on the possibility of refunctioning elements of the metaphysical tradition, without, however, buying into its dogmatic side. To put it differently, Adorno assumes that philosophical discourse can no longer be grounded in first principles, nor can it rely on universal concepts deduced from these principles (*ND*, 136; *GS*, 6:140). Consequently, a positive concept of totality is no longer available. This leaves philosophy with an arduous task for which it is not quite adequately equipped: to discover how concepts and "the nonconceptual" (*das Nichtbegriffliche*) come together (*ND*, 137; *GS*, 6:141).

At this juncture we have to focus on Adorno's literary essays of the 1950s and 1960s, which approach the same problem from a different angle. Their center is, of course, precisely *das Nichtbegriffliche* in works of art, the moment that escapes conceptual construction. This opposition is crucial for Adorno's music criticism, but in his literary criticism it comes into the foreground as the problem of language. The problem articulates itself in two different ways. First of all, art criticism is concerned with the epistemological status of art and literature: can art and literature contain cognitive truth, or are they (exclusively) expressive? Second, given the difference between literary and philosophical discourse, how can criticism articulate the nonconceptuality of the artwork?

Adorno's famous essay on the essay, "Der Essay als Form" ("The Essay as Form") addresses primarily the latter question by arguing for a nonsystematic treatment of aesthetic issues, but it also speaks to the larger problem of the truth content in works of art and the difference between conceptual claims and *das Nichtbegriffliche* as the Other, which does not seem to fit traditional philosophical discourse. Adorno directs his essay (typically enough for the 1950s) against the scientific and systematic claims of traditional academic criticism, which is concerned with both the factual aspects of the artwork and the aesthetic features of the individual text. Like the early Lukács, Adorno underscores the special character of the essay: its deliberate incompleteness, the fragmentary quality that resists the demands of systematic treatment and refuses to take its cues from philological research. Taking the factual side for granted, the essay concentrates instead on the moment of reflection; it is concerned with precisely those aspects that tend to get lost in scientific or philosophical approaches. Still, we have to note that Adorno does not give up on the conceptual element in criticism. His scorn for the journalistic feuilleton and the fashionable existentialist criticism of the 1950s (Heidegger) is unmistakable: "With a peasant cunning that justifies itself as primordiality, it refuses to honor the obligations of conceptual thought, to which, however, it had subscribed when it used concepts in its propositions and judgments. At the same time, its aesthetic element consists of merely watered down, secondhand reminiscences of Hölderlin or Expressionism" (*NL*, 1:6–7; *GS*, 11:13).

More rigorously than the young Lukács, Adorno insists on the difference between the essay form and poetry (*Dichtung*), notably in their use of language. The pseudo-poetic, an attempt to lose itself in its object by imitating its language, is the temptation (*Versuchung*) of the essay. For Adorno, the essay must preserve a precarious balance between conceptual and poetic language. But this formulation does not quite do justice to his radical notion. It leaves out the moment of transcendence: "In the emphatic essay thought divests itself of the traditional idea of truth" (*NL*, 1:11; *GS*, 11:18). The essay does not state truth, nor is it merely a matter of (poetic) expression; rather, it "seeks the truth contents (*Wahrheitsgehalte*) as themselves historical. It does not seek any primordial given, thus spiting a societalized (*vergesellschaftete*) society that, because it does not tolerate anything that does not bear its stamp, tolerates least of all anything that reminds it of its own ubiquity" (*NL*, 1:11; *GS*, 11:19).

Adorno's rigorous defense of conceptual criticism, however, must not be confused with a return to a traditional philosophical discourse. For him, concepts fulfill a different function in the essay: they may remain undefined; they approach truth by forming a specific configuration through which the nonconceptual Other can be articulated. In this context he offers a crucial formulation for the character and use of concepts: "In actuality, all concepts are already implicitly concretized through the language in which they stand. The essay starts with these meanings, and, being essentially language itself, takes them farther; it wants to help language in its relation to concepts, to take them in reflection as they have been named unreflectingly in language" (*NL*, 1:12; *GS*, 11:20). The essay form takes back and reverses the linguistic ossification implied in scientific discourse. Thus, the essay presents a paradox: a process of defining its particular object through nondefinitions, thereby creating a nonfetishized language. What Adorno celebrates is not only the essay's open form and conscious lack of a dogmatic position but ultimately its lack of intellectual security, its lack of an affirmative ideal of truth. The anti-Cartesian tendency is unmistakable.

It is not accidental, of course, that Adorno refers to Leibniz's concept of the monad in order to suggest how language and truth may be related. He defines this relationship as a configuration that does not follow the conventional distinction between the parts and the whole. The essay, as Adorno notes, does not allow a search for its elements or for origins. Its moments are not strictly derived from its totality, nor do its individual parts lead to the whole. As an anti-Cartesian form (and method), Adorno stresses, the essay does not instrumentalize its own language. Instead, it allows and encourages a full articulation of the object through a linguistic differentiation that radically appropriates contradictions and discontinuities. The essay form, Adorno notes, is characterized by breaks and gaps, following the breaks and gaps of reality itself; it reaches its unity by acknowledging these moments rather than by harmonizing them.

In its antisystematic mode, the essay form frees itself from the pressure to use language as a means of identification. In fact, the essayist's awareness that representation through language is not identical with the object (*Sache*) provides the essay with critical energy. For Adorno, essayistic language is critical language par excellance—not because it defines a position but because it refuses to define a position, because it undercuts all positions including its own. As a consequence, truth cannot be defined as the correspondence (*Übereinstimmung*) of language and reality. In the essay, Adorno suggests, and the suggestion could be extended to critical writing in general, truth can and must be articulated through untruth.

The essay's defiance of discursive logic, its keen interest in associations and equivocations (*Äquivokationen*), brings it close to aesthetic language. The essay, Adorno submits, partakes of the possibilities of the nonconceptual without becoming art. This means that concerns for "rightness" (*Stimmigkeit*) are of greater importance than rules of discursive logic. Does this indicate that Adorno returns to a romantic position, which celebrates art at the expense of rational philosophical arguments? The proximity to the romantic fragment is obvious enough. But there is no attempt to restore the ideology of originality as embodied in the artistic genius. Hence, Adorno does not mean to reinforce an irrational idea of poetic language as pure expression; rather, he sees poetic language as an objective structure following its own internal logic.

In "On Lyric Poetry and Society" Adorno offered the first analysis of this structure by emphasizing the social aspect of poetry. By and large, that essay has been read as Adorno's contribution to a sociological method; less attention has been paid to the essay's equally important emphasis on language, epecially since this topic receives a more thorough and more differentiated treatment later in *Aesthetic Theory*. Methodologically speaking, the essay on poetry owes its force to the dichotomy of the particular (poem) and the general (society), which is subsequently unfolded dialectically. Adorno wants to demonstrate the universal quality in the individual poem. More relevant in our context, however, are his remarks about the character of poetic language. Adorno underscores its noncommunicative nature: "Not that what the lyric poem expresses must be immediately equivalent to what everyone experiences. Its universality is no *volonté de tous*, not the universality of simply communicating what others are unable to communicate" (*NL*, 1:38; *GS*, 11:50). Instead, he suggests, the poem is expected to preserve the individual moment, the moment that has not yet been subsumed under the concept. In doing so, in concentrating on the particular, the poem reaches the level of the universal (*Allgemeine*).

Adorno's polemic against theories of communicative poetic language, however, does not cancel a model of poetic language as expression (*Ausdruck*). What he wants to eliminate is the traditional use that directly links the poem and the emotions of its author; he sees the language of the poem rather as the objective correlate of its specific social conditions. This means that for Adorno there is a referent outside the semiotic system but a referent that cannot be communicated directly. Only a mediated correspondence is possible: the speaking subject of the poem can suggest meaning through a specific configuration of words. "The 'I' whose voice is heard in the lyric is an 'I' that defines and expresses itself as something opposed to the collective, to objectivity; it is not immediately at one with the nature to which its expression refers" (*NL*, 1:41; *GS*, 11:53). For Adorno, both poetry and society are mediated through language (*NL*, 1:43; *GS*, 11:56). By emphasizing the expressive aspect of poetry, which crystallizes in language, Adorno brings together a subjective and an objective model of language. He describes language as a twofold phenomenon (*Doppeltes*), that simultaneously molds the subjective reactions and feelings and articulates concepts along with their relationship.

The core of Adorno's concern is his interest in redemption (*Versöhnung*): that is, his interest in nonreified language. In the poetry essay this means first and foremost a critique of Heidegger's ontological conception of language, which celebrates poetry as the language of Being. Adorno's concept of poetic language, by contrast, reintegrates—at least in its moment of redemption—subject and linguistic system. In this respect, the poetry essay reiterates a concern that Adorno had already expressed in the early 1930s: the need for a language theory that does not simply reflect the actual reification of language in modern society. In *Aesthetic Theory* he more rigorously unfolds these questions, although even there he does not offer a systematic treatment.

Aesthetic Theory does differentiate two aspects of the concept of language that were not separated in the poetry essay: language as a means of communication, and language as artistic expression. The poetry essay defined them dialectically; *Aesthetic Theory* emphasizes their fundamental distinction. It is characteristic for the work of art, Adorno suggests, to transcend the language of communication; in fact, it is no longer compatible with communication. "The true language (*Sprache*) of art is speechless (*sprachlos*). Art's speechless moment has priority over the signifying one of poetry—a moment which is not entirely lacking even from music" (*GS*, 7:171; *AT*, 164). The expressive moment of art, aesthetic articulation, does not coincide with its conceptual aspect. Hence, the language of art moves to a metaphorical level—at least from the point of view of modern linguistics. Yet for Adorno this metaphorical use is the older and more fundamental mode: a prediscursive, mimetic use in which the work of art has a special affinity to the subject. For expression does not communicate the subject's concerns; rather, works of art "reverberate with the prehistory of subjectivity—that of ensoulment [*Beseelung*]" (*GS*, 7:172; *AT*, 165). Hence, for the late Adorno the concept of poetic language cannot be exhausted by rational and logical considerations; its core is the element of mimesis "as imagining objectivity" (*GS*, 7:172; *AT*, 165). *Aesthetic Theory* underscores the nondiscursive character of the artwork. "Only by withholding its verdict does art judge, that is the defense for great naturalism" (*GS*, 7:188; *AT*, 181). The implication is that works of art cannot be pinned down to define their truth content. It is the peculiar nature of their linguistic code that they cannot be decoded; they are like hieroglyphs whose code is unknown or lost. "Works of art speak only as handwriting [*Schrift*]" (*GS*, 7:189; *AT*, 182).

More than before, the late Adorno emphasizes the enigmatic character (*Rätselcharakter*) of the artwork, its incompatibility with discursive knowledge. But at the same time, he insists on the element of truth in the work of art, which cannot be dismissed simply as reflection (imitation) or illusion, as much as these elements do play a significant structural role. The mode of art is disclosure without the certainty of disclosure. "As a mimetic struggle against taboo, art attempts to give the answer and gives it as an answer free of judgment-but then again not; thereby, the answer becomes enigmatic, like the dread of the primordial world which changes, but does not disappear" (*GS*, 7:193; *AT*, 85). It is precisely this enigmatic character of art that calls for philosophical reflection and thereby reintroduces discursive language. Only philosophical reflection, which must rely on concepts, can articulate the truth content of art. The artwork also needs to be deciphered, and that deciphering is the task of criticism.

This solution seems to bring us back to a hermeneutic model: the disclosure of truth in the artwork can be achieved through interpretation; in the process of close reading the truth content can be disclosed—though only indirectly. As Adorno notes: "The truth content of works of art is not something to be immediately identified. Just as it is only discerned in a mediated manner, so is it in itself mediated" (*GS*, 7:195; *AT*, 187). This suggests that art and philosophy ultimately converge insofar as the truth of the artwork is no other than the truth of philosophical reflection; what Adorno initially separated in *Aesthetic Theory* finally comes together again.

This integration is not without problems, however, since Adorno's most radical formulations about the nature of the work of art, in particular its existence as *Schrift* (writing), make it difficult to superimpose philosophical reflection as a means of revealing the truth content. *Schrift* remains elusive and ambiguous vis-à-vis conceptual cognition. Adorno achieves the integration by conflating the two concepts of language that he uses in *Aesthetic Theory*. Insisting that language always contains a universal aspect, he postulates the convergence of art and philosophy in a collective subject that clearly transcends the individual aesthetic experience. This (metaphysical) grounding allows him to bridge the gap between the discourse of philosophy and the language of the artwork. But this solution does not take into account that, for Adorno, the language of the work of art is not compatible with identifying judgments. Hence, the truth content of the artwork must remain a paradox: "Works of art are in the most extreme tension with their truth content. While the nonconceptual truth content does not appear otherwise than in the product, it negates the product" (*GS*, 7:199; *AT*, 191). The truth content is not, as one might expect, simply contained in the work of art; rather, artwork and truth content remain in a state of extreme tension. The truth content, Adorno suggests, although it must appear through the product, negates the artwork as a product. To put it differently, the truth content is conceived of rigorously as a negation of the product (*das Gemachte*). The integration of the artwork and philosophical language can be achieved, as Adorno underscores, only by admitting this hiatus. Consequently, the artwork's authenticity is always problematic—not so much because it only "imitates" reality as because it postulates what is not there and what therefore must be illusion.

As I have argued, the ultimate testing ground for Adorno's theory of language is the work of art. It is here that he forces together conceptual discourse and aesthetic expression in the concept of the truth content (*Wahrheitsgehalt*). Ultimately, this construct is bound to fail because it must conflate two incompatible notions of language: Whereas conceptual language cannot escape the moment of identification in the process of making judgments (*Urteile*), the logic of the artwork is exclusively based on the configuration of its material. The more Adorno underscores its "lack of conceptuality" (*Begriffslosigkeit*), the more he widens the gap. Hence, he must postulate a rapprochement between art's immanent logic and discursive thought; he does so either via the idea of negation or through the analogy with mathematics (*GS*, 7:205; *AT*, 197–98), which integrates formal logic and pure configurations without referent. Yet Adorno does not want to cancel the referent, for without empirical reality, art would lose its counterweight and, hence, its authenticity. Therefore, *Aesthetic Theory* must attempt to resolve this dilemma and undermine its solution at the same time. Even as he celebrates the undecidability of art, Adorno insists on the possibility of its redemption in philosophical reflection.

More than other members of the Frankfurt School, such as Horkheimer or Marcuse, Adorno was keenly aware of the embeddedness of philosophy in language, especially of the linguistic constraints of philosophical discourse. In this respect he was indebted, without explicitly saying so, to Nietzsche's critique of traditional metaphysics and its linguistic models. Insofar as Nietzsche's philosophy has provided a new linguistic paradigm, traditional models of signification have become problematic: the quest for truth is no longer firmly grounded in concepts. Clearly, however, Adorno did not follow Nietzsche's path of language critique, which foregrounds the arbitrary nature of signs. As much as he questioned the legitimacy of traditional philosophical discourse and stressed the problem of the copula in any judgment (*Urteil*), Adorno did not want to sever signifiers, meaning and referents. In other words, Adorno did not follow modern linguistics as it was developed by Saussure and then radicalized in poststructuralist thought. The structuralist model had no appeal for him because it separates semiotic and semantic aspects, whereas Adorno maintained the need for concepts and categories as modes of conveying thought. Although skeptical of conventional philosophical language, he did not share the fundamental doubt that philosophical categories are the mere result of language: that is, the result of an effect produced in a particular language such as Greek or German. With Kant and Hegel, he maintained the legitimacy of reason against radical nominalism and positivism.

Still, Adorno was neither a Kantian nor a Hegelian in any dogmatic sense. His affinity to German idealism, I suggest, was not based on dogmatic faith in Kant's and Hegel's positions; rather, it reflected his commitment to rational conceptual operations—despite their problematic nature. At the same time, he emphasized the deficiency of traditional logic in its desire to impose identity at the expense of both the subject and the object. This distancing from traditional logic is already clearly present during the early 1940s in his discussions with Horkheimer, and it is also strongly articulated in *Dialectic of Enlightenment* (1944). Adorno's resistance to the philosophical discourse takes the form of foregrounding an oppositional discourse, which he found almost exclusively in art and literature. As Susan Buck-Morss has suggested, his counterdiscourse or countermodel was deeply indebted to Benjamin's writing of the 1920s, notably the study of the German *Trauerspiel*.[9] The logic of mimesis (*unsinnliche Ähnlichkeit*) complements and corrects conceptual logic.

Benjamin's pre-Marxist texts rely on mystical inspiration rather than on modern linguistic theory. As he remarks in his essay "On Language as Such and on the Language of Man," for Benjamin "every expression of human mental life can be understood as a kind of language."[10] More important, Benjamin stresses the distinction between spiritual character (*geistiges Wesen*) and strictly linguistic character (*sprachliches Wesen*), which serves as a tool to express and communicate the spiritual character. But insofar as the spiritual essence can be communicated, it becomes identical with its linguistic character, which means that "all language communicates itself."[11] For Benjamin, persons and things articulate themselves *in* language rather than *through* language. The distinction is crucial because it separates the conventional theory of language, which defines the word as a tool, and a theological theory in which God's creation becomes complete when humans give names to things. Ultimately, for Benjamin, the nature of language can be understood only in the context of a theological model grounded in sacrifice.

It seems that Adorno was less interested in the theological aspects of Benjamin's work than in its implicit critique of conventional secular linguistic theories. Furthermore, for Adorno the music critic, Benjamin's notion of a variety of languages (painting, sculpture, poetry) was particularly important because it enabled him to relate music to the discourse of philosophy. More specifically, the symbolic nature of artistic languages (expression)—for Benjamin the supplement of communication (*Mitteilung*)—allowed the articulation of that which cannot be communicated (*das Nicht-Mitteilbare*). In this context the idea of mimesis played an important role in Adorno's late writings. Especially in *Aesthetic Theory*, he relies on the notion of mimesis in order to differentiate between conceptual language and the language of art, which he sees as an older, even archaic mode of expression.[12]

Adorno underscores the mimetic element in modern art as well: works of the avant-garde are involved in the transformation of communicative language into mimetic language (*GS*, 7:171; *AT*, 164). Although he never offers a formal definition of mimesis, his frequent use of the term in *Aesthetic Theory* suggests a sharp distinction between the "language" of the artwork—which remains without language (*sprachlos*)—and any form of discursive language. Mimetic language precedes—in archaic as well as modern art-works—the split between subject and object implied in the signifying use of discursive language. For Adorno, mimesis invokes the primal history of the subject and its link to nature. Hence, he suggests the proximity of the aesthetic to mimesis in archaic art and underscores the link between magic and mimesis. In magical praxis the agent seeks not to imitate but to approximate nature, thereby creating a moment of close affinity. Through mimesis the work of art remains connected to nature beyond the principle of imitation. The act of mimesis is bound up with art's prespiritual aspect (*das Vorgeistige*), while the spiritual moment is linked to the aspect of construction in the artwork. Both are indispensable. In art, Adorno argues, mimesis enables expression not as an arbitrary articulation of the subject but as an alternative form of knowledge (*GS*, 7:87; *AT*, 80–81). Where Benjamin emphasized the religious ground, Adorno stresses the dualistic nature of language: its conceptual nature on the one hand, and its mimetic moment on the other. For Adorno this dualism remains an unresolved dialectial opposition. Each mode of language validates the other without the possibility of synthesis.

ABBREVIATIONS

AE: Theodor W. Adorno, *Against Epistemology: A Metacritique*, translated by Willis Domingo (Cambridge: MIT Press, 1983).

AT: Thedor W. Adorno, *Aesthetic Theory*, translated by C. Lenhardt (London: Routledge and Kegan Paul, 1984).

GS: Theodor W. Adorno, *Gesammelte Schriften*, edited by Rolf Tiedemann (Frankfurt: Suhrkamp Verlag, 1973–).

ND: Theodor W. Adorno, *Negative Dialectics*, translated by E. B. Ashton (New York: Continuum, 1987).

NL: Theodor W. Adorno, *Notes to Literature*. 2 vols, translated by Shierry Weber Nicholson (New York: Columbia University Press, 1991–92).

NOTES

1. See Walter Benjamin, *Reflections* (New York: Harcourt Brace Jovanovich, 1978); Richard Wolin, *Walter Benjamin. An Aesthetic of Redemption* (Berkeley: University of California Press, 1994), 31–47; Michael W. Jennings, *Dialectical Images: Walter Benjamin's Theory of Literary Criticism* (Ithaca, NY: Cornell University Press, 1987), 82–120.

2. Theodor W. Adorno, "Why Philosophy," in *Man and Philosophy*, ed. Walter Leifer (München, 1964), 15 (*GS*, 10[2]:463).

3. See n. 2 above, 17 (*GS*, 10[2]:465–66).

4. See n. 2 above, 18 (*GS*, 10[2]:466).

5. See n. 2 above, 23 (*GS*, 10[2]:471).

6. Theodor W. Adorno, "The Actuality of Philosophy," *Telos* 31 (Spring 1977):131.

7. See Susan Buck-Morss, *The Origin of Negative Dialectics* (New York: The Free Press, 1977).

8. "Certainly the immanent critique of epistemology itself is not exempt from the dialectic. While philosophy of immanence—the equivocation between logical and epistemological immanence indicates a central structure—can only be ruptured immanently, i.e., in confrontation with its own untruth, its immanence itself is untruth" (*AE*, 25; *GS*, 5:32).

9. See n. 7 above.

10. Walter Benjamin, "On Language as Such and on the Language of Man," in *Reflections*. For a rigorous reading of Benjamin's theory of language see also Winfried Menninghaus, *Benjamins Theorie der Sprechmagie* (Frankfurt am Main: Suhrkamp, 1980), esp. 9–11.

11. Benjamin, "On Language," 316.

12. In the writings of Benjamin mimesis plays an equally important role. In more general terms, he defines mimesis as *unsinnliche Änlichkeit* (nonsensual similarity); more specifically, he understands mimetic language as the capability of approximating nature, ultimately becoming one with nature. In "On the Mimetic Faculty" (*Reflections*, 333–36), Benjamin argues that writing (*Schrift*) consists of an archive of nonsensual correlations between sign and nature. Therefore, he also suggests the possibility of reading nature as a configuration of hieroglyphs. See Josef Früchtl, *Mimesis. Konstellation eines Zentralbegriffs bei Adorno* (Würzburg: Königshausen und Neumann, 1986), 17–29.

Chapter 4

Mass Culture as Hieroglyphic Writing: Adorno, Derrida, Kracauer

Miriam Bratu Hansen

The vicissitudes of Adorno's reception in English-language cinema and media studies make a well-known and tedious saga. In its latest chapter, marked by the dissemination of British Cultural Studies in American academic institutions and publishing, the invocation of Adorno's writings on film and mass culture amounts to little more than a ritualistic gesture, reiterating the familiar charges of elitism, pessimism, and high-modernist myopia.[1] The trouble with such accounts is not that they are critical of Adorno—there is much to be critical about—nor even that they use him as a foil against which to assert the identity of a new paradigm or to defend the legitimacy of a field of study which Adorno himself, at his darkest, considered as little more than an appendix of political economy. The trouble is that such accounts effectively preclude critical engagement with the body of thought in question. They do so, for one thing, because they limit themselves to a rather well-trod and narrow basis of texts (narrower even than the amount of writings available in English, whatever problems there may be with the translations). More importantly, they evade the challenge posed by any historical theory of film and mass culture: how to discuss the theoretical claims made in these earlier texts without neutralizing their historical distance and contingency; and, by the same token, how to enlist their very historicity in theorizing the break, as well as the links, between earlier forms of mass culture and our own.

The more interesting critics of Adorno's writings on film and mass culture all, in one way or another, tend to take up this challenge. They try to engage his writings as "a living thought" by historicizing them, by tracing their concerns in relation to ours, by mobilizing disjunctions and contradictions in the texts themselves.[2] Whether reading "Adorno in reverse," "against the grain," or in the spirit of "redemptive critique," such revisionist approaches seek to defamiliarize the well-known arguments, both about him and his own, and to make the texts articulate problems for which they themselves may not have an answer. (Admittedly, this is more difficult in the case of Adorno than it seems for Benjamin. The latter's ostensible endorsement of cinematic technology's inherent political potential has earned him the status of good object in the same canon that dismisses Adorno—the status of a bourgeois theorist who could nonetheless envision a democratic, class-conscious appropriation of mass and consumer culture. Yet, if we wish to learn more from Benjamin than what merely confirms our intellectual-political desire, there is no question that this account needs to be defamiliarized as well.)

One strategy of redeeming Adorno's position on mass culture, in particular film, has been to highlight tropes of "writing"—the graphic, the scriptural—in those texts in which he attempts to conceptualize an aesthetics of film, irrespective of its industrial-technological context of exploitation.[3] To recall the familiar argument, Adorno's reservations about film are rooted in the photographic basis of cinematic representation which subtends its seemingly unmediated doubling of empirical reality; in semiotic terms, its indexically grounded iconic character, that is, a form of signification that claims a perceptual likeness between sign and referent. In the context of Adorno and Horkheimer's chapter on the "Culture Industry" in *Dialectic of Enlightenment*, this iconicity is seen as a major source of the cinema's ideological complicity, because it allows the filmic image to function as an advertisement for the world "as is." But even where Adorno begins to think about film in terms of an alternative artistic practice, as in *Composing for the Films* (written with Hanns Eisler, 1947) or "Transparencies on Film" (1966), the philosophical problem remains: that, in its very specificity, (live-action) film conflicts with the Biblical ban on graven images (*Bilderverbot*) which, as Gertrud Koch and other scholars have emphasized, constitutes a regulative idea in Adorno's aesthetic theory.[4] For film to become art, in Adorno's view, it would have to inhibit the photographic iconicity of the image flow by means of cinematic techniques that make it "resemble the phenomenon of writing," that would fracture the illusionist self-identity of the moving image and make it an object of immanent construction, figuration, and deciphering. As Koch points out, the search for a specifically cinematic form of "determinate negation" finds one answer in the principle of montage which, according to Adorno, "arranges [things] in a constellation akin to writing"[5]—that is, discontinuous editing in the widest sense (which for Adorno and Eisler includes sound/image relations).

In a similar vein, Tom Levin defends Adorno against the charge of a Luddite and mandarin hostility toward the mass media by shifting the discussion to Adorno's writings on the gramophone record. Adorno could display a remarkably open, even enthusiastic attitude toward this particular medium of technical reproduction, Levin argues, because he saw in it an indexical, that is, materially motivated, form of inscription (acoustic waves etched into a vinyl plate) that was not hitched, as in film, to an iconically asserted surface resemblance and hence to false immediacy and facile intelligibility. Adorno goes so far as to justify the reification of the live performance by means of the phonograph record on the grounds that it reestablishes "an age-old, submerged and yet warranted relationship: that between music and *writing*." For the phonograph record replaces the arbitrary conventions of musical notation with a form of nonsubjective writing that is at once motivated and unintelligible, a language of "determined yet encrypted expressions." Adorno explicitly links this kind of writing to Benjamin's early speculations on language, in particular the *Trauerspiel* book's vision of a "last remaining universal language since the construction of the tower," and Levin in turn links both to the Romantic tradition of a "hieroglyphics of nature."[6]

Whether in the context of film aesthetics or the ontology of record grooves, writing for Adorno (as for Benjamin or, for that matter, Derrida) clearly means something different from the notation systems of phonetic languages. In both media, it refers to a form of inscription that is fixed and motivated in its discrete signs, yet is not immediately accessible and requires deciphering. For both film and the phonograph, the emphasis on writing implies a form of reception closer to the activity of "reading" than to the automatic consumption excoriated by Adorno in "The Fetish Character of Music and the Regression of Listening" and elsewhere. If this were indeed the case, we should be able to extrapolate from Adorno's writings on film aesthetics and the phonograph not only an alternative practice of filmmaking and composition, but also a different vision of collective reception.

To emphasize Adorno's investment in the scriptural character of the technological media is, I think, a valid and necessary argument. It occludes, however, the negative valence that the terms writing and reading have for Adorno in the context of mass culture, nowhere as strongly as in his notion of film and other media as hieroglyphics. Focusing on the latter, I will ask what kinds of writing and reading, what processes of signification and reception are involved in that comparison. Among other things, this raises the question of the subject(s) and situations of reading, in particular the relationship of the critical theorist to both the mass-cultural hieroglyph and its "ordinary" consumers. Moreover, if we find that Adorno may have captured something about processes of mass-cultural identification for the period in which he was writing—that is, Hollywood at its most classical, American mass culture at its most Fordist and homogenizing—what does this analysis tell us about postmodern, post-Fordist media culture and its seemingly obverse strategies of diversification? Finally, Adorno's untimely negativity may encourage us to rethink the possibility and necessity of critique, even if today we are likely to invest greater confidence in the ability of mass-cultural publics to reappropriate industrially manufactured meanings in diverse, oppositional and collective ways: the stakes and methods of manipulation may have changed, but postmodern media culture is still a far cry from any emphatic, radically democratic notion of the "popular."

In his 1953 essay, "Prolog zum Fernsehen" (Prologue to Television), Adorno speaks of mass culture as a "language of images" (*Bildersprache*), "pictographic writing" (*Bilderschrift*) or "hieroglyphic writing" (*Hieroglyphenschrift*). This language of images lends itself to the "will of those in charge," all the more so as it attempts "to pass itself off as the language of those whom it supplies":

> By giving visual representation to what slumbers in the preconceptual layers of their minds, [this language of images] simultaneously shows them how to behave. While the images of film and television strive to conjure up those that are buried in the viewer and indeed resemble them, they also, in the manner of their flashing up and gliding past, approach the effect of writing: they are grasped but not contemplated. The eye is pulled along by the shot as it is by the written by the printed line and in the gentle jolt of the cut a page is turned. As image, this pictographic language is the medium of regression in which producer and consumer collude; as writing, it displays the archaic images of modernity.[7]

The analogy between mass-cultural images and hieroglyphic writing is grounded, at first sight, on the level of psychoanalysis, in the affinity of filmic/televisual discourse with pre- and unconscious modes of thought. Accordingly, Adorno footnotes an article by two Italian psychoanalysts who belabor that affinity drawing mainly on Freud's *Interpretation of Dreams*.[8] But where these authors celebrate the pictographic and prelogical quality of filmic images as the ideal of "pure cinema," Adorno discerns a powerful mechanism of ideology, reminiscent of Leo Lowenthal's quip about the culture industry as "psychoanalysis in reverse." By mimicking the figurations of unconscious or preconscious phantasy, Adorno argues, mass-cultural hieroglyphics actually spell out a behavioral script; by disguising the very fact that they were written, and with it their heteronomous origin, they create the regressive illusion of a common discourse. Similar to film theorists of the 1970s such as Metz and Baudry, Adorno ascribes this ideological effect to the configuration of the apparatus, the psychotechnical conditions of film reception, rather than a particular mode of film practice.[9]

The regression that Adorno sees facilitated by the hieroglyphics of mass culture, however, is not just a matter of individual or even social psychology. The statement that, "as writing," they display "the archaic images of modernity" points to another context—the historico-philosophical framework of the *Dialectic of Enlightenment*. In the note citing the psychoanalytic article, Adorno primarily refers the reader to his (and Horkheimer's) use of the term hieroglyphic writing in the long-time apocryphal sequel to the chapter on the culture industry, entitled "Das Schema der Massenkultur" (not published until 1981). In that context, the notion of mass culture as hieroglyphics ties in with the familiar themes of the *Dialectic of Enlightenment*: the reversion of Enlightenment into myth and the resurfacing of the archaic in modern forms of domination; the dissociation of image and sign, and the concomitant instrumentalization of language and reification of aesthetic expression; the double character of mimesis; and the false identity of individual and social totality under monopoly capitalism, advanced by a cultural economy of commodity fetishism, repetition and regression.

In "The Schema of Mass Culture," the interpretation of mass culture as hieroglyphics seems to confirm the most problematic aspect of Horkheimer and Adorno's indictment of the culture industry, the thesis of total manipulation and delusion, compounded with the system's timeless, perennial quality. Like the fascist resurrection of archetypes, the ostensibly consumer-engendered dream production of Hollywood is seen as a manufacturing of archaic symbols on an industrial scale; like the former, these function as allegories of domination: "In the rulers' dream of the mummification of the world, mass culture serves as the priestly hieroglyphic script which addresses its images to those subjugated, not to be relished but to be read." Predicated on repetition and effect, such pictographic language culminates the historical "transition from image to writing" or "script" (*Übergang von Bild in Schrift*), the absorption of mimetic capabilities by monopolistic practice.[10]

The term "priestly hieroglyphics" refers back to the opening chapter of *Dialectic of Enlightenment* in which Horkheimer and Adorno elaborate the imbrication of myth and enlightenment in terms of a genealogy of language. Here hieroglyphics is introduced as a "symbolic" language, mediated by "the doctrine of the priests," but one in which the functions of word and image still converged. The core of the symbolic is the mythical conception of nature as cyclical, endlessly renewable and permanent. The historical process of disenchantment, in Horkheimer and Adorno's account, inevitably entails a dissociation of verbal and pictorial functions. In the division of labor between science and the arts, language degenerates, on the one hand, into a "mere system of signs," into an instrument of recognizing nature by renouncing any similarity with it; as image (*Bild*), on the other, language is made to resign itself to the function of copy, imitation or reflection (*Abbild*), to become all nature but renounce any claims to recognize it.[11] Implied in this historico-philosophical construction, however, is another genealogy, which traces the fall of language as a movement from an originary *written* language to a demythologized language described in *phonological*, Saussurian terms. This implies further that the *mimetic* capability of language is conceived as belonging to its originary form as (hieroglyphic) writing, rather than the spoken word. With the shift to a phonocentric concept of language, mimetic capability recedes into the realm of the image, the preverbal layers of aesthetic expression. But inasmuch as that realm too, in monopolistic culture, is increasingly subject to reification, it reverts to a state of writing, in the sense of allegorical mortification. Thus, in the universal idiom of modern mass culture, the ancient hieroglyphs return to consummate mimetic desire with a vengeance. With the technologically enhanced transition from image to writing the reversal of enlightenment into myth has come full circle.

As an instance of the progressive reification of aesthetic expression, the notion of mass-cultural hieroglyphics merely elaborates for film and television what Adorno had stressed earlier in his critique of popular music, in particular his writings on jazz and his essay on Wagner. There he traced the reification of musical expression into formulaic fragments that could be endlessly replicated, corresponding to the reduction of listening to hearing only what one has heard before. Instead of exposing or refiguring the effects of reification, alienation, and fragmentation, popular music, following Wagner, works to cover them up, to rehumanize and provide an affective "glue" for irrevocably sundered social relations.

By a similar logic, aggravated by the iconicity of the visual media, the hieroglyphics of mass culture exert a regressive appeal, in Horkheimer and Adorno's account, not because they would reflect the general state of reification ("the mummification of the world") but, on the contrary, because they mask that state, disguising script as pure image, as natural, humanized presence. In the emphasis on false concreteness, the notion of mass-cultural hieroglyphics echoes Marx's troping of the commodity as a "social hieroglyph," his attempt to locate the "magic" of the commodity in its simultaneously sensual and hypersensual quality.[12] If the commodity beckons the consumer as a real thing, its value, its "real" meaning, is determined by its abstraction of labor and position within a total system of exchange. Similarly, the "secret doctrine" communicated by the hieroglyphics of mass culture is not the historical truth of reification, but the "message of capital." Its secrecy, its encryptment, however, has nothing to do with the enigma of the nonintentional, transsubjective language of aesthetic images; rather, it is a ploy of total domination to keep itself invisible: "no shepherd and a herd."

Simulating immediacy, individuality, and intimacy, the "characters" of mass culture spell out norms of social behavior—ways of being, smiling, and mating. Regardless of the explicit messages touted via dialogue and plot, the viewer is ceaselessly asked to transcode image into script, to read the individual appearance of a star as an imperative of identity—"to be like her"—and to articulate the most subtle nuances in terms of the binary logic of "do and don't" (*GS*, 3: 333; *CI*, 81). While we might expect this to happen to a supposedly passive viewer under the spell of diegetic absorption, Adorno and Horkheimer rather impugn mass culture's specific forms of hermeneutic pleasure, that is, narrative and generic conventions that encourage the viewer to second-guess the apparent mysteries of plot or construction. It is in the shift of the viewer's attention to the "how" by which the trivial resolution is achieved, "the rebus-like detail," that the "hieroglyphic meaning flashes up in him or her." In other words, Horkheimer and Adorno ascribe the effectivity of mass-cultural scripts of identity not simply to the viewers' manipulation as passive consumers, but rather to their very solicitation as experts, as active readers.[13] The identification *with* the stereotype is advanced by the appeal to a particular type of knowledge or skill predicated on repetition: the identification *of* a familiar face, gesture or narrative convention takes the place of genuine cognition.

In "Prologue to Television," Adorno gives the hieroglyphic imperative of identity a somewhat subtler twist by qualifying it as the culture industry's cynical recommendation, "become what you are."

> Its lie consists in the repeated affirmation and rigidification of mere being, of that which the course of the world has made of human beings. . . . Instead of paying tribute to the unconscious by elevating it to consciousness so as to fulfill its urge and at the same time pacify its destructive force, the culture industry reduces human beings to their unconscious behavior even more than the conditions of their existence do all along. (*GS*, 10, 2:514)

The ideological effect of mass-cultural hieroglyphics is not so much a matter of administering positive (or negative) models but, rather, of preventing human beings from changing, from being different, from distinguishing their own wishes and needs from those imposed upon them by distribution from above. As Adorno says in a later text, analyzing the myth of "consumer-oriented art": "By reproducing [the reified consciousness of the audience] with hypocritical subservience, the culture industry in effect changes this consciousness all the more, that is, for its own purposes: it actually prevents that consciousness from changing on its own, as it deep down, unadmittedly desires. The consumers are made to remain what they are: consumers" (*TF*, 205).

In "Schema," Horkheimer and Adorno see the identificatory spell of the mass-cultural hieroglyph linked to the return of mimesis, as I suggested earlier, coupled with the resurfacing of archaic writing. "Mimesis," they propose, "explains the mysteriously empty ecstasy of the fans of mass culture."

If this is clearly a perverted form of mimesis, it still feeds on its utopian opposite, the possibility of reconciliation. What "drives human beings into the movie theaters," Adorno and Horkheimer observe, as it were, in the same breath, may be "the deeply buried hope" that one day the hieroglyphic "spell be broken." (*GS*, 3: 334; *CI*, 82).

"Mimesis" notably is a central category in Adorno's thought and a notoriously difficult one at that.[14] Like many of his key categories, mimesis has a number of different, possibly conflicting meanings depending on the constellation in which it is used—meanings to which I can only allude here in a rather reductive manner. In the anthropological-philosophical context of *Dialectic of Enlightenment*, the concept of mimesis is derived from magic and shamanistic practices as well as zoological forms of mimicry. It involves making oneself similar to the environment; a relation of adaptation, affinity, and reciprocity, a nonobjectifying interchange with the Other; and a fluid, pre-individual form of subjectivity. In this sense, the concept of mimesis assumes a critical and corrective function vis-à-vis instrumental rationality and the identifying logic of conceptual language which distances subject from object and represses the nonidentity of the latter. Since, however, the historical subjugation of nature has irrevocably transformed nature and sundered its relations with society, mimetic practice can be thought of only in a utopian mode. As a utopian category, mimesis prefigures the possibility of a reconciliation with nature, which includes the inner nature of human beings, the body and the unconscious.

By the twentieth century, mimetic experience in the utopian sense is conceivable only in the realm of art, specifically art that inscribes the historical disfigurement of human, social relations with nature. In the context of Adorno's *Aesthetic Theory*, mimesis marks a form of aesthetic expression that differs from traditional (Platonic) notions of mimesis as imitation, in particular Marxist theories of reflection.[15] Mimesis for Adorno does not pertain to the relation between sign and referent; it is not a category of representation. Rather, it aims at a mode of subjective experience, a preverbal form of cognition, which is rendered objective in works of art, summoned up by the density of their construction. Such moments of trans-subjective expression constitute art's *promesse de bonheur*, the unfulfilled promise of reconciliation. At the same time, throughout modern art history, the mimetic impulse has also objectified itself in the bent toward imitation, in the futile attempt to close the gap with the object by doubling it.[16]

To the extent that it is patterned on zoological forms of "mimicry," Adorno's concept of mimesis involves the slippage between life and death, the assimilation to lifeless material (as in the case of the chameleon) or feigning death for the sake of survival. This paradox, indebted to Freud's theory of the death drive, structures the dichotomies of the mimesis concept in significant ways. In an unreflected form, mimesis as mimicry converges with the regime of instrumental reason, its reduction of life to self-preservation and the reproduction of domination by the very means designed to abolish it. In that sense, mimesis entails what Michael Cahn calls "a deadly reification compulsion" that perpetuates the state for which Adorno likes to cite Kürnberger's apothegm, "Das Leben lebt nicht" (life is not alive). In the context of aesthetic theory, however, this mimesis onto the reified and alienated (*"Mimesis ans Verhärtete und Entfremdete"*), the world of living death, is a crucial means of negation available to modern art—as an "admixture of poison," a pharmakon that allegorizes the symptoms though it necessarily fails as a therapy.[17]

In the context of the culture industry, the concept of mimesis is obviously dominated by the negative connotations of both an unreflected mimicry onto reified and alienated conditions and the misguided aesthetic investment in imitation. But it is important to remember that even at this low point of its dialectics, mimesis does not concern a semiotic relation between sign and referent, but the social relations between subjects and commodities. These are determined by a reification compulsion that enjoins economic and psychoanalytic senses of fetishism in the "I-know-quite-well-but-all-the-same" of enlightened consumption. The "triumph of advertising in the culture industry," the chapter on the culture industry concludes, is made possible by "the compulsive mimesis of the consumers onto the cultural commodities, even as they see through them."[18]

In "Schema of Mass Culture," Horkheimer and Adorno elaborate on this remark in terms of the hieroglyphic analogy. As hieroglyphic signs, the characters of film and television rehearse the compulsive assimilation of human beings to the commodity. In the very assertion of individuality, every face, every smile congeals into a mask, a grimace: "The face becomes a letter by freezing that which brings it to life—laughter." The secret of the "keep smiling" is that it transforms the horror over the possibility of such fixation "into obedience before the mortified face." In the economy of perverted mimesis, reification is not just a metaphor: mass culture "literally makes the human beings it reproduces resemble things, even where their teeth do not signify toothpaste, even where the lines of grief in their faces do not conjure up a laxative."[19] By identifying with such images, the viewers surrender their mimetic desire to the universe of death, accepting a false social identity in place of the genuine collectivity and reciprocity they secretly hope for in the experience of mass culture.

This expectation is not entirely a matter of (self-)deception. Horkheimer and Adorno grant at least the potential for true mimetic experience to silent film as a medium or apparatus. For the tendency toward hieroglyphics, they argue, reached its full force only with the transition to sound: the masks of mass culture are all the more terrifying once they begin to talk, once they are naturalized by synchronized dialogue. In silent film, the alternation between written titles and images, as antithetical materials, allowed the images to retain some of their imagistic, mimetic quality. This dialectic, however, was incompatible with the culture industry's bent toward amalgamation and homogeneity. It altogether collapsed with the advent of sound, when written language was "expelled from film as an alien presence [*Fremdkörper*], but only to transform the images themselves into the writing which they in turn absorbed" (*GS*, 3:333; *CI*, 81). The material heterogeneity of silent film thus harbors a moment of resistance which, once eliminated, makes technological progress all the more a catalyst of regression.

In a similar movement, Adorno's "Prologue to Television" affirms his case against the bad present by highlighting the critical difference of similar conventions in the past. In this essay, he contrasts the stereotypes of the mass-cultural hieroglyphic with stereotypical figures in earlier forms of popular art which, "in the spirit of allegory," registered and hyperbolized objective developments. Unlike the character masks of the modern mass media, "the highly stylized types of the Commedia dell'arte," for instance, "were so removed from the everyday existence of the audience that it would not have occurred to anyone to model their own experience after the mask-like clowns" (*GS*, 10, 2:515).

But is this objectifying "spirit of allegory," clearly indebted to Benjamin, not to some extent still present in the hieroglyphics of mass culture, in the very metaphor of hieroglyphics? The reified idiom of mass-cultural products is, after all, also the condition of their critical readability; only as figurations of writing can the naturalized images of mass culture be deciphered, can their "secret code" be cracked. As Adorno and Horkheimer assert in the introduction of *Dialectic of Enlightenment*, echoing Benjamin's programmatic transformation of myth into allegory: "Dialectical thought interprets every image as writing. It teaches how to read in its own features the admission of its falsity so as to deprive it of its power and appropriate it for truth" (*GS*, 3:41; *DE*, 24). The same double vision seems to inform Adorno's approach to mass-cultural hieroglyphics, specifically in the phrase quoted earlier: "As image, this pictographic language is the medium of regression in which producer and consumer collude; as writing, it displays the archaic images of modernity."

Alas, not quite. It is easy to misread this phrase in light of the poststructuralist aura of writing and reading, and I have done so myself by mistranslating the verb, "*zur Verfügung stellen*," as "display" instead of "supply" or "make available." A more adequate translation would therefore be: "as writing, [this pictographic language] supplies the archaic images of modernity," or alternatively, if we read "*der Moderne*" as a dative case, "supplies archaic images to modernity."[20]

There are actually, at least, two kinds of writing, and two kinds of reading, involved in Adorno's notion of mass-cultural hieroglyphics. Indeed, his argument hinges upon the distinction between a literal and a figurative, that is, between a complicit and a critical form of reading.[21] Himself a critical reader, Adorno discerns the emergence of a different type of reading, a mode of enlightened viewer response which amounts to little more than predetermined picture-puzzle solving, based on a shortcircuit between mass-cultural conventions and the consumer's disfigured unconscious.

Adorno's concept of writing is just as ambivalent, and relative to constellations, as his concept of mimesis, to which it is intimately linked. In the context of the culture industry, writing apparently means script in the sense of *Vorschrift* or prescription, a discourse that masks itself in iconic images and familiar sounds. In the context of aesthetic theory, however, writing becomes *écriture*, the nonsubjective, indirect language of modern music and abstract painting. In its renunciation of traditional imitational and even expressive elements, this *écriture* is profoundly historical. Adorno explicitly links the scriptural character of modern art to a "seismographic" capacity, a "breaking through of early mimetic behavior" comparable to physical irritations, by which such art registers the tremors of distant, even future, catastrophes.[22] More generally, Adorno joins writing, and tropes of graphicity such as "cipher" and "hieroglyph," with the character of art as enigma (*Rätsel*). "All works of art are scripts [*Schriften*] . . . that is, hieroglyphic ones whose code has been lost and whose substance [*Gehalt*] not least depends on the fact that their code is missing" (*GS*, 3:189). The enigmatic character of artworks is constitutive and unsolvable; the secret of mass-cultural hieroglyphics, by contrast, translates into a singular meaning—which in turn can be decoded only by the critical reader.

The ambivalence of Adorno's notion of writing may be yet another symptom of the split between his aesthetic theory and the analysis of culture as commodity and industry in the *Dialectic of Enlightenment*.[23] It would therefore make sense that the section on the mass-cultural hieroglyphic does not follow the rhetorical strategy of the culture industry chapter, that is, the pairing of particular aspects of mass-cultural practice with particular concepts of bourgeois aesthetics (such as "*Gesamtkunstwerk*," "catharsis," or the Kantian "purposefulness without purpose") which the culture industry at once mocks and consummates. The opposition between script and *écriture*, between secret code and enigma has to remain implicit, because the absent counterpart belongs to a different register (as well as to a later phase of Adorno's work).

By the same token, however, it could be argued that, especially in Adorno's postwar texts, the distinction between writing as *écriture* and writing as script all too often coincides with the institutional divisions between high art and popular culture. The problem with this linkage is not so much the insistence on an aesthetic dimension (to which I will return), but the way it circumscribes the position of the critical theorist toward mass-cultural phenomena, in particular his relation to the "ordinary" consumers. Notwithstanding the principle of immanent critique, Adorno's attitude toward mass culture involved a notorious gap, if not an unreflected hierarchy between the critical intellectual and the subjects of consumption, the "slow-witted" or "batrachians" (*Lurche*). While it would be foolish to deny Adorno's "mandarin" sensibility, the issue is more complicated. For it raises the question as to the possibility of an alternative discourse on mass culture that is simultaneous receptive and critical, nonelitist and yet not simply "popular." Bound up with this question is the larger one of whether and how mimetic-aesthetic experience can be generalized, that is, democratized, even under the conditions of late-capitalist, electronic media publics. I will return to these questions via a detour through other concepts of film and mass culture as hieroglyphic, with a focus on Derrida and Kracauer.

The comparison between cinema and hieroglyphics appears rather early and frequently in discourse on film throughout the silent era; with the transition to sound, the analogy became less obvious and less opportune. In France, commentators like Victor Perrot celebrated film for its restoration of "humanity's first writing system" (1919) and filmmakers like Abel Gance claimed that the cinema would save the cultural heritage for the future by returning to the ancient Egyptian language of images.[24] In the United States, the poet Vachel Lindsay advertised film as a new "American hieroglyphics" as early as 1915, resuming the fascination with the Egyptian hieroglyph in the writings of Whitman, Emerson, Poe and Thoreau as well as a popular undercurrent ranging from hieroglyphic Bibles to children's books like *Mother Goose in Hieroglyphics*. D. W. Griffith, at home in the tradition of the American Renaissance, was certainly familiar with Lindsay's slogan when he made *Intolerance* (1916), a film that put the hieroglyphic analogy into practice and thus aimed to affiliate itself with this particular tradition in American culture.[25]

In most commentaries during the silent era, the comparison between cinema and hieroglyphics is celebratory, if not apologetic; the underlying concept of hieroglyphics is one of a language of mystical correspondence and visual self-evidence, reincarnated in the new universal language of film. Yet there is another direction of conceptualizing film as hieroglyphic, or ideographic writing in a wider sense. In a famous essay of 1929, Sergei Eisenstein illustrates his argument for "intellectual montage" (the signification of an abstract meaning by juxtaposing two separate visual representations) with reference to the Chinese ideogram and its composition from pictographic elements (which he calls hieroglyphics). During the 1930s, he abandoned this basically constructivist model in favor of a more complex notion of film as ideographic writing based on the psycholinguistic concept of "inner speech," a topic explored by the Bakhtin circle at the time.[26] The analogy between filmic writing and the process of association and figuration in the human mind, a process that mixes images, words, and symbols, entailed an emphasis on the composite character of the cinematic sign, its mixing of figural, graphic, and phonic matters of expression. If the filmic hieroglyph is thus conceived as fundamentally heterogeneous, however, its mode of signification is anything but self-evident, self-identical and universal.

It is in this sense that the hieroglyphic analogy has been revived, in the more recent past, by Derridean film theory.[27] The key text for this endeavor is notably *Of Grammatology* where Derrida traces the suppression of writing in the name of speech through the vicissitudes of the hieroglyph. In particular, he elaborates on the epistemological shift in the conception of the hieroglyphic sign, from the longstanding Western idealization of the hieroglyph as a form of mystical correspondence between sign and referent to the eighteenth-century discovery of the hieroglyph's simultaneously phonetic and nonphonetic mode of signification which enabled the deciphering of the Rosetta Stone. For Derrida, the conceptualization of "the organized co-habitation, within the same graphic code, of figurative, symbolic, abstract, and phonetic elements" emblematizes the moment at which "a systematic reflection upon the correspondence between writing and speech could be born."[28] The hieroglyph assumes a further paradigmatic function for Derrida in his reading of Freud, especially with regard to the pictographic writing of dreams which "exceeds phonetic writing and puts speech back in its place."[29]

Derrida's notion of hieroglyphics is no doubt more complex than Adorno's because, ironically one might say, Derrida historicizes the very concept of the hieroglyph which Adorno assumes as a given. While they converge in the critique of hieroglyphics as a "natural language," Derrida draws more radical conclusions from the irreducible heterogeneity of the hieroglyphic sign. Granting it an indeterminacy and indirection that Adorno reserves only for works of autonomous art, Derrida shifts the question of meaning from the sign to the reader: the hieroglyphic is ultimately not a property of the text but a method and metaphor of interpretation.

As a struggle of interpretations, the history of the hieroglyph exemplifies the indissociable relationship between writing and power. In his reading of Bishop Warburton's 1744 essay on Egyptian hieroglyphs, Derrida focuses on Warburton's contention that hieroglyphics were not originally a sacral, esoteric script but a natural medium for preserving knowledge and civil organization, and that its deflection from common usage came about by a historical and political act of encryption which rendered writing a secret and reserved knowledge in the hands of the priests. While Derrida predictably questions the naturalist origin of the hieroglyph posited by Warburton, he stresses the latter's insistence that the hieroglyph's encryptment came about as a political event or strategy (rather than a divine mystery as earlier accounts would have it). Spinning out the dual figure of priest and hieroglyph, Derrida traces the net that binds writing to the production, circulation and contestation of meaning and knowledge, and both in turn to a "caste" of intellectuals and institutions that ensure "hegemony, whether [their] own or that of special interests."[30] Unlike Warburton, Derrida sees the "crypto-politics of writing" as a necessary and inevitable process, inseparable from the effort to undo the "discriminating reservation." "Whenever a code is inverted, disencrypted, made public, the mechanism of power produces another one, secret and sacred, 'profound.' " Thus writing is never outside or independent of power, just as power cannot be grasped, or indicted, as a unitary and general principle; rather, it is a matter of "struggles and contending forces" that set up and permeate "writings and counter-writings." Nor is any form of writing or power originary. The cryptographic maneuver of intellectuals and politicians "*does not consist in inventing new religions but in making use of the remanence*," Derrida concludes, quoting Warburton, "*in 'taking advantage of those that they . . . find already established.'* "[31]

Such reasoning places Derrida in surprising vicinity with cultural theories indebted to Gramscian notions of hegemony or, closer to the Frankfurt School, with conceptions of the public sphere as a multiple, hybrid and antagonistic horizon such as we find in Negt and Kluge. This strand of Derrida's thinking on the gnoseo-politics of writing, however, seems to have had little impact on Derridean approaches to film and the electronic media. Marie-Claire Ropars-Wuilleumier, for instance, the most eminent Derridean film critic in France, limits her elaboration of "filmic writing" (*cinécriture*) to certain "hieroglyphic texts"—Eisenstein's *October*, films by Resnais, Duras, and Godard—and thus to a canon inspired by literary modernism. On the other end of the spectrum we have Gregory Ulmer's attempt to popularize Derrida in *Applied Grammatology*, a book that celebrates the electronic media in McLuhanesque fashion as the last nail on the coffin of the metaphysics of the "Book": "The pedagogy of grammatology is, finally, an educational discourse for an age of video."[32] In either case, there is hardly any reflection on the institutional parameters of film/video writing (and the hegemonic valorization of image over writing), its contestation within particular public spheres, its imbrication with networks of profit and power. By privileging "graphicity" as such, these adaptations perpetuate, to paraphrase Derrida, the "mystification" of the "singular abstraction," of Writing as much as of Power, "fostering the belief that one can do otherwise than to oppose powers to powers and writings to other writings."[33]

Moreover, Derridean film theory lacks a historical perspective that would relate the emergence of the mass media, as a rather specific form of writing, to the cultural, economic and political transformations associated with modernity or, for that matter, postmodernity—to the emergence of new forms of subjectivity and knowledge, domination and resistance. One could argue that Adorno's indictment of mass-cultural hieroglyphics is just as ahistorical, unspecific and abstract as the Derridean valorization of Writing, and therefore just as inadequate to the tasks of critical media theory and practice. If the object of critique is the culture industry as "system" and totality, there is no space for concepts of cultural difference and contestation and hence no way to conceptualize historical change.

In each paradigm, the hieroglyph functions as an allegory of signification itself: in one case demonstrating the irreducible heterogeneity internal to the sign which undermines fictions of identity, unity, linearity, priority; in the other, rehearsing the script of reification that veils itself in moving images. These tropological structures inform the very styles of reading and reasoning. If catachresis is the master trope of deconstruction, Adorno reasons in figures of paradox and contradiction. For instance: "Every peal of laughter resonates with the blackmailer's threat and the comic types are written characters [*Schriftzeichen*] for the disfigured bodies of the revolutionaries."[34] Or: "The photographic assertion that the trees are green, the sky is blue and that the clouds are moving already turns these images [of nature] into cryptograms of factory chimneys and gas stations"—cryptograms, that is, of a double violation of nature, the industrial one as well as the cultural denial of such disfigurement in the industrial imaging of nature as pure (*GS,* 3:171; *DE,* 149).

From a deconstructionist point of view, such statements flaunt a moral pathos that impairs their analytic claims. But they also illustrate a crucial difference of cognitive interest, not just between Derrida and Adorno but between deconstruction and Critical Theory in a wider sense. If the former seeks to demonstrate the epistemic primacy of language over history, the latter is concerned with the historical inscription of the present, as the juncture of economic, social, political forces that are not outside or before language yet also cannot be explained solely in terms of the problematic of language.[35] The dissociation of language and experience, like the dialectic of writing and mimesis, itself becomes a mark of historicity, linked to the advent of modernity, even if—as in Adorno and Benjamin—modernity is seen as entering into peculiar constellations with prehistory.

The question of the historical place of modernity leads me to my last example, an alternative concept of mass culture as hieroglyphic in the context of Critical Theory. In his articles and reviews of the 1920s and early 1930s, Siegfried Kracauer reads the ephemeral, unnoticed and culturally marginalized phenomena of everyday life as configurations of writing, resorting to scriptural figures such as hieroglyph, "ornament," "rebus," or "arabesque." With his turn to the quotidian and neglected, Kracauer belongs to a larger tradition, related in turn to the philosophical program of "the readability of the world."[36]

In the crisis as which modernity was perceived, this program finds a particular inflection in the work of Jewish intellectuals—Simmel, Benjamin, Bloch, Franz Hessel, to mention only a few—who direct reading skills developed in the interpretation of sacred and canonical texts to the spaces and artifacts of modern urban life, trying to decipher a hidden subtext that is referred to redemption. Like Adorno, Kracauer realized the importance of Benjamin's study on the Baroque _Trauerspiel_ for the contemporary situation, particularly the latter's redefinition of allegory in the framework of _Naturgeschichte_. But Kracauer also insisted that Benjamin's own allegorical method, "the dissociation of immediately experienced unities," would not reach its "detonating" force unless actually applied to the present.[37]

Kracauer's recourse to scriptural metaphors, like his entire emblematic mode of reading, seems initially motivated by an apocalyptic sense of withdrawal of meaning from the world, which blends contemporary theories of alienation and reification (Weber, Simmel, Lukács) with the imagery of Jewish Messianism and Gnosticism.[38] Adorno, reared on the same discourse, was wont to imagine the social reality of reification in images of mortification, rigidification and death by freezing (_Kältetod_)—the most negative form of mimesis. Kracauer, using similar imagery, visualized the effects of reification simultaneously as a process of dissociation, as a "disintegration of the world" (_Weltzerfall_). Once he moved beyond a history of decline, Kracauer saw the fracturing of all familiar relations and shapes increasingly (that is, before 1933) as a chance—to point up the "_preliminary_ character of all given configurations,"[39] to watch the fragments reconfigure themselves, perhaps into something new. The crystallization of the social environment into scriptural figures is no more the "authorless script" of a metaphysical History than it is an invitation to random readings. From the mid-1920s on Kracauer conceives of this process quite concretely in terms of the effects of capitalist rationalization, specifically, the abstraction of human labor and bodies; the progressive detemporalization and discontinuity of perception and experience; and a turn to the "surface," the tendency toward "pure externality" he discerned in the emerging mass culture of entertainment and consumption.[40] Like many Weimar intellectuals, Kracauer welcomed mass culture as a practical critique of the remnants of bourgeois high culture and philosophical attempts to patch up the actual state of disintegration and disorder. The figuration of the "mass as ornament," for instance, which Kracauer observed in musical revues and sports displays, objectivates the "exodus of the human figure from sumptuous organic splendor and individual shape into anonymity" and thus promotes the demise of concepts such as personality and the self-identical subject.[41]

Above and beyond this iconoclastic, allegorizing function, however, the mass ornament remains profoundly ambiguous—as ambiguous as the historical process that it congeals into legibility. On the one hand, the anti-organic tendency of such figurations has a utopian dimension for Kracauer in prefiguring a state in which only those remnants of nature prevail that do not resist reason. On the other, the mass ornament encapsulates the dialectic of capitalist rationality (which points in the direction of the *Dialectic of Enlightenment*): instead of emancipating humanity from the forces of nature, capitalist rationality perpetuates society as mere nature and thus reverts into myth; reproducing forms of economic and social organization that do not include the human being, the process of disenchantment stops halfway, arresting thought in empty abstraction and false concreteness.[42] While the mass ornament achieves a measure of (aesthetic) abstraction and succeeds in inspiring in the spectating mass a measure of spontaneous recognition (of their own reality), its patterns ultimately remain "mute," renaturalized, unpermeated by reason. Kracauer's distress seems to be far less over the parallel between chorus line and assembly line, as is often claimed, than over the "muteness" of the mass ornament, its lack of (self-)consciousness, its inability to read itself. But the answer, as Kracauer asserts here as in other contexts, is not evasion or critical rejection: "the process leads right through the middle of the mass ornament, not back from it."[43]

Not all of Kracauer's scriptural tropes are that clearly defined or decoded in historico-philosophical terms. More often, the figures he traces are writerly attempts to register a multiplicity of phenomena that are as yet unnamed; the very image of the "turn to the surface" is an effort to trope them into legibility. What these phenomena share is an increased focus of perception on the visual, a "primacy of the optical" that Adorno found characteristic—and problematic—in Kracauer's own mode of thinking.[44] It is no coincidence that so many of his essays traverse sites and media of visual fascination: photography, film and movie theaters, hotel lobbies, bars, streets, squares, arcades, department stores, city maps, neon lighting, amusement parks, circus, and variety shows. Visuality itself becomes a cipher of modernity, a trope for the possibility of new configurations that resist a decoding in terms of traditional meanings and values. "In these swarms of light," Kracauer writes of the electric advertisements in the Paris sky, "one can still recognize signs and scripts, but signs and scripts are here relieved of their practical goals, their insertion into the colorful variety has fragmented them into glittering particles which recompose themselves according to different laws than the habitual ones. The advertising drizzle dispensed by economic life congeals into constellations in a strange sky. . . . The elements of a familiar language are assembled into compositions whose meaning can no longer be deciphered."[45]

But the historical process not only brings forth emblems of glamor or excesses of information. What Kracauer understood like hardly any of his contemporaries is how a society that "externalizes" itself in terms of visuality and visibility defines what remains repressed, hidden from public view. In his 1930 essay on Berlin unemployment agencies, he rejects the official debates and interpretations of statistics in favor of a reading of unemployment as an arrangement of social space, as a spatial hieroglyph:

> Every typical space is produced by typical social relations which it expresses without the distorting intervention of consciousness. Everything denied by consciousness, everything studiously ignored participates in the construction of such a space. The images of space [*Raumbilder*] are the dreams of society. Wherever the hieroglyph of a spatial image is deciphered, it displays the foundation of social reality.[46]

Notwithstanding the epistemological optimism, this hieroglyph is anything but unitary. Kracauer maps the dreams of society in terms of the nightmares of those who have been ejected from it. What makes his account so poignant is not only his description of the misery, psychic as well as physical, that congregates in these spaces; it is his tracing of the ways in which society administers that misery, through signs, directions, and instructions that speak the ideology of property and propriety. "This is, after all, the genius of language: that it fulfills orders which it was not given and that it erects bastions in the unconscious" (*GS*, 5.2:189).

As one might imagine, Adorno was rather disturbed by this text and accused Kracauer of having accepted "Benjamin's formula of buildings as the dreams of the collective—just without using the word collective which I can't stand either."[47] Kracauer was quick to distance himself from Benjamin's "romantic" notion of the city as "a dream of collectivity": he was using the word "dream" merely in the sense of uncensored manifestations, as opposed to an "epoch's judgments about itself."[48] And yet, if one reads Kracauer's essays side by side with Benjamin's, one cannot help feeling that Adorno's critique of Benjamin's concept of the "dialectical image" to some extent also aired his misgivings about Kracauer's hieroglyphic readings; the epistemological shortcut he observes in the one could as well be held against the other:

> The notion of collective consciousness was invented to divert attention from true objectivity and its correlate, alienated subjectivity. It is up to us to polarize and dissolve this "consciousness" into a dialectical relationship of society and individual, rather than galvanize it as an imagistic correlate of the commodity character.[49]

One can see how Adorno himself came to use the metaphor of the mass-cultural hieroglyph—as "an imagistic correlate of the commodity character"—in such a singularly condemnatory sense, all the more so since he was increasingly convinced that any existing collectivity could only be false. In the systematic analysis of the culture industry, the hieroglyph epitomized modes of reception and identification assumed to manipulate people other than oneself; its particular meanings, accordingly, were predetermined by a critique of ideology.

Like Benjamin, Kracauer was not primarily interested in a critique of ideology (though he considered that too his task, especially in his work as daily reviewer for the *Frankfurter Zeitung*); his impulse was rather to discern the unknown, as yet untheorized phenomena of modern life with a view to critical redemption. Nor was he primarily concerned with the relation of individual and society or, for that matter, the question of collectivity, at least not from the mid-1920s on. The more pressing issue for Kracauer, I believe, was the fate of the public sphere: the bifurcation of public life into a traditional, dominant sphere of culture and politics, and the emerging horizon of the new media of consumption, of new forms of subjectivity, fantasy, and pleasure—new possibilities of experience, expression, and self-reflexion but also new forms of ideology that easily coalesced with the old myths of authority, militarism, and nationalism. As the dominant public sphere became increasingly repressive and retrograde, Kracauer saw the decisive battle being fought on the deterritorialized grounds of the new media and, accordingly, the task of the intellectual as one of engaging their contradictions, complicities, and missed opportunities. Still, much as this engagement, especially toward the end of the Weimar Republic, mandated a critical perspective, Kracauer never ceased to consider himself a member of the spectating mass—and, as an employee, potentially one of the unemployed—rather than a consciousness apart from, or above, the battleground of publics and counterpublics.

What is at stake, then, in reading the scriptural figurations of modernity is a question of, to borrow Derrida's term, the "gnoseo-politics" of the public sphere. Kracauer's distress over the muteness of the mass ornament has to do with the blockage of its rationalizing force: it fails to include the mass it abstracts in the process of cognition. Just as Kracauer, as I have argued elsewhere, knows himself to be vulnerable to the lure of mass-cultural fascination, he proceeds on the assumption that, in principle, the capacity for critical reading is available to others as well, including those who are the target of—and in practice often complicit with—capitalist manipulation.

The possibility that consumers could relate to the scriptural condensations of modern life in a simultaneously receptive and critical manner distinguishes Kracauer's reading politics from Horkheimer and Adorno's analysis of mass-cultural hieroglyphs and their single-minded customers. For Adorno, the dialectic of mimetic experience and critical reflection that characterizes Kracauer's—and Benjamin's—approach to mass culture is reserved only for works of autonomous art, and only insofar as these works acknowledge their precarious status, the price of their autonomy. To the extent that aesthetic experience becomes the refuge of an individuality alone capable of critique, it runs the risk of functioning as a "discriminating reservation." The problem is not just that this aesthetic double standard led Adorno to hypostasize the opposition between the subject of mass manipulation and critical subjectivity, but that it also prevented him from imagining alternative—and unpredictable—engagements with the hieroglyphics of mass culture; in other words, that he denied the mass-cultural hieroglyph even the potential of indeterminacy and ambiguity that he assumed for the hieroglyphic *écriture* of modern art.

Or did he? Earlier in this essay, I referred to efforts to revise Adorno's position on film and mass culture with recourse to moments in his oeuvre in which he himself crosses the dividing line between aesthetic theory and the critique of the culture industry. Among those moments (which are far more numerous than generally assumed) his 1966 essay "Transparencies on Film" has been singled out as his most systematic attempt to redeem film as an aesthetic medium. In a key passage of that text, Adorno recommends that an aesthetics of film should base itself on a subjective form of experience which it resembles: "A person who, after a year in the city, spends a few weeks in the mountains abstaining from all work, may unexpectedly experience colorful images of landscape coming over or through him in dreams or daydreams." Elaborating on this type of experience, Adorno resumes his earlier comparison of film as writing and film viewing as reading. In its discontinuous movement, he observes, the flow of these involuntary mental images resembles the phenomenon of writing, "similarly moving before our eyes while fixed in its discrete signs." "As the objectifying recreation of this type of experience," he concludes, "film may yet become art. The technological medium *par excellence* is thus intimately related to the beauty of nature [*dem Naturschönen*]" (*TF,* 201).

As Gertrud Koch has shown, the imbrication of mimetic experience with writing permits Adorno to envision techniques of immanent aesthetic construction that would permit film to negate its technologically grounded violation of the *Bilderverbot*; to achieve mimetic expression by filmic means of "enscriptment" (*Verschriftung*) such as montage.[50] However, in light of the problematic of writing I have tried to unfold, this aesthetic redemption leaves crucial questions untouched. While it is an important contribution to theorizing avant-garde and feminist film practice (as Koch suggests), it also reproduces the split between modernist *écriture* and mass-cultural script on another level, by making the possibility of critical difference in cinema a matter of whether and how film can "yet become art."[51]

To make the imbrication of mimesis and writing productive for a theory of cinema and mass culture we need to complicate both terms, writing and mimesis, with the negative connotations they have in the critique of the culture industry. For a film aesthetics that brackets the institutional conditions of production and reception remains an aesthetics of film rather than one of cinema or mass culture. By the same token, however, a cinema and media theory that jettisons the question of aesthetic difference ultimately resigns itself to rationalizing existing practices in the name of reception studies.[52]

To theorize the nature of the aesthetic experience that, to echo Benjamin, people have a right to expect from film, the concept of mimesis needs to be expanded beyond the individualistic bent that characterizes Adorno's notion of experience in relation to art, as in the passage from "Transparencies" cited above. To recall an earlier point, mimesis in its perverted form animates the mass-cultural script not only by the reduction of the image to iconic doubling, but also in the consumers' adaptation to the false image, the reification compulsion operating in the hieroglyphic spell. This form of mimesis, however baleful, is a collective one, grounded in the institution of cinema, its economic origins as much as its public mode of reception. Under the conditions of the culture industry, the collectivity enacted is a mirage, enhancing the false identification of individual and social totality. Yet in "Transparencies," Adorno himself attributes an intrinsic collectivity to film, mediated by the "mimetic impulse" of its movements, which gives it an affinity with music. He even goes so far as to speak of "the constitutive subject of film as a 'we,' " albeit a rather vague collective id/it that lends itself to ideological misuse. "The liberated film would have to wrest its *a priori* collectivity from the mechanisms of unconscious and irrational influence and enlist this collectivity in the service of emancipatory intentions" (Ibid., 203–204). If this entails the possibility of a filmic *écriture* that would give expression to collective experience, then one would also have to conceive of this collective as a plural, heterogeneous term, capable of diverging readings and interpretations. Such pluralization would shift the potential for resistance, which Adorno occasionally grants the isolated, damaged subject, to an intersubjective agency of readings and counter-readings, publics, and counter-publics.[53]

It is not surprising that Adorno's concept of mimesis has been claimed, within the tradition of the Frankfurt School, for a theory of communicative reason, notably by Habermas in his *Theory of Communicative Action* (1982). This adaptation involves removing the category from the language philosophy underpinning the *Dialectic of Enlightenment*—which, in Albrecht Wellmer's words, places mimesis in a position "extraterritorial to the sphere of discursive reason"—and conceptualizing it instead as "a mimetic-communicative dimension *internal* to discursive reason."[54] It also means turning Adorno's utopia of a reconciliation with nature (which pertains to relations within the subject, between subject and object, and among objects) into a regulative principle for the communication *between* or *among subjects*, that is, intersubjective action and the organization of the public sphere. But, as Josef Früchtl and others have cautioned, such adaptation of Adorno's mimesis concept cannot be accomplished without a paradigm shift. Not only was Adorno adamantly opposed to a subjective, let alone intersubjective grounding of reason but, to the extent that he could think of mimesis as an intersubjective relation at all, it was mediated by objective forms of communication, such as the noncommunicative language of art.[55]

From the perspective of a theory of cinema and mass culture, I share these reservations, not necessarily to preserve the purity of Adorno's legacy, but because the communicative inflection of his mimesis concept tends to occlude the relation between mimesis and writing, which I consider one of Adorno's key insights into film. This is not to collapse the two terms: on the contrary, the tension between expressive and constructive elements in filmic *écriture* is essential to preventing their bad convergence in the mass-cultural hieroglyphic. Yet, while the preverbal or, rather, nonverbal qualities of the mimetic may or may not be diametrically opposed to language as speech, they are definitively not outside or other to writing, but part of it. This is important with regard to film and the mass media for two reasons.

One, film and other forms of mass culture have given rise to more and more mediated, deterritorialized forms of *Öffentlichkeit*: publics that crystallize around texts which are always already written, fixed by means of their—indexical and often iconic—technology, and whose dissemination, as commodities, increasingly exceeds the boundaries of local and even national space. These publics can no longer be theorized in terms of an ideal of communication modelled on face-to-face relations, but require a concept of the public that accounts for the profoundly changed organization of social experience.[56] Two, to think of the mimetic as an element of filmic writing implies conceiving of the filmic sign as irreducibly heterogeneous, whether in a Derridean sense or that of inner speech, a heterogeneity Adorno himself stressed when reflecting on the critical potential of silent film versus the practice of synchronized sound. On the level of the public sphere, this corresponds to an irreducibly composite, hybrid make-up of twentieth-century "publicity," its mixing of industrial-commercial, bourgeois and popular, global and local, technologically generated and live elements. According to Negt and Kluge, such volatile mixture makes for unexpected fissures, conjunctures, and alliances—and thus provides the conditions for the formation of counterpublics.

This argument returns us to a question raised earlier, concerning the historicity of Adorno's observations. If his analysis of the hieroglyphic mechanisms of identity captures something about cinema and mass culture during the 1940s and 1950s, how does it help us understand analogous processes in the present? Postmodern culture has not only blurred the divisions between high and popular art, but also replaced the Fordist principles of standardization and homogenization with new strategies of differentiation on a global scale. Whether the diversity of this new culture of consumption will set into play the conditions of a "new cultural politics of difference" (Cornel West),[57] or whether it represents just another, more subtly disguised form of subjection and stabilization, remains to be seen. If we "relativize" Adorno's critique of mass culture as hieroglyphic (in the spirit of Wellmer's proposal for a relativization—not moderation—of his critique of reason),[58] it could help us formulate critical perspectives that would keep both these possibilities in view. Thus the split between mass-cultural script and modernist *écriture* could be mobilized into a stereoscopic vision that spans the extremes of contemporary media culture: on the one hand, an instrument for the ever more effective simulation of presence and relentless reinscription of difference and identity; on the other, a matrix for a postmodern culture of difference, for new, syncretistic forms of experience and unpredictable formations of public life.

Finally, if the split between mass-cultural script and modernist *écriture* today acquires a different meaning, it is not in the name of the foolish assertion that postmodernism has abolished aesthetic distinctions. This shift is indicated, rather, by developments within mass-cultural practices, in particular with the proliferation of video and its impact on cinema—developments that have decisively weakened the reality or doubling effect, film's insistence on its iconic character, that Adorno abhorred. In "Prologue to Television," Adorno himself observed how television deviated from cinematic standards of verisimilitude, speculating that "the public" must be unconsciously aware of the discrepancies: "The suspicion will grow that the reality that is being served up is not what it pretends to be" (*GS,* 10, 2:510). Contemporary film and television practice abounds with examples of such "discrepancies," with highly stylized, ironic, hyperbolic forms of representation, from camp to overt parody and excentric fantasy. To modify Adorno's point about the allegorical quality of the Commedia dell'arte: even if, unlike the latter, television programs purport to relate the everyday existence of the audience, it is questionable whether viewers would *model* their experience after the mask-like characters of soap operas, although they are likely to use them to *interpret* their own lives. However problematic the nexus of media and corporate power remains, the institutional weakening of iconicity would permit mass-cultural hieroglyphics to become *écriture,* to generalize the possibility of mimetic experience and memory within and against the very institutions that promote their reification. This *écriture* may not look like the modernist one theorized by Adorno; it may have many different faces and styles. Its distinction from the mass-cultural script can only be relative, impure and conjunctural; its difference will remain, at any rate, a matter of readings and counter-readings.

ABBREVIATIONS

CI: Theodor W. Adorno, *The Culture Industry: Selected Essays on Mass Culture,* edited by J. M. Bernstein (London: Routledge, 1991).

DE: Max Horkheimer and Theodor W. Adorno, *Dialectic of Enlightenment,* translated by John Cumming (New York: Continuum, 1994).

GS: Theodor W. Adorno, *Gesammelte Schriften,* edited by Rolf Tiedemann (Frankfurt: Suhrkamp Verlag, 1972–).

TF: Theodor W. Adorno, "Transparencies on Film," translated by Thomas Y. Levin, *New German Critique* 24–25, 1981–82, 199–205.

NOTES

1. For a recent example of such rhetoric, see Jim Collins, *Uncommon Cultures: Popular Culture and Post-Modernism* (New York, London: Routledge, 1989). The following is a slightly revised version of an essay published in *New German Critique* 56 (Spring–Summer 1992) and is part of a larger research project which has been generously supported by the Alexander von Humboldt-Stiftung. Unless otherwise indicated, translations are my own.

2. See, for instance, Andreas Huyssen, "Adorno in Reverse: From Hollywood to Richard Wagner" (1983), rpt. in *After the Great Divide: Modernism, Mass Culture, Postmodernism* (Bloomington: Indiana University Press, 1986); Bernard Gendron, "Theodor Adorno Meets the Cadillacs," *Studies in Entertainment,* ed. Tania Modleski (Bloomington: Indiana University Press, 1986); Richard Allen, "The Aesthetic Experience of Modernity: Benjamin, Adorno, and Contemporary Film Theory," *New German Critique* 40 (1987):225–240; Gertrud Koch, "Mimesis und Bilderverbot in Adornos Ästhetik: Ästhetische Dauer als Revolte gegen den Tod," *Babylon* 6 (1989):36–45 (for a slightly revised, English version see *Screen* 34.3 [Autumn 1993]:211–222; Thomas Y. Levin "For the Record: Adorno on Music," *October* 55 (1990):23–47; the quotation is from Fredric Jameson, *Late Marxism: Adorno, or, The Persistence of the Dialectic* (London, New York: Verso, 1990), 7.

3. See Koch and Levin, as well as my introduction to Adorno's "Transparencies on Film," *New German Critique* 24–25 (1981–82):186–198.

4. Koch 39ff.; Adorno, *Ästhetische Theorie, Gesammelte Schriften* (in the following abbreviated as *T* and *GS*), ed. Rolf Tiedemann, (Frankfurt: Suhrkamp, 1970), 7:106, 416, and passim. This is the place to reiterate Kluge's paraphrase on Adorno's iconophobia: "I love to go to the movies: the only thing that bothers me is the image on the screen." Klaus Eder and Alexander Kluge, *Ulmer Dramaturgien: Reibungsverluste* (Munich: Hanser, 1981), 48.

5. Adorno, "Transparencies on Film" (1966), trans. Thomas Y. Levin, *New German Critique* 24–25 (1981–82):199–205, 201 (in the following abbreviated as *TF*).

6. Levin, "For the Record," 35–41; Adorno, "The Form of the Phonograph Record" (1934), trans. Thomas Y. Levin, *October* 55 (1990):56–61.

7. Adorno, "Prolog zum Fernsehen" (1953), *GS,* 10, 2:513–514.

8. Angelo Montani and Giulio Pietranera, "First Contribution to the Psycho-Analysis and Aesthetics of Motion-Picture," *Psychoanalytic Review* 33 (1946):177–196.

9. Cf. Jean-Louis Baudry, "Ideological Effects of the Basic Cinematic Apparatus," and "The Apparatus," rpt. in Theresa Hak Kyung Cha, ed., *Apparatus* (New York: Tanam Press, 1980); Christian Metz, *The Imaginary Signifier* (Bloomington: Indiana University Press, 1982); Teresa de Lauretis and Stephen Heath, eds., *The Cinematic Apparatus* (London: Macmillan, 1980).

10. "Das Schema der Massenkultur," *GS,* 3:332; for a recent (not entirely reliable) translation by Nicholas Walker, see Adorno, *The Culture Industry: Selected Essays on Mass Culture,* ed. J. M. Bernstein (London: Routledge, 1991), 53–84; (in the following abbreviated as *CI*).

11. *GS,* 3:33–34, 41; *Dialectic of Enlightenment,* trans. John Cumming (New York: Seabury, 1972) 17–18 (in the following abbreviated as DE). The sentence containing the distinction between language and "a mere system of signs" is omitted from the translation, DE 41.

12. Karl Marx, *Capital* (New York: International Publishers, 1975) 1:74–75; on the structure of this Marxian trope see also W. J. T. Mitchell, *Iconology: Image, Text, Ideology* (Chicago, London: University of Chicago Press, 1986) ch. 6.

13. This observation ties in with Horkheimer and Adorno's analysis of the peculiar fetishism of enlightened consumption which I discuss below. The critique of this kind of active reading has implications for attempts, such as David Bordwell's, to counter psychoanalytic views of the spectator as passive and manipulated with a conception of the spectator as an active participant "in creating the illusion," patterned on the "hypothesis-checking" unitary subject of cognitive psychology. Bordwell, Janet Staiger, and Kristin Thompson, *The Classical Hollywood Cinema* (New York: Columbia University Press, 1975), 7, 9; Bordwell, *Narration in the Fiction Film* (Madison: University of Wisconsin Press, 1985), 30. Horkheimer and Adorno's skepticism regarding consumerist expertise should also make us think twice about the *type* of knowledge generated by studio and fan publicity, discourses frequently touted by Cultural Studies as "resistant" practices, as well as the vexed issue of Hollywood's "self-reflexivity."

14. Josef Früchtl, *Mimesis: Konstellation eines Zentralbegriffs bei Adorno* (Würzburg: Königshausen und Neumann, 1986); Michael Cahn, "Subversive Mimesis: T. W. Adorno and the Modern Impasse of Critique," in *Mimesis in Contemporary Theory,* ed. Mihai Spariosu (Philadelphia, Amsterdam: John Benjamins, 1984), 27–64; see also Susan Buck-Morss, *The Origin of Negative Dialectics* (New York: Free Press, 1977), 87ff.

15. In its opposition to contemporary advocates of realism or naturalism, Adorno's concept of mimesis converges with Benjamin's, specifically as developed in "The Doctrine of Similarity" (1933), trans. Knut Tarnowski, *New German Critique* 17 (1979):65–69, and the second version of this essay, "On the Mimetic Faculty" (1935), trans. Edmund Jephcott, in *Reflections* (New York: Harcourt Brace Jovanovich, 1978). Like the latter, though with significant distinctions, Adorno opposes any surface resemblance of representation in favor of what Benjamin called a "non-sensual similarity," a mimetic "affinity" achieved only through materially specific techniques of determinate negation; like Adorno, Benjamin associated this nonsensual similarity with the phenomenon of writing.

16. *GS,* 7:169ff., 424–425 and passim.

17. Cahn 32–33; Adorno, *GS,* 7:39, 201ff. and passim.

18. "Das ist der Triumph der Reklame in der Kulturindustrie: die zwanghafte Mimesis der Konsumenten an die zugleich durchschauten Kulturwaren." *GS,* 3:191; in the translation, *DE,* 167, the word "mimesis" is dropped from the text.

19. *GS,* 3:333–334; in the English version, *CI,* 82, the word "Laxativ" is translated as "cosmetics."

20. The subsequent sentence further eliminates any possible ambiguity in the word "writing" here: "As magic that has lost its enchantment, they [the archaic images of modernity] no longer convey any secret but are models of a behavior that corresponds as much to the gravitation of the total system as to the will of those in control" (*GS* 10, 2:514).

21. There is a third notion of reading in Adorno, on which he comments in conjunction with Hegel's writings, a "kind of gestic or curve-like writing" that makes the signifying function withdraw in favor of a mimetic one which compels the reader to retrace the thoughts with a "speculative ear as if they were musical notations." "Skoteinus oder Wie zu lesen sei," *GS,* 5:353ff.

22. "Über einige Relationen zwischen Musik und Malerei," *GS,* 16:628–642. Adorno explicitly adopts the term *écriture* from Daniel-Henry Kahnweiler to whom the essay is dedicated.

23. This is what Jameson argues, quite convincingly, in *Late Marxism* (107–108, 145), although I think he underrates the complex and problematic ways in which the concept of mimesis brackets both projects. See Albrecht Wellmer, *Zur Dialektik von Moderne und Postmoderne: Vernunftkritik nach Adorno* (Frankfurt: Suhrkamp, 1985); *The Persistence of Modernity,* trans. David Midgley (Cambridge: MIT Press, 1990).

24. Abel Gance, "Le temps de l'image est venu" (1927), cited in Christian Metz, *Language and Cinema,* trans. Donna Jean Umiker-Sebeok (The Hague: Mouton), ch. 11.

25. Vachel Lindsay, *The Art of the Moving Picture,* 2d. ed. (New York: Liveright, 1970); John T. Irwin, *American Hieroglyphics: The Symbol of Egyptian Hieroglyphics*

in the American Renaissance (Baltimore: Johns Hopkins University Press, 1983); Miriam Hansen, *Babel and Babylon: Spectatorship in American Silent Film* (Cambridge: Harvard University Press, 1991), ch. 8.

26. Sergei Eisenstein, "Beyond the Shot," *Writings 1922–34*, ed. and trans. Richard Taylor (London: BFI; Bloomington: Indiana University Press, 1988) 140ff.; on the concept of "inner speech" see essays by Stephen Heath and Paul Willemen in *Cinema and Language*, ed. S. Heath and Patricia Mellencamp, American Film Institute Monograph Series, 1 (Frederick, MD: University Publications of America, 1983).

27. Marie-Claire Ropars-Wuilleumier, *Le texte divisé* (Paris: Presses Universitaires de France, 1981); "The Graphic in Filmic Writing: *A bout de souffle*, or the Erratic Alphabet," *Enclitic* 5.2/6.1 (1981–82):147–161; Gregory Ulmer, *Applied Grammatology* (Baltimore: Johns Hopkins University Press, 1985); and, more recently, Tom Conley, *Film Hieroglyphs: Ruptures in Classical Cinema* (Minneapolis, Oxford: University of Minnesota Press, 1991). Also see D. N. Rodowick, "The Figure and the Text," *Diacritics* 15.1 (1985):34–50; Peter Brunette and David Wills, *Screen/ Play: Derrida and Film Theory* (Princeton, NJ: Princeton University Press, 1989), ch. 4.

28. Jacques Derrida, *Of Grammatology*, trans. Gayatri Chakravorty Spivak (Baltimore: Johns Hopkins University Press, 1976), 81.

29. Derrida, "Freud and the Scene of Writing," in *Writing and Difference*, trans. Alan Bass (Chicago: University of Chicago Press, 1978), 218. For Freud's own use of the term, see *The Interpretation of Dreams, Standard Edition* 4:277–278; 5:341; and "The Claim of Psychoanalysis to Scientific Interest," *SE*, 13:177.

30. Derrida, "Scribble (writing-power)," trans. Cary Plotkin, *Yale French Studies* 58 (1979):117–147, 124. Warburton's Essay is the French translation of a part of the second edition of *The Divine Legation of Moses demonstrated* (London, T. Cooper 1742).

31. "Scribble" 140, 138, 117ff., 147.

32. Ulmer, *Applied Grammatology* 265. I am aware that this is a caricature of Derridean film theory, highlighting an idealistic tendency in the adaptation of the hieroglyphic analogy; for a critique of Ulmer, see Brunette and Wills, 125.

33. See n. 31 above, 117, 144.

34. "Schema," *GS*, 3:335; *CI*, 82. This statement is part of Adorno's desparate argument with Benjamin who valorized the collective laughter inspired by slapstick comedy and Disney cartoons as an "antidote," a "therapeutic detonation" of technologically created mass psychoses and violent tensions; see earlier versions of the Artwork Essay, *Gesammelte Schriften* 1, 2:462; 7:376ff.; Adorno, letter to Benjamin, March 18, 1936, trans. Harry Zohn, in Fredric Jameson, ed., *Aesthetics and Politics* (London: New Left Books, 1977), 123ff.

35. This difference gets lost, for instance, in DeManian readings of Benjamin that tend to reduce the promiscuous and contradictory quality of Benjamin's texts to a single, doctrinal core—a tendency rehearsed in de Man's own ingenious reading of "The Task of the Translator," *Yale French Studies* 69 (1985), 25–46.

36. The phrase is from Hans Blumenberg, *Die Lesbarkeit der Welt* (Frankfurt: Suhrkamp, 1986). Also see Benjamin's programmatic invocation of Hofmannsthal's phrase: "to read what was never written." *GS,* 1, 3:1238.

37. Siegfried Kracauer, "Zu den Schriften Walter Benjamins" (1928), *Schriften* 5, vol. 2, ed. Inka Mülder-Bach (Frankfurt: Suhrkamp, 1990), 123; trans. forthcoming in Thomas Y. Levin, ed. and trans. *The Mass Ornament* (Cambridge, MA: Harvard University Press, 1994). On the tension between violence and redemption that characterizes this secularized Jewish reading program, see Anson Rabinbach, "Between Enlightenment and the Apocalypse: Benjamin, Bloch and Modern German Jewish Messianism," *New German Critique* 34 (Winter 1985):78–124.

38. Miriam Hansen, "Decentric Perspectives: Kracauer's Early Writings on Film and Mass Culture," *New German Critique* 54 (1991):47–76; also see Inka Mülder, *Siegfried Kracauer—Grenzgänger zwischen Theorie und Literatur: Seine frühen Schriften 1913–1933* (Stuttgart: J. B. Metzler, 1985), 19ff.

39. "Die Photographie" (1927), *Schriften* 5, 2:97; trans., in *Mass Ornament*.

40. "Cult of Distraction" (1926), trans. Thomas Y. Levin, *New German Critique* 40 (1987):91–96. On Kracauer's own "turn to the surface," see Inka Mülder-Bach, "Der Umschlag der Negativität: Zur Verschränkung von Phänomenologie, Geschichtsphilosophie und Filmästhetik in Siegfried Kracauers Metaphorik der 'Oberfläche,'" *Deutsche Vierteljahresschrift* 61.2 (1987):359–373. Also see David Frisby, "Deciphering the Hieroglyphics of Weimar Berlin: Siegfried Kracauer," in Charles W. Haxthausen and Heidrun Suhr, eds., *Berlin: Culture and Metropolis* (Minneapolis and Oxford: University of Minnesota Press, 1991), 152–165.

41. "Das Ornament der Masse" (1927), *Schriften* 5, 2:64; "The Mass Ornament," trans. Barbara Correll and Jack Zipes, *New German Critique* 5 (Spring 1975):67–76. New trans. forthcoming, *Mass Ornament*.

42. Obviously, Kracauer had a slightly more optimistic view of the Enlightenment than Horkheimer and Adorno, as he did of the emancipatory possibilities of capitalism. Thus, against romantic anticapitalists who seek to overcome alienation by restoring a *Gemeinschaft*, he insists that the problem with capitalism is not that "it rationalizes too much but *too little*" (*Schriften* 5, 2:62).

43. *Schriften* 5, 2:67.

44. Adorno, "The Curious Realist: On Siegfried Kracauer" (1964), trans. Shierry Weber Nicholsen, *New German Critique* 54 (Fall 1991):163.

45. "Lichtreklame," *Frankfurter Zeitung* 15 January 1927, *Schriften* 5, 2:19–20. Also see his article "Internationaler Tonfilm?," *Europäische Revue* (Januar–Juni

1931), rpt. in Karsten Witte, ed., *Schriften* 2 (Frankfurt a.M.: Suhrkamp, 1984), 469–473, where he emphasizes the tension between readability and undecipherability in the "languages" of silent versus sound film.

46. "Über Arbeitsnachweise: Konstruktion eines Raumes" (1930), *Schriften* 5, 2:186.

47. Adorno, letter to Kracauer, July 25, 1930; quoted in Mülder, *Kracauer,* 181.

48. Kracauer, letter to Adorno, August 2, 1930; quoted ibid.; "Ornament," *Schriften* 5, 2:55; "Mass Ornament," 67.

49. Adorno, letter to Benjamin, August 2, 1935; trans. Harry Zohn, in Jameson, ed., *Aesthetics and Politics,* 113 (trans. modified).

50. Koch (n. 2, above), 44. It should be added here that, notwithstanding his own endorsement of montage in *Composing for the Films*, Adorno remained skeptical as to the aesthetic scope of the procedure; see *TF,* 203 and *AT, GS,* 7:90, 231–234.

51. In a lecture on "Art and the Arts," delivered the same year as "Transparencies," Adorno himself calls the "question as to whether or not film is art," a "helpless" question, inasmuch as film (and here Adorno invokes Benjamin's Artwork Essay) has paradigmatically challenged that distinction. Yet, unlike Benjamin, Adorno concludes: "Whereas, by its immanent laws, film tries to rid itself from any resemblance to art—as if that contradicted its own aesthetics—by its very rebellion it becomes and expands art. This contradiction, which film is prevented from acting out in a pure form by its dependency on profit, is the vital element of all truly modern art," "Die Kunst und die Künste," (1967), *GS,* 10, 1:451–452. That the reservation is phrased in economic rather than technological terms may make it less absolute: if film cannot act out the contradiction "purely," it could just as well do so in an impure form.

52. To the extent that Cultural Studies approaches have privileged the area of mainstream reception to the exclusion of alternative practices and a critique of production they could be said to repeat, on the level of analysis, the negative-mimetic adaptation to reified conditions that Adorno observed in the consumers themselves.

53. Huyssen, (n. 2 above), 26.

54. Wellmer, (n. 23 above), 97.

55. Früchtl, (n. 14 above), 190ff., 235–240.

56. See Hansen, "Foreword," Oskar Negt and Alexander Kluge, *Public Sphere and Experience* (Minneapolis: University of Minnesota Press, 1993).

57. Cornel West, "The New Cultural Politics of Difference," in Russell Ferguson, Martha Gever, Trinh T. Minh-ha, Cornel West, eds., *Out There: Marginalization and Contemporary Cultures* (New York: New Museum of Contemporary Art; Cambridge, London: MIT Press, 1990), 19–36.

58. Wellmer, (n. 23 above), 99.

Chapter 5

Adorno, Modernity, and the Sublime

Albrecht Wellmer

I.

"Art is true to the degree to which it is an illusion of the non-illusory," (*Warheit hat Kunst als Schein des Scheinlosen*) Adorno says in a crucial passage of his *Aesthetic Theory*.[1] Somewhere else he says: "The question of the truth of art comes into view when a non-existent is seen to rise as if it were real" (*AT*, 122). And: "Art's Utopia, the counterfactual yet-to-come, is draped in black. It goes on being a recollection of the possible with a critical edge against the real: it is a kind of imaginary restitution for that catastrophe, which is world history; it is freedom which did not come to pass under the spell of necessity and which may well not come to pass ever at all [. . .] Aesthetic experience is the experience of something which spirit does not have yet either of the world or of itself. It is the experience of the possible, as promised by its impossibility. Art is the promise of happiness, a promise that is constantly broken" (*AT*, 196).[2]

These sentences express the core of Adorno's interpretation of artistic beauty in the horizon of a philosophy of reconciliation. The truth content of the artwork consists in its becoming the "mirror writing" (*Spiegelschrift*) of an absolute which is veiled in black, the mirror-writing of reconciliation. By the same token, art is the illusion of the nonillusory (*Schein des Scheinlosen*). This illusion of an epiphany of the absolute is part of a "genuine aesthetic experience" with regard to "authentic works of art" (AT 152): the truth content of art is inseparable from its creating a semblance of reconciliation. The constitutive relationship between truth and semblance (illusion) determines two aporetic constellations, which according to Adorno are characteristic for modern art: the first of these aporetic constellations concerns the relationship between art and philosophy; the second one concerns the conditions of the possibility of art itself: that is, the possibility of art under conditions of "completed negativity" of the modern world.

Adorno points to the first of these aporetic constellations, the one concerning the relationship between art and philosophy, when he says: "The truth of discursive knowledge is without veil—but for this reason discursive knowledge does not have its truth; the knowledge embodied in art has its truth, but as something incommensurable to it" (*AT,* 183).[3] That which aesthetic experience, which loses itself in an emphatic "now," *has,* is the intuition of the world in the light of redemption; however, caught in the illusory character of artistic beauty, aesthetic experience does not understand what it experiences: it does not understand the oblique reference of the artwork to something not present, to a nonbeing; in short, aesthetic experience does not understand the semblance to which it succumbs. For this reason philosophical reflection must come to the aid of aesthetic experience; only philosophical reflection can inform aesthetic experience about what it is that it experiences; only philosophy can decipher the mirror-writing of the Absolute in the semblance of artistic beauty and thereby articulate the truth content of the artwork which *as* a truth content is incommensurable to the immediacy of aesthetic experience. And yet philosophy also cannot really articulate in words what the truth content of aesthetic experience is; bound to the medium of "identifying" conceptual thought, philosophy cannot express the Absolute—the idea of reconciliation—it can rather only point toward the Absolute—something which has no being and yet is not Nothing—it can only try to make this Absolute indirectly, ex negativo, visible as the vanishing point of all that can be said and thought. In contrast to Kant, for Adorno not only the representation and the cognition of the Absolute, but the mere thought of the Absolute has become problematical. Although Adorno follows Kant in maintaining that each thought, that the very idea of truth contains an unavoidable, if only oblique reference to the Absolute—and therefore to the idea of reconciliation—at the same time he shows (notably in his *Negative Dialectics*) that this unavoidable reference point of all thinking cannot itself be thought, that it defies the possibilities of conceptual articulation. The Absolute is that which has no being and yet, as the unavoidable presupposition of all thinking, is not nothing. Metaphysics for Adorno is the thinking of the Absolute as that which has being in the fullest sense; what Adorno postulates as "solidarity with metaphysics in the moment of its downfall" at the end of *Negative Dialectics* is a thinking of the Absolute in the moment where it has become unthinkable, a thinking of God and his kingdom after the death of God. The absolute *is not*; here Adorno agrees with Nietzsche. But only at the price of a self-negation of spirit could we avoid trying to think the unthinkable as that which is yet to come into being: here Adorno sharply disagrees with Nietzsche. If, however, philosophy—for the reasons indicated—cannot really spell out the Absolute, the idea of reconciliation, and therefore the truth content of the artwork, then philosophical reflection is in need of aesthetic experience as much as aesthetic experience is in need of philosophical reflection: philosophy and art need *each other* if their common truth content is not to be lost. Both are related to each other as concept and intuition are in Kant's philosophy; except that now the relationship between concept and intuition concerns the sphere of ideas, that is, that Absolute which defies the faculty of intuition as much as it does the faculty of conceptual thought. Only in the aporetic constellation of mutual reference from aesthetic experience to philosophical reflection and from philosophical reflection to aesthetic experience can the weak traces of a nonillusory Absolute (*eines scheinlos Absoluten*) become visible.

The second of the two aporetic constellations of which I spoke is one inherent in artistic production itself. The constitutive relationship between truth and semblance in the work of art has, for Adorno, increasingly become an *inner-aesthetic* problem of modern art. For the sake of its possible authenticity, modern art is compelled to come to grips with this problem as an aesthetic problem; this problem, one might say, determines the law of artistic progress in the period of modernity. The aspect of blindness, of illusion, of a lack of comprehension, which philosophical reflection uncovers in the immediacy of aesthetic experience, increasingly comes to trouble artistic production as an *aesthetic* problem from the inside, as it were. For the sake of truth artistic production is driven toward a revolt against aesthetic illusion, while aesthetic illusion, at the same time, remains the condition of the possibility of art, a condition which art cannot escape without negating itself. Truth *and* semblance (illusion) signify the two poles of what Adorno calls the "*Stimmigkeit*" (the aesthetic coherence) of the artwork; however, truth and semblance, at the same time, militate against each other. Great art wants to be true, as Adorno insists; aesthetic coherence (*Stimmigkeit*) is possible only under the condition of the artwork's being true—therefore art must turn itself against aesthetic illusion, against everything which is illusory about it. Nevertheless art tries in vain to get rid of this illusory character, since what constitutes art as art—aesthetic coherence, in more traditional terms: beauty—is inseparable from an element of semblance, from its illusory character. This, according to Adorno, is the antinomy of modern art which, at the same time, determines the laws of artistic progress.

II.

Through its reference to the Absolute, which is "veiled in black", modern art for Adorno becomes an art of the sublime. This has been repeatedly pointed out by commentators, notably by W. Welsch in a recent publication.[4]

"The sublime," Adorno says, "which Kant reserved for nature, has after Kant become a historical constituent of art itself. The sublime draws the line of demarcation between art and what later was called 'arts and crafts.'" (*Kunstgewerbe*) (*AT,* 281). In contrast to Welsch, however, I do not believe that the category of the sublime signifies a strand of Adorno's philosophy which stands in opposition to his philosophy of reconciliation; I rather believe that it occupies a central place *within* his aesthetics of reconciliation: this aesthetics, as an aesthetics of reconciliation, is, at the same time, an aesthetics of the sublime. This also means that the "beautiful" and the "sublime" are not opposed to each other in Adorno's aesthetics in the same way as they are in Kant's; they are rather opposed to each other as the two poles of aesthetic coherence (*Stimmigkeit*) are, of which I have spoken, that is, as semblance and truth. Instead one might say that the sublime signifies for Adorno a condition of the possibility of what under conditions of modern art production might still be called "beauty"; the sublime becomes a *constituent* of artistic beauty. Prima facie this idea of Adorno's appears to have a strong affinity to J. F. Lyotard's rehabilitation of the category of the sublime, the decisive difference being that in Adorno the category belongs to a context of a philosophy of reconciliation, while for Lyotard it is part of a postmodern philosophy which is directed *against* the idea of reconciliation. Things are not so simple, though. For although I believe Lyotard is right if he tries to take the category of the sublime out of the context of a philosophy of reconciliation, Adorno's procedure is in one decisive respect more convincing than Lyotard's, since he does not simply try to rehabilitate the Kantian category of the sublime, but, at the same time, shows how the "internal composition" of this category has changed since the premises of Kant's critical metaphysics were put into question. Adorno develops his theory of the sublime in modern art through a critique of Kant's critical metaphysics. I think that any attempt to give a "postmetaphysical" account of the sublime in art has to take this critique seriously. Only in this way will it be possible to save the productive implications of Adorno's idea, while taking them out of the context of a philosophy of reconciliation. The idea of reconciliation—this much is true about "postmodernist" critiques of utopian and totalizing modes of thinking—indicates a strong metaphysical residue in Adorno's philosophy. The difficulty is that this metaphysical residue in Adorno's philosophy is intimately connected with many of his best insights. For this reason a "deconstructive" reading of Adorno, which would also be a "reconstructive" reading, is not easy to achieve. In a sense the coordinate system of Adorno's philosophy has to be set in motion as a whole. I have once spoken of the need for a "stereoscopic" reading of Adorno. The following reflection may be understood as an attempt toward such a stereoscopic reading of Adorno, focused upon his category of the sublime.

It is of basic importance for Adorno's interpretation of the sublime that this sublime—as I have indicated above—could become a constituent of modern art only through a change of what Adorno called its "internal composition" (*AT*, 283, trans. false). "Transplanted into art, the Kantian definition of the sublime expands beyond its original confines" (*AT*, 281). By way of a comment, Adorno refers to the famous dictum of Napoleon, that there is only a step from the sublime to the ridiculous:

> Originally this phrase was meant to puncture stylistic grandeur and inflated reproduction that was unable to fulfill what it promised and which therefore opened the door to the pedestrian and the comic. Actually, the offenses pierced by that dictum take place in the concept of the sublime itself. Sublimity was supposed to be the greatness of man as a spiritual being and as nature's tamer. However, once the experience of the sublime turns out to be man's self-conscious realization that he is natural, the internal composition of the category of the sublime changes [translation altered]. Even in the context of the Kantian formulation, sublimity was tinged by the nulllity and transience of man as an empirical being that was to have thrown in relief the eternity of his universal destination, i.e. spirit. If, however, spirit is reduced to its natural scale, then the destruction of the individual can no longer be said to be positively sublated (negated) in his spiritual nature [translation altered!]. With the triumph of the intelligible in the individual, who spiritually withstands death, man puffs himself up, pretending to be absolute as a bearer of spirit after all. This makes him appear comical. Advanced art rewrites tragedy as comedy, commingling the sublime and play. (*AT*, 283)[5]

The idea of spirit being itself a part of nature signifies the basic thrust of Adorno's critique concerning Kant's distinction between the empirical and the intelligible (noumenal) world. Adorno has developed this critique in particular in the "Meditations on Metaphysics," the last part of his *Negative Dialectics*. Kant's conception of the noumenal, Adorno shows here, is incompatible with a conception of spirit which is bound to individuated beings, and therefore to the body and language of human beings. This is Adorno's version of a critique of metaphysics, by which his thought corresponds with much that has been written on this theme from Nietzsche to Derrida. The concept of the noumenal, the concept of a noumenal Ego is here revealed as a phantasmagoria of conceptual thought; not only being without empirical reality, but already inconsistent as something merely thought. It is here that, for Adorno, the moment of truth within the empiricist, naturalistic side of the Enlightenment can be found. What Adorno will nevertheless attempt to save from within the concept of the Noumenal is the utopia of an unreconciled spirit; but the Absolute, which would have to include within itself the ideas of freedom, immortality, and a kingdom of ends, is, as I have already emphasized, an aporetic concept for Adorno, "to be thought only negatively."

The "remembrance of nature in the subject" which the *Dialectic of Enlightenment* had already postulated as a figure of reconciliation between spirit and nature, assumes an ambiguous meaning in the later Adorno's critique of Kant's critical metaphysics. This "remembrance" no longer only signifies the emphatic hope for a resurrection of nature in the medium of spirit, but also, at the same time, man's being "surrendered" (*verfallen*) to nature, that is, the fragility, finitude, and non-utopian materiality of spirit. It is the latter of which Adorno is speaking in the passage I quoted above. While for Kant the noumenal realm of spirit was exempt from the fragility and mortality of the natural side of human existence, this noumenal realm is now revealed as being itself affected by the conditions of fragility and mortality. That which really surpasses the sphere of a finite spirit—which is bound to the body and language of human beings—is not a noumenal world in the sense of Kant; it is rather a natural world devoid of meaning; an abyss, as it were, which opens itself in the midst of the human world as it is disclosed through language, an abyss within the world of language, of linguistic meaning. Adorno rehabilitates the category of the sublime in the spirit of Beckett. The experience of the fragility of the empirical subject, of the impotence of its (his/her) imaginative or practical faculties vis-à-vis the greatness and power of nature—for Kant the essential "negative" ingredient in the feeling of the sublime—is now transformed into the experience of the fragility of the noumenal subject itself. Adorno is alluding to the lawsuit against this noumenal Ego in Beckett's "Endgame with subjectivity" when he points to the convergence of tragedy and comedy, of the sublime and the playful in advanced art. But how can a new concept of the sublime, how can the sublime of modern art result from the destruction of the polarity of the empirical and the noumenal subject, which for Kant was the source of the feeling of the sublime? Adorno gives two answers to this question. With his first answer he remains within the horizon of a philosophy of reconciliation; the second answer is based on a postmetaphysical interpretation of modernity. Both of these answers are related to each other through the concept of "withstanding" (*Standhalten*) in which the pathos of Kant's concept of the sublime still resonates. For Adorno, actually, the two answers signify only two different aspects of one and the same answer; a stereoscopic reading is needed to make two different answers recognizable in this single one.

According to the first answer—the answer given from within the aesthetics of reconciliation—the place of the modern sublime would be the tension, grown to unmeasurable proportions, between the reality of the modern world and a utopia veiled in black, between a state of complete negativity and a state of reconciliation. Here, one might say, it is the work of art which, by uncompromisingly taking the negativity of the world into its own complexion, withstands the superior power of a meaningless reality in the name of an Absolute that has no being yet, that is, in the name of a reconciled spirit. As Adorno puts it: "If works of art are to survive in the context of extremity and darkness, which is social reality, and if they are to avoid being sold as mere comfort, they have to assimilate themselves to that reality. Radical art today is the same as dark art: its basic color is black" (*AT,* 58). That Adorno is speaking here of the sublime in modern art becomes obvious in the following quote: "Radical negativity, as bare and non-illusory as the illusion promised by the sublime, has become the heir of the sublime" (*AT,* 284).

In contrast, Adorno's second answer to the question posed above locates the sublime of modern art in the field of tension between what Adorno has called the "explosion of metaphysical meaning"[6] in modernity, on the one hand, and the emancipation of the subject, on the other. The two poles of this field of tension signify two different aspects of what Adorno has thematized as the "progress of consciousness" in the modern world. What is at stake here is not a dialectics of subjectification and reification, that is, the Dialectics of Enlightenment; it is consequently not the polarity of complete negativity and reconciled spirit. What is at stake is rather the price which modern individuals who have emancipated themselves from tradition and convention have had to pay for their emancipation. What is at stake is the internal connection between the emancipation of the modern subject and the loss of objectively binding systems of meaning and of world interpretation. It is to this second answer of Adorno's that I want to refer in what follows. For the moment I shall neglect the fact that Adorno himself has tried to establish a conceptual link between his two perspectives on the modern sublime, that is, between the explosion of metaphysical meaning and the realization of a state of complete negativity in the modern world. I have criticized this conceptual "short circuit" in Adorno's philosophy in another place.[7] Adorno did not develop an adequate conception of the intersubjectivity of language which would have allowed him to connect the disenchantment of the world—the explosion of metaphysical meaning—with a gain in communicative rationality. As soon, however, as one allows for the possibility of such a connection—arguments for such a connection can be found particularly in the work of Habermas— the two answers given by Adorno prove to be rather different. The second answer, understood correctly, does not imply the first one, which rests on the premises of a philosophy of reconciliation; the second answer rather contains the elements of a postmetaphysical conception of the sublime through which Adorno's *Aesthetic Theory* opens itself up to an interpretation in terms of a theory of communication. To be sure, such an interpretation will ultimately also shed new light on Adorno's first answer, that is, on his conception of a state of complete negativity: The state of complete negativity that corresponds to an Absolute which is veiled in black, is the state of the world after the explosion of metaphysical meaning, a world which is cut off from reconciliation; but this being cut off from reconciliation, if seen in the right way, is not the catastrophe of spirit which Adorno saw in it. It rather signifies the condition of a spirit that has come to recognize itself as finite; a spirit that has come to recognize both delight *and* terror, both reconciliation and disunification as the colors of its own finitude and that recognizes and unfolds its potentials as that of a communicative reason on the basis of this insight. Retrospectively, Adorno's critique of "identifying thought" could be read as an exercise of such a new discovery and unfolding of finite spirit as communicative reason.

III.

Adorno spoke of a "transplantation" of the sublime into art; he dates this move toward a specifically modern art at the end of the eighteenth century (*AT,* 280). The invasion of the sublime into art puts art into an "increasing conflict with taste," and therefore with standards of beauty in the sense of an idealist aesthetics. Three determinations of the sublime in art, through which the work of art violates the desiderata of taste, are repeatedly pointed out by Adorno: an energetic, a structural, and a "dynamic" characteristic. All three determinations actually touch upon aspects of the sublime in the sense of Kant.

From an energetic point of view the sublime appears as shocking, shattering, moving, overpowering. If one understands the moment of aesthetic experience as one of a condensed presence, through which the temporal continuum of ordinary experience is suspended, the experience of the sublime may be characterized by an additional element of violence, a violence which bursts into the interior space of aesthetic distance, shaking up, dislodging, or disquieting the subject, generating a tremor, a vertigo, loosening the confines of the experiencing ego. To be sure, this happens *under conditions* of aesthetic distance: the shaking up of the subject, its stepping out of itself is part of an *aesthetic* experience only where the subject, at the same time, remains with itself in a state of utmost concentration: "If the ego wishes to look beyond the walls of the prison that it is, it needs not distraction, but utmost concentration. This concentration prevents tremor from being regressive even though it is spontaneous behavior. In his aesthetics of the sublime Kant faithfully depicted the strength of the subject as being a precondition for the sublime" (*AT,* 347–348).

Structurally speaking, the sublime in art is the negation of flawless or "harmonious" aesthetic synthesis, that is, of a perfect interpenetration of sensuous and spiritual elements in the sense of the idealist conception of beauty. It is a negation of formal beauty, that is, of measure, of balance, of flawless unity, of harmony, in short: of beautiful semblance (*des schönen Scheins*). "It is the scars of damage and disruption," Adorno says, "that guarantee the authenticity of the modern work of art" (*AT*, 34).[8] Through these scars of disruption a reality comes to appearance in the work of art which no longer corresponds to the desiderata of a closed universe of meaning. The contingent, the meaningless, the absurd, that which is excluded from the world of linguistic meaning, the disparate, the heterogeneous, the nonsensical other side of a world that is disclosed through language—all this modern art takes up in "unmitigated negativity," as Adorno would say, making visible the cracks and fractures in the texture of reality, the "fissure which runs through the soul and through the world as a whole," as Monika Steinhauser has put it with reference to the paintings of Caspar David Friedrich.[9] Art opens itself toward an experience of the world which no longer understands itself through the anticipation of a totality of meaning, but rather faces the presence of what is non-sense, the abyss of meaninglessness within the world of sense. Art illuminates the darkness of the world not by reconciling the contradictions but by articulating them, putting them into words, as Adorno says (*AT*, 282), by "communicating the incommunicable." By withstanding and articulating the darkness, the fragility and the horror of existence, by making it communicable, modern art becomes an art of the sublime, transforming the negativity of the world into a source of aesthetic delight.

> Actually, the ideal of darkness does no more and no less than postulate that art properly understood finds happiness in nothing except its ability to stand its ground. This happiness illuminates the sensuous phenomenon from the inside. Just as in internally coherent works of art spirit penetrates even the most impermeable phenomena, redeeming them sensuously, as it were, so blackness too—the antithesis of the fraudulent sensuality of culture's facade—since Baudelaire has a sensual appeal. There is more pleasure in dissonance than in consonance—a thought that metes out justice to hedonism, measure for measure." (*AT*, 59)

From a dynamic point of view, finally, referring to the internal logic of artistic progress, the invasion of the sublime into art signifies a tendency toward a progressive "spiritualization" of art. This tendency toward spiritualization corresponds to an increasing incorporation of "a-semantic" materials and layers of experience into art, to a tendency toward *de*-spiritualization, as it were. To put it in different terms: the opening up of art toward that which is farthest from spirit, from the world of linguistically articulated meaning, its opening up toward the meaning*less* other side of the world of linguistic sense, signifies, at the same time, an increasing reflexivity of art and an increasing importance of its constructive elements. In these reflexive and constructive aspects of modern art the strength of an emancipated subject manifests itself which has become capable of surrendering itself, unprotected by aesthetic conventions, to the experience of the nonidentical for the sake of aesthetically objectifying it. Spiritualization therefore also means an increasing tension between the spiritual and the nonspiritual, between the constructive and the mimetic, between the reflexive and the barbaric or chaotic elements in modern art. For Adorno, modern art, in its individual productions as well as in the variety of its productions as a whole, is a dynamic process going on between these two extreme poles, the spiritual and the non- or antispiritual.

> Rimbaud's postulate of radical modernity is met by an art which moves in the field of tension between *spleen et ideal*, between spiritualization and obsession with anti-spirit. The primacy of spirit in art and the lifting of old taboos are two sides of the same coin [. . .] Spiritualization is not brought about when art propagates ideas. It comes to pass when it has sufficient strength to penetrate non-identical layers (of experience), layers that are inimical to the sphere of ideas. This is one of the reasons why that which is socially tabooed and excluded from communication has tempted artistic genius time and again. The new spiritualization in art prevents the continued sullying of art by the true, the beautiful, and the good—the ideals of philistine culture. (*AT*, 137–138)

From the perspective which Adorno is suggesting, modern art indeed appears as the aesthetic realization of what Kant meant by the concept of the sublime: "Kant's theory of the sublime, sketched in reference to the beautiful in nature, anticipates that spiritualization which only art can actualize. What is sublime in nature, Kant says, is the autonomy of spirit in the presence of a prepotent empirical world, and that autonomy comes into its own only in the spiritualized work of art" (*AT*, 136–137). Adorno locates the autonomy of spirit not in a noumenal ego, but in the authentic work of art and therefore, as I shall try later on to show, implicitly in a structure of intersubjective communication—of which the work of art is a part—that is, in a world of *finite* spirit. What will have to be shown yet is how such a seemingly paradoxical transformation of a Kantian idea can be justified.

What has usually been missed in interpretations of Adorno's aesthetics is that Adorno's theory of modern art—in contrast to basic theses which were developed in the *Dialectic of Enlightenment*—construes an *internal* connection between the emancipation of the modern subject, the decay of objectively binding aesthetic traditions and conventions, and an increasing self-consciousness of spirit as being a part of nature. The progress of consciousness, through which the end of metaphysics is indicated, also means a progress of spirit toward a heightened self-awareness of itself as finite and as part of nature. Modern art is the remembrance of nature in the subject, tied to the strength of a subject which is capable of sustaining the experience of its own finitude as spirit.

> The unleashing of elemental forces was identical with the emancipation of the subject and hence with the self-consciousness of spirit. This self-consciousness qua nature spiritualized art. By the same token, art's spirit became a reflection on the naturalness of spirit. The more art assimilates a non-identical, that which is directly contrary to spirit, the more it must become spiritualized. Conversely, spiritualization incorporated something into art that had always been taboo, because it was ugly and repulsive to the senses; the sensually unpleasant has an affinity to spirit. (*AT,* 280–281)

A peculiar relationship between the invasion of the sublime into modern art and the emancipatory impulses of modernity becomes visible here. The opening up of art, its constant revolt against its traditional limits, which Adorno analyzes under the heading of its spiritualization, corresponds to that opening up of ordinary discourses, which Habermas has diagnosed in the communicative thawing ("making fluid") of traditions, and in what he calls the communicative "rationalization" of the life world. Moreover: both of these processes are geared to a process of increasing individuation, by which alone that decay of socially binding meaning systems can be compensated for which is the precondition for the emancipation of the subject—in a moral and cognitive as well as in an aesthetic sense. With respect to the generation of aesthetic meaning the spiritualization of art, therefore, also signifies the need for an "increasing individuation" of the single work of art. The experimental, constructive and reflexive traits of modern art are the medium of such an individuation for Adorno, as the experimental, discursive and reflexive traits of a "rationalized" life world are the medium of *social* individuation for Habermas. In the subtext of Adorno's *Aesthetic Theory*, precisely at those points where Adorno analyzes the invasion of the sublime into modern art, the contours of an alternative to the main thesis of the *Dialectic of Enlightenment* become visible. According to this alternative thesis the dialectical relationship between subjectification and reification would have to be replaced by an internal relationship between aesthetic, cognitive, and moral-practical enlightenment. Modern art, modern science, and philosophy, and a modern form of democracy based on universalist moral principles move into a relationship of mutual correspondences and mutual complementarity: aesthetic, cognitive, and moral-practical enlightenment become visible as different spheres into which the emancipatory impulse of modernity has differentiated itself. Contrary to the main thesis of the *Dialectic of Enlightenment* this differentiation process cannot *as such* be interpreted as a victory of instrumental reason. If, however, the spiritualization of art and therefore the emancipation of the subject in Adorno's sense are related to changes in the communicative relationships *between* the individuals in a post-traditional society, the assimilation of new layers of experience and of reality through modern art, layers of experience and reality which Adorno describes as being "inimical" to spirit, may be seen as carrying a potential for opening up the communicative relationships between the individuals as well their relationships to themselves: an opening up toward the meaningless, tabooed, socially excluded, and heterogeneous aspects of their own world. The emancipation of art could then be related to a possible communicative opening up of social relations as well as of the self-relation and self-understanding of the individuals: not as prefiguring a utopia of reconciliation, but as a medium as well as a manifestation of that progress of consciousness which Adorno related to the invasion of the sublime into modern art.

The three characteristics of the modern sublime which I find in Adorno's account jointly signify a tendency of art toward its self-transcendence under conditions of its autonomy. As far as artistic techniques are concerned, this tendency implies a constant drive toward innovation, through which the production of art communicates with capitalist commodity production. "Explosion is one of its invariable traits," says Adorno. "Antitraditional energy becomes a voracious eddy that consumes everything" (*AT,* 34). The compulsion to innovate, however, has a non-technical aspect as well: time and again modern art is driven to transcend the limits of the existing *concept* of art, as it has been sedimented in those of its previous productions which have been culturally assimilated and thereby "neutralized." Great art never was merely beautiful semblance; under conditions of its autonomy, however, art must try to organize that surplus by which it had always transcended the desiderata of taste and formal beauty, by its own aesthetic means. Art must revolt against its own concept, question the limits of its autonomy, as long as it wants to redeem those emphatic claims which it must maintain, lest the demarcation lines between art and mere entertainment, or between art and what has been called "arts and crafts," are to be blurred. The avante-garde movements of modern art have often misunderstood this felt necessity toward a self-transcendence of art as a demand for a sublation of art into life. Even Adorno still thought—and it is exactly here that his philosophy turns into a philosophy of reconciliation—that "the historical perspective of the end of art is the idea of each single work of art" (*AT,* 91).

But Adorno knew that an "end" of art, instigated by art itself under existing historical conditions, could never imply a final sublation of art = reconciliation, but rather merely art's adaptation to that which is. He thus insisted, *rebus sic stantibus*, on the autonomy of art as the condition for art's continuing "methexis in reconciliation." Yet the alternatives here seem to be in themselves false ones: we can no more interpret the necessity of a selfovercoming of art from the perspective of a final reconciliation than we can regard it at all meaningfully as an imperative for the self-overcoming of art in the context of life. It would rather be a question of thinking art's impulse toward transcendence together with the autonomy of art; not as an impulse that aimed toward a magical transformation of society as a whole, but rather an impulse by means of which that potential peculiar to art, a potential for an ever-renewed magical transformation of the world, can be kept alive. And if this impulse toward transcendence cannot aim toward an absolute beyond, toward a world in a state of redemption, then this means that transcendence and immanence, negation and affirmation, must be thought together within it: overcoming and transformation of the world as the self-transcendence and self-affirmation of a finite spirit.

If one stops taking this self-transcendence of art as a *final* self-transcendence, then Adorno's thesis of an irreconcilable opposition between authentic art and mass culture in advanced modernity loses its philosophical foundation as well. For Adorno's comparisons "authentic art = negation = truth," and "mass culture = affirmation = falsehood" hide a moment in which philosophy predetermines aesthetic criticism; a moment that does not stand up to full aesthetic experience. An art whose impulse toward transcendence doesn't aim toward some wholly other, or reconciliation, but turns itself back critically and affirmatively toward the historical world from which it arises, will also no longer be able to accept any fixed boundaries between "higher" and "lower" culture. That these boundaries (which in reality are often diffuse, variable and porous in the advanced modern) also constitute the difference between what is potentially aesthetically successful and what is a priori an aesthetic failure, between the authentic and the inauthentic, between truth and falsehood—this too is a historical-philosophical assumption that cannot be validated through aesthetic experience. Thus these boundaries can also become a provocation, for advanced art, to transgress them.[10]

However, art's movement of self-transcendence can have no other aim than that of keeping alive art *as* autonomous: only as autonomous can art still generate that surplus by which for moments the world in a state of disenchantment may be re-enchanted again, by which the dried riverbeds of ordinary communication may be flooded and the meaning-structures of the everyday world be shaken up. Given what I have said so far, it is tempting to characterize this surplus of art in terms of the sublime as contrasted to the merely beautiful; in terms of a spiritual element in contrast to the merely sensual pleasing; in terms of a shocking or shaking impact of art in contrast to that which is merely tasteful. However, as is well known, Kant's conception of artistic beauty already contains such a surplus over a merely formal conception of beauty. Artistic beauty as an expression of aesthetic ideas does not coincide in Kant's aesthetics with the beautiful in the sense of the analytic of taste. "Spirit"—*Geist*—is already that category through which Kant distinguishes artistic beauty from what is merely tasteful. Even the idea of communication of the incommunicable, of the representation of the unrepresentable, as it becomes for Adorno—and after Adorno for Lyotard—the characteristic of the sublime in art, is already implied in Kant's idea of artistic beauty. Moreover, there seem to be good reasons why it is that for Kant, as far as artworks are concerned, the concept of beauty retains its priority over the concept of the sublime: Works of art, as being made, are neither without limit nor without form; and they also are not objects of actual fear. Whatever may be called sublime in works of art, such works, as limited and formed "objects," are subject to conditions under which aesthetic delight will be, in the first place, a delight in the specific sensuous configuration as presented by the artwork, and therefore a delight in its beauty. Even for Adorno the category of the beautiful retains its primacy inasmuch as for him the creation of the artistic sublime is tied to the condition of aesthetic coherence: the sublime is a modification, an intensification of the beautiful, not its actual negation as in Kant. As a last step in our considerations we should therefore ask more specifically, by what arguments Adorno's reference to Kant's conception of the sublime might be justified.

IV.

I have claimed before that Adorno tries to rehabilitate the category of the sublime in the spirit of Beckett. Beckett's *Endgame*, as interpreted by Adorno, is the aesthetic objectification of the explosion of metaphysical meaning, that is, "an aesthetic construction of meaninglessness." Such an aesthetic construction of meaninglessness for Adorno is an act of withstanding the negativity of the world, and therefore a paradigm of the sublime. Prima facie therefore the reference point of the sublime in modern art is not an Absolute which cannot be represented (i.e., an Absolute in the Kantian sense), but the disappearance of the Absolute, the death of God. In two well-known formulations Nietzsche has related the sublime to the "horrible" and the "unintelligible":[11] this corresponds in Baudelaire to the image of the abyss. The horrible, the unintelligible, the abyss: these words no longer signify an overpowering, threatening and infinite nature, which under the gaze of the intelligible subject is then reduced to small proportions; they rather signify a natural world which even encompasses the intelligible subject and the noumenal world of pure reason. The abyss is an abyss of the meaning*less* in the midst of the world of linguistic meaning. This abyss signifies a negative Absolute, Nothingness, the empty place, as it were, which was left by the Absolute of metaphysics. As already in the theology of St. Paul, for Adorno the name of this negative absolute is death. Death as something ultimate is the crisis of meaning; as a crisis of metaphysical meaning it is, at the same time, the crisis of all linguistic meaning: by the explosion of metaphysical meaning all the conditions are put into question, which are constitutive of the life of linguistic meaning; conditions through which the life of linguistic meaning is connected with the ideas of truth, of reason, and of autonomy. It is precisely this Nietzschean perspective which Adorno adopts and which, at the same time, he rejects as unbearable. Through this double gesture of affirming and rejecting a Nietzschean perspective, Adorno becomes a philosopher of reconciliation. As he puts it dramatically in the *Negative Dialectics*: "If death were that absolute which philosophy in vain tried to conjure positively"—here, of course, Adorno is referring to Heidegger—"everything is nothing; all that we think, too, is thought into the void, none is truly thinkable."[12] For Adorno this means, as emphasized above, that withstanding the negativity of the world is only possible in the name of an Absolute, which, although it is veiled in black, is not Nothing. Between Being and non-Being of the Absolute there remains an infinitely narrow crack through which a glimmer of light falls upon the world: light from an Absolute, which is yet to come into being. And what holds for the Absolute, equally holds for the individual Ego; its fragility and illusory character (*Nichtigkeit*) is not to be the last word. The word I is the name of a utopian hope. Nothing existing corresponds to this hope; only in the state of redemption would individuals be justified to say "I" to themselves. This is the aporetic constellation in which the sublime finds its place in Adorno's aesthetics of reconciliation.

What remains of this concept if we cut off the philosophy of reconciliation that forms the crown of Adorno's thought; if we cut through the roots through which this thought nourishes itself from a missing Absolute? There is a polarity that is constitutive of the sublime in all its variants; a productive tension between a constitutively threatened, overburdened ego, and an ego that affirms itself, with pleasure, precisely in these experiences of fragility, horror, and vertigo. Kant interpreted this polarity as that between the empirical and the intelligible ego. Concerning art at least, it is nevertheless easy to see that this Kantian sense of an intelligible ego doesn't require the idea of an Absolute to make this polarity conceivable. In the successful aesthetic articulation of negativity, of the "power of the negative," subjects have an immediate experience of their own power of articulation, communication, and world-formation; a power that stands *in opposition to* this power of the negative. *This* is why the experience of the negative can transform itself into aesthetic pleasure. Nietzsche already saw it in this way: in the successful artistic articulation of the meaningless and the gruesome, horror transforms itself into aesthetic pleasure. And in essence Adorno sees it the same way: the pleasure of the sublime is the happiness of the act of withstanding; the communication of the incommunicable. The idea of reconciliation falls out of this equation. The category of the modern sublime does not require the idea of reconciliation; it's rather Adorno's radical concept of negativity that makes reconciliation into its correlate. Adorno's opposition to Nietzsche is a matter of ethics, not aesthetics. Nietzsche understood his own destruction of metaphysics also as a destruction of the ideas of the true and the morally good. This is where Adorno opposes Nietzsche: at the end of *Negative Dialectics* he postulates a "solidarity with metaphysics at the moment of its fall" in the name of just these ideas. But his attempt at a critical redemption of metaphysics leaves Adorno hostage, in a peculiar way, to the premises of Nietzsche's destruction of metaphysics. For the sake of the idea of truth and of the right life, and so to speak in a gesture of helpless protest, he must maintain against Nietzsche that the historical reference to a place of reconciliation beyond history, is, despite everything, the truth of metaphysics; it was against this that Nietzsche had maintained, with good reason, the argument that this place of reconciliation beyond history could be nothing other than Nirvana. In the end, this comes down to a pair of false alternatives: both thesis and antithesis, Nietzsche's antimoral affirmation of finitude as well as Adorno's negativist recourse to theology, remain bound up in the problematic premises of the modern philosophy of subjectivity. Only in overcoming this philosophy can we find a place beyond metaphysics for Kant's concept of the intelligible; and only in this way can we also overcome the false alternatives which emerge in Adorno's opposition to Nietzsche. I will return to this point in a moment.

But what does this have to do with the problem of aesthetics and the sublime? Here the question becomes how the aesthetic subject, who undergoes the experience of the sublime, stands in the world of communicatively shared meaning. Kant's response is clear: in the feeling of the sublime, subjects sense their freedom as moral subjects. Nietzsche and Adorno see in this a metaphysical illusion or, what amounts to the same thing, a bourgeois ideology. Only their conclusions are different: while Nietzsche parts company with the ideas of truth and freedom, Adorno tries to rescue them as utopian hope. This is the false alternative that I spoke of earlier; namely the alternative of aestheticism or messianism. It is a false alternative concerning the meaning and the status of the aesthetic, and hence the place of art within modernity. Therefore, we cannot explain the concept of a modern sublime, or the place of the sublime in aesthetic modernism, until we have resolved and moved beyond this false alternative. This brings me back to the question of what place can be found beyond metaphysics for what Kant thought in the concept of the intelligible.

In a certain sense, I think, Adorno was right to search for a place for the Absolute, for the intelligible Ego, between Being and non-Being. But the subject-object dialectic here permits a third moment only the idea of a *future* Being. Kant had already (prior to every critical metaphysics) convincingly determined this place between Being and non-Being as that of *practical* Being: There "is" freedom in the world, insofar as we are capable of acting under the idea of freedom. This being of freedom does not describe a state of reconciliation as much as it describes the mode of being of the world of meaning disclosed through language, which must remain inaccessible to objectifying cognition in a strict sense, and which can only appear to it as a nonbeing. To be sure, in Kant's philosophy this fruitful idea remains enmeshed in the conceptual presuppositions of the philosophy of consciousness; only in recent philosophy—I am thinking above all of Heidegger, Wittgenstein, and the American pragmatists—do we find the presuppositions for both the reformulation and generalization of this Kantian idea, through a philosophy of language. According to this idea—formulated in a particularly clear form in Habermas—the being of linguistic meaning, of freedom, of truth, of reason, is a *performative* being, one that only constitutes itself in the performative attitude of linguistically communicating subjects, and only maintains itself in them. Habermas has characterized this performative being of language as a network of validity claims, assumptions and relations of recognition that are constitutive for linguistic communication. We cannot communicate linguistically without acknowledging one another as beings capable of speech and action; conversely, it is precisely this mutual recognition as beings capable of speech and action that is constitutive for our capacities for speaking and acting. To this belongs the exchangeability of the perspectives of I and "Thou": only in the medium of recognition through others can I—as the Other of the Other—return to myself, understand myself as an I to whom rationality is attributed and who is held accountable for my actions. We cannot, moreover, communicate linguistically without raising mutual validity claims which, through their own meaning, are simultaneously context-dependent and context-transcendent; which therefore are unconditioned *in* their contextuality, directed, one could say, toward an ideal—in the sense of an unlimited—communication community.

We can clarify the performative being of linguistic meaning with the example of the understanding of utterances and texts and of the relation between meaning and validity. This is the field of study wherein modern philosophy of language —in Wittgenstein no less than in someone such as Gadamer—the critique of the objectivistic misconception of the being of linguistic meaning was first initiated in the philosophy of language. Gadamer's thesis concerning the moment of application in understanding, as well as Wittgenstein's elaborations of the meaning of words through their use in language, refer to the performative Being of linguistic meaning: There is such meaning only from the perspective of speakers, who come to an understanding *with* one another *about* something and *in* language, so to speak from out of a practical perspective that is oriented toward validity. Linguistic meaning is formed and preserved in the success and failure of linguistic communication. Thus there are no external criteria of such success or failure that stand apart from the performative being of language, but rather only the internal correctives of linguistic praxis itself: the success of linguistic communication must prove itself beyond its own context and from out of the perspective of a third, that is, in the context of life, just as much as in the forum of an (in principle) unlimited communication community. Through the idea of truth, a critical standard is built in to the world of linguistic meaning; a critical standard, however, that means neither an ideal Being beyond language nor an ideal form of linguistic understanding, but rather one that describes nothing other than the self-transcending force of a reason that is embodied in a respective language. What we presuppose in the performance of linguistic communication—the possibility of coming to understanding and the transparency of meaning—must not be misunderstood as the prefiguration of a "final" understanding, a meaning that has become perfectly transparent, or a final reconciliation. This misunderstanding is metaphysics: an objectivistic misinterpretation of the performative Being of linguistic meaning; perhaps also—so Derrida sees it, at any rate—a transcendental illusion that burdens the life of linguistic meaning.

The performative Being of linguistic meaning is the sphere of that which Kant named the Intelligible. This realm of the Intelligible—if we wish to continue to use the Kantian expression—is in fact a realm beyond nature, insofar as by "nature" we understand objectifiable Being in Kant's sense. At the same time, however, it is also a part of nature, because it is bound to the intersubjectivity of finite, "natural" beings.

The performative Being of spirit, and therefore the sphere of the Intelligible, is finite, limited by death. It lacks the messianic power to illuminate the darkness of the world as a whole or to "sublate" the experiences of contingency, of moral or existential meaninglessness, of existential failure, of irresolvable conflict, or of the fragility of the subject and of all intersubjective relationships in a higher or "meta"-meaning. The intelligible subject only has being as an empirical subject, fragile even in its subjectivity and in its moral character, threatened by death and without hope for redemption.

Nevertheless this *empirical* subject—as an empirical subject—only exists as an individuated I inasmuch as it has grown into the "intelligible" world of linguistic meaning and sustains itself in this world: it is exposed to the demands of reason and morality which are constitutive of its being a subject of speech, and from which it can never completely withdraw without jeopardizing the conditions of the possibility of its empirical existence as an individuated I. What Kant called the sphere of the Intelligible is not a sphere of being outside and above the empirical world; it is rather a structural feature of that empirical world into which human beings are born, in which they live their lives and into which they disappear again: the intersubjective, public world of speech and action which is opened up through language. Humans are thus actually citizens of two worlds: it is only that the intelligible world, that is, the public, intersubjective world of linguistically disclosed meaning is embraced and surrounded by the world of nature, one could say, with Heidegger, "towered through" (*durchragt*) by the earth. The "earth" here should stand for the sensible (*Sinnliche*) within linguistic meaning, the sensible ground of meaning (*sinnliche Boden des Sinns*) just as for the Other of meaning, the abyssal of meaning. The other of meaning—Nature—is the ground and the abyss of the meaningfully disclosed world (*sinnhaft erschlossenen Welt*).[13] Nature itself has the double character of the redemptive and the abyssal. As abyss of meaning, however, it is a perpetual threat to the world of communicatively shared meaning, the mark of its fragility.

If one wanted to stick to a concept of the sublime which is still conceptually related to the Kantian idea as well as to its reinterpretation by Adorno, I think its place would be here: the opposition, the polarity, the irresolvable tension which gives rise to the feeling of the sublime would be one in the intelligible subject itself: namely the tension between the experience of an abyss of meaninglessness or non-sense, through which the subject of speech becomes aware of its own fragility, on the one hand, and on the other hand the subject's resistence to the superior force of negativity, through which the subject is able to sublate the experience of its own negligibility within the world of communicatively shared meaning and, in this manner, lifts itself out of its negligibility. The place of the sublime would not be in the opposition between the empirical and the intelligible I, not in the opposition between sensibility and reason, but rather in an opposition within the intelligible I itself, which is at once both a nullity and sublime.

In the scars of disintegration and disruption, which according to Adorno are the marks of authenticity in modern art, the artwork expresses the truth that the world can no longer be understood as a totality of meaning. By doing it aesthetically, however, being a medium of a reflexive delight, the artwork, at the same time, brings the colors of the world of communicative meaning to glow. And by transforming the fragile, broken-off, and abysmal characters of the world of meaning into aesthetic sense, the artwork illuminates this world, communicating the noncommunicable. The subjects of aesthetic experience are, after all, the ordinary subjects of a common world of speech and action. If for a moment they step out of the temporal and the meaning-continuum of this world, they will also return to this world; what happens to them aesthetically, happens to them also as subjects of a communicative praxis, which in turn will be affected by aesthetic experience: an experience which has the power to illuminate, shake up, transform and enlarge the world of communicatively shared meaning. Art is part of the world of meaning, a part through which this world opens itself up to its borders and abysses, remembrance of nature in the subject; by transforming the terror of what is unintelligible into aesthetic delight, it widens, at the same time, the space of communicatively shared meaning.

However, if the modern sublime is no longer understood in the light of an anticipated redemption, it becomes questionable whether authentic modern art can be equated with an art of the sublime. Actually, the interplay of ecstatic and contemplative aspects which is characteristic of genuine aesthetic experience is not necessarily tied to the condition that the world of art sensuously represent and exorcise the "unintelligible as the horrible," to use Nietzsche's phrase. Communication of the incommunicable, representation of the unrepresentable are rather characteristics of art through which art can deal with all possible aspects of our experience of the world. The disclosing, presencing, and transforming power of art is manifested in its ability to gather, condense and transform those traces of sense and non-sense which are scattered through our ordinary experience, to objectify the ephemerous and fleeting moments of this experience, to say what resists being said, to make visible what has never been seen and to make audible what has never been heard. In this sense one might certainly say that art is concerned with the obverse side of that world of meaning which at any given time is disclosed through language. However, that other side of discursive reason, the abyss of meaning, is not only the unintelligible as the horrible, but also nature as a source of delight beyond all meaning. In the abyss of meaninglessness which opens up in the midst of the world of meaning happiness is waiting as well. The terror and the delight of finitude do not exist one without the other; in this Nietzsche was right against Adorno. To be sure, Adorno was right against Nietzsche in maintaining that the public world of speech and action, that the world of communicative praxis must become hell if the web of relationships of mutual recognition is torn apart. This is a possibility which we can never exclude; the only power which can prevent this possibility from coming true is the power of reconciliation which is embodied in the world of meaning *in spite of* its fragility: a power of reconciliation which today can only maintain and renew itself in the institutions and habits of post-conventional, democratic forms of life. Adorno, however, since he construed the state of the modern world from the vantage point of Auschwitz, failed to identify those powers of reconciliation which, after the explosion of metaphysical meaning, can alone prevent that the whole world is formed in the image of Auschwitz: the hope for redemption, the hope for a coming absolute, devalues all *possible* reconciliation. Reconciliation, however, or that which we can think of as possible reconciliation, is not without disunification: Adorno accepted this truth of Hegel and Hölderlin only as a truth about art; for this reason he could understand aesthetic dissonance only as the virtual negation of real dissonances, as a "withstanding negation" through which modern art for him became an art of the sublime.

If, in contrast, one tries to reconstruct Adorno's concept of the modern sublime in the light of the internal connection between the explosion of metaphysical meaning and the emancipation of the subject, the thesis can no longer be maintained that the basic color of modern art is black. To be sure, the arts in an age of postmetaphysical modernity can no longer conform to an idea of beauty which was meant to be the "sensuous shining forth of the idea", which was meant to embody a reconciliation of contradictions, a higher Meaning beyond ordinary meaning. In this sense the sublime may be a constituent of all modern—or postmodern—art. If the sublime is understood in this way, however, the basic color of authentic art does not need to be black— no more than a life without the hope for an ultimate redemption means despair. That "the sublime converges with play" in the aesthetic construction of the meaningless, as Adorno says, can be understood in another sense than Adorno's, who relates this thought to the black comedy of Beckett. It might, for example, mean that in art the play of the world comes to appearance, that the space of history is transformed back into the space of nature, in such a way that the abysmal character of linguistic meaning is rendered experiencable not just in its negativity, but in its productivity as well. The experience of such an art could also be the ecstatic experience of a *transgression* of meaning: art as the imitation of natural beauty. Within the tradition of modern music there is a line of development that connects Debussy with Stravinsky, Messiaen and Ligeti, a line of development which Adorno—because of his preoccupation with the German-Austrian tradition of dynamic-expressive constructivisim—was never quite sure how do deal with. The deeper reason for this might be that Adorno held firm to a Hegelian conviction concerning music, according to which music is rooted in the expressive vocal gesture of human speech.[14] However, it is characteristic of the music of this other traditional line that in it, to speak with Hegel, it is not the "sphere of subjective interiority" that expresses itself tonally, not the subject, but rather the things are brought to expression in sound, and the world emerges as a sound-space. As opposed to the finality of a subject-centered temporality, a no longer finalized object-like character of art moves colors, rhythmic complexities, and the spatiality of music into the foreground; the natural space of history is made audible, and music tends toward the imitation of natural beauty— even if it is a mathematically-technically generated "natural beauty," like the "fractals" in the case of Ligeti.[15] And yet this music satisfies all the desiderata of modernism in Adorno's sense as well: it is highly constructive and individuated both in its language and its technical procedures, and it has opened up entirely new levels of musical experience and material, in particular those from non-European cultures. Moreover, the lines of demarcation between these two traditions of modern music have long become blurred; I have distinguished between them above all because Adorno tended to exclude one of these two from the canon of modern art. Places like this show that in the end the aesthetics of negativity is bound up not just with philosophical blinkers, but with aesthetic ones as well. Other examples—as in Adorno's notoriously distorted relationship with jazz and film—make the same point.

Of course, the idea of an imitation of natural beauty in the work of art is Adorno's own. One might be tempted to say that all the elements of a postmetaphysical aesthetics of modernity are assembled in Adorno's work, only in an order that is distorted by the perspective of a philosophy of reconciliation. Adorno's aesthetics is a hesitation, to speak in popular terms, at the threshold of postmodernism; in more serious terms, at the threshold of a postmetaphysical conception of modernity. This aesthetics is still superior to all postmodern aesthetics. However, it can be made fruitful today only if it is resolutely read against the grain; pushed beyond that threshold where it hesitates: the threshold of a postmetaphysical modernity. This would be a modernity that recognized in the fall of metaphysics not just a loss but also an emancipation: the liberation from the illusions and the terror of a somehow objectively finalized, all-encompassing Meaning; a modernity that would *need* metaphysics the less, the more it would have preserved and negated (*aufgehoben*) the truth of metaphysics in the structures of its worldliness.

NOTES

1. Theodor W. Adorno, *Aesthetic Theory* (London and New York: Routledge and Kegan Paul, 1984), 191. (In what follows I refer to *Aesthetic Theory* as *AT*.)

2. Translation changed.

3. Translation changed.

4. Wolfgang Welsch, "Adornos Ästhetik: eine implizite Ästhetik des Erhabenen," in C. Pries ed., *Das Erhabene* (Weinheim: VCH, Acta Humaniora, 1989).

5. Translation changed.

6. "Noten zur Literatur," in *Gesammelte Schriften*, vol. 11 (Frankfurt/Main: Suhrkamp, 1974), 282.

7. Cf. "Truth, Semblance, Reconciliation," in A. Wellmer, *The Persistence of Modernity* (Oxford: Polity Press, 1991).

8. Translation changed.

9. Monika Steinhauser, "Im Bild des Erhabenen," in *Merkur* 487–488, September–October 1989, 824.

10. This much is legitimate in the postmodern questioning of the boundaries between "higher and lower" art, between the avante-garde and mass culture.

11. F. Nietzsche, *Werke* vol. 1, ed. K. Schlechta, (Darmstadt: Wissenschaftliche Buchgesellschaft, 1960), 49, 238.

12. Theodor W. Adorno, *Negative Dialectics* (New York: Seabury Press, 1973), 371.

13. Christoph Menke-Eggers (in *Die Souveranität der Kunst*, Frankfurt: Suhrkamp 1988), relates the double figure of the "ground-abyss" (*Grund-Abgrund*) to the *beautiful* ("The beautiful that we experience both as ground and as abyss of our efforts of aesthetic understanding," 167). This is connected to the thesis that "the aesthethic experience of negativity . . . brings the subversion of the possibility of comprehensible experience itself to experience" (240). Aesthetic experience itself signifies the crisis of meaning. My difference with Menke-Eggers' brilliant reflections concerns the construction of the relationship between aesthetic negativity and communicatively shared meaning.

14. Cf. Georg Wilhelm Friedrich Hegel, "Vorlesungen über die Ästhetik III," in *Werke*, Bd. 15 (Theorie-Werkausgabe) (Frankfurt a.M., Suhrkamp 1970), 144ff., 149–152.

15. Cf. Denys Boulaine, "Stilisierte Emotion. György Ligeti im Gespräch," in Musik-Texte (March 1989), 28–29. Denys Boulaine, "Geronnene Zeit und Narration. György Ligeti im Gespräch," in *Neue Zeitschrift für Musik* #49, (May 1988).

Chapter 6

Kantian Snapshot of Adorno: Modernity Standing Still

Wilhelm S. Wurzer

FICTIONING SPINOZA'S *NATURA*

For Adorno, legitimacy in philosophy resides beyond metanarratives in the aesthetic experience of natural beauty. Appealing explicitly to *das Naturschöne*, Adorno rewrites modernity without yielding to a Hegelian aesthetics in conformity with a phenomenological absolute. His rewriting of modern spirit involves a praxis of negation, paradoxically, an aesthetic deformation of Spinoza's *natura*—a work without end. In painting Spinoza's *Ethics* parergonally, that is, aesthetically, spirit is no longer rendered as eternal substance but as nonidentitary expression out in the open. This temporal orientation disrupts the Spinozistic legacy of modernity, a classical ethics of nature *and* spirit. Providing an idiosyncratic aesthetic theory, Adorno paints spirit falling into the beautiful-in-nature, underlining a Kantian extension of history into realm of the inexpressive.

Adorno paints Spinozistic nature by circumventing a mimesis of the ideal, nonetheless, in a specular mimetic becoming: "Art imitates neither nature nor individual natural beauty. What it does imitate is natural beauty in itself" (*AT*, 107). The image of nature becomes unimaginable in spirit's deconstructive itinerary, leading to a constellation of philosophy and art.[1] Within this unique constellation, we pass from nature as absolute identity to the beautiful-in-nature as imageless *Bild*, ultimately challenging the sublime darkness of capital, a certain persistence in modernity. Clearly, Adorno subverts the unity between metaphysics, art, and society. While these subtexts comprise modernity's textuality, his rewriting thereof leaves us with an aesthetic abyss. Neither art nor metaphysics or society are ever reconciled. With the beautiful-in-nature as site of a possible reconciliation, Adorno's thought marks the "strange" hope of spirit straying into a series of mimetic finites. In short, the task of philosophy is to dispel the dialectic of substance whose subject has ruled modernity from Spinoza to Marx. Adorno presumes to do this by virtue of a different nature—*das Naturschöne*—a "reflective" dimension, which, nonetheless, opens up to the nonconceptual. After Hegel, the concept permeates philosophy *and* art in a manner no longer constrained by subjectivity's *fabula* of pure representation. Modernity, therefore, slips out of metaphysical spirituality into monadic works of art, concrete, finite explosions of possible social horizons.

Adorno rewrites modern philosophy from the perspectives of the problematic itinerations of spirit, nature, and art. He draws upon resources throughout the tradition of modernity, revamping Spinoza's metaphysics into a radical aesthetic deconstruction of Kant's philosophy of nature. The details of this claim must be left aside at this time. It should be noted, however, that there is still a metaphysical ghost in Adorno's configurations of the concept of *das Naturschöne*. Another spirit links history and nature to a negative *interieur*, an echo of subjectivity.[2] This idiosyncratic *interieur* is named "second reflection" and recognized as an allegorical operation, a reflective painting of "the place of spirit in art" (*AT*, 129). Second reflection is parergonal, continually transforming modernity into a sublime praxis of "first nature."[3] First nature marks something yet to be. It does not refer to what may or may not have happened in the past. It is not nostalgic but futural. From this point of view, second nature takes on the inhuman form of capital. Adorno's myth of capital's evil belongs very much to the historical rhythm of subjectivity. His texts invariably lead the reader back to the scene of exchange. Spirit, however, is truly free only in the world of art. The intervention of the beautiful-in-nature enables spirit to pass over into an aesthetic realm of freedom. Art, therefore, is the terrain in which truth does not accommodate an absolute will. Yet, while Adorno disturbs the phenomenological model of spirit, which claims to show how spirit ought to be, he is unable to liberate spirit from negative individuation, that is, from the eternal return of a certain *interieur*. The explosive quality in works of art makes it possible to respond dialectically to social reality without ever seriously changing it. His aesthetic praxis is in principle unassignable. The eleventh thesis on Feuerbach is, therefore, brushed aside.[4] What counts most in Adorno's painting of *natura* is the beautiful as sublime abyss in a spirit coming out of its own double, its former subject/ substance concept.

Without replicating Kant's transcendental idea of the beautiful, Adorno's concept of individuation is inspired by the beautiful-in-nature itself, an inverse aestheticization of Spinoza's substance. *Natura* is taken out of its objectivity and inscribed into the *interieur*, a mimetic/monadic terrain of critical imagination. Imagination is freed from transcendental subjectivity for history's free play in which art unfolds its social and imaginal content. Yet, is this gesture not metaphysical? The different sounds of Adorno's textual melodies, in which one can hear with clarity the metaphysical songs of Spinoza, Leibniz, Kant, and Schelling, are only distinguished by a change of rhythm. We encounter negative variations of a familiar theme: individuation, apparitions, fireworks, art imitating the inimitable, the incomparably beautiful beyond society in nature itself.

"Spirit is present in art solely through the principle of individuation" (*AT*, 62). Withdrawn from the metaphysical frame of conceptual manipulation, spirit installs itself in art as second reflection. Philosophy's task is to interpret this determinate negation of the universal. Paradoxically, the truth of this nomadic monadology lies in the very dissolution of completeness and totality. "At a deeper level, aesthetics has to be a response to the open-endedness of works of art. They call for mental exercises such as commentary and critique" (*AT*, 468). "Shapes of spirit," commentary and critique rewrite *fabula philosophiae*. Adorno's subversion of modernity is not a reconstruction of metaphysics: "We cannot reconstruct something in aesthetics that has gone down to defeat in philosophy" (*AT*, 471). Rewriting, to recall Lyotard, means resisting the writing of metaphysics and that of supposed postmodernity.[5] Adorno's speculative desire is to resist the impact of what is modern and postmodern, if that impact rests upon the former's totality and the latter's undisciplined particularity. This resisting, however, is not to be misconstrued as a logocentric negation of reification in the Marxist sense. Adorno's aesthetics is ultimately more of a desistance rather than resistance of modernity. Desistance marks a standing away from, a standing down of, a ceasing to proceed in the manner of, a letting go of, even, finally, a fictioning of a certain textual metaphysics of nature which commences with Spinoza's *natura* and culminates in Kant's "free play of the subject in nature."[6] Adorno's negative dialectics in *Aesthetic Theory* marks a transition from a post-Marxist resistance to a post-Kantian desistance. The concept of the beautiful-in-nature is responsible for this transition.

KANTIAN MONTAGE

The genealogy of Adorno's allegorical *Naturschöne* can be traced to Kant's intriguing rewriting of aesthetic modernity.[7] In the *Critique of Judgment*, Kant introduces a radically different way of regarding a mere thing and a work of art. The concept of thing is freed from its epistemic confinement to phenomenal-noumenal difference. Indeed, from the perspective of a poet's radiant eye (*Augenschein*), *das Ding* is neither a phenomenon nor a thing in itself but rather a thing that is freely beautiful. "A natural beauty," Kant writes, "is a *beautiful thing* (*CJ*, 179)."[8] And works of art are not perceived culturally as something present at hand but as so many pathways along a free imagination, invariably open to an ever-wider trajectory of judging. This marks "a new ground" for judgment and art, "a supplementary shining" (*Erscheinen*) which is not anchored in subject or object. Indeed, a culture of pleasure "founds" the pure work of art in imagination's reflective rhythm. A peculiar mirroring occurs which draws judgment into the imaginal regions of art. In regarding an individual artwork, judgment *begins to see* what it does not see in its dialectical service to understanding, namely, that it is intimately linked to imagination; that it moves imagination at the level of a pure work of art, surprisingly, in its response to each concrete work of art.

Kant's perspective on aesthetic judgment introduces a dimension of anti-art into aesthetics.[9] Something appears that is not dependent upon the existence of the artwork's object. An aesthetic slashing of the particular and the universal is linked to a supplementary shining in works of art. A peculiar appearing, not a "phenomenon," subverts the appearance of a thing in itself. There is no artwork itself. Art is always already a matter of imagination, in judging or creating. An artwork's reflexive pronoun darkens in the very interplay of art and judging. This darkening or aesthetic eclipse of judgment marks, nonetheless, an opening (i.e., clearing) in imagination for judgment.

An imaginal play of judging, consequently, provides an *appearing* beyond appearances or things in themselves.[10] Indeed, matters of beauty and art "exist" in that very appearing. Artworks, in turn, appear through imagination's reflective play beyond the metanarrative constraints of a phenomenal-noumenal world. A new ground of appearing, which no longer presents nature as an object of cognition, shines upon artworks as pure instances of judgment.

So art engages in an imaginal venture which reason imitates. Still, reason's desire for the infinite is not abandoned. On the contrary, it is strengthened in judgment's imaginal free play which reveals the infinite in art rather than in the realm of noumenon. Extricated from a metaphysics of nature, the infinite is inscribed into a peculiar aesthetic enterprise. Reason thus descends to imagination in order to become in relation to the pure work of art what it cannot become in relation to objects of cognition. Mimesis is now aligned to a new ground, a reflective judging, notably, a pure work of art.

Discovering "itself" again, reason moves within the realm of pure aesthetic pleasure, invariably consistent with Kant's imaginal theory of free purposiveness. What is pure, that is, free in an artwork is the anti-art, precisely that which points away from a particular work's charm and seduction. Nothing is taken away from an artwork's material configurations. Instead, the focus is mainly on anti-art, that is, on a power of judging prompted, nonetheless, by a concrete work of art.[11] Art, therefore, opens up to judgment's play with individual artworks ("anti-art"). And on Kant's view art is not something that happens primarily in historico-cultural spaces. Nor is it merely the product of a subjective aesthetics which Kant questions in his tactic of letting judgment be aesthetically free and open. Art, essentially conceivable within a "schema of imagination," relates the mental faculties to individual works of art without integrating their objective existence into aesthetic judgment. As semblance of the universal (that is not given), art (resembling nature in its beauty), serves as "primal image" of imagination which judgment relates to a natural thing or a concrete work of art. So, even though it is judgment which correlates the pure work of art (i.e., imagination's free play) with matters of art in particular, art is not extracted from reflective judgment. On the contrary, judgment merely highlights imagination's free play of relations.

To bring this into sharper focus: Art consists in the very relations that make imagination's free play possible. These relations, however, concern more than the harmony of our mental powers. More importantly, they concern the relation in and between the very relations of works of art. These works evoke a manner of judging that invites the repetition of an as-yet unrealized future for philosophy and art. What matters, then, is not the nature of art itself nor even that of judgment in general but rather *how* art and judgment interact in imagination's play. This question is most important when one considers Kant's emphasis on the relation of judgment and culture. Throughout the *Critique of Judgment*, he views judgment according to the subject's aesthetic propensity for culture. Indeed, culture is the thread that binds art and judgment beyond what is merely historically given as society to date. Culture is nature's ultimate purpose in imagination. It is, one might say, imagination's sublime desire to be purposive without falling into purpose. Hence it corresponds to a play of forms in which teleological moments of judging do not establish teleological structures. This is possible when culture is regarded as "producing in a rational being an aptitude for purposes generally" (*CJ*, 319). No mere culture is adequate for achieving this aesthetic freedom, only the culture of a pure work of art, simultaneously, a certain aesthetic ideal which in expressing a free imagination, stirs an universally communicable attitude. The mental powers, therefore, are exposed to a form of purposiveness in the reflective interplay of art and judgment. This interplay yields to *das Naturschöne* which "constitutes the sociability that befits humanity and distinguishes it from the limitation of animals" (*CJ*, 231).

What is at issue here is the aesthetic quest for freedom. The subjective/objective debate about art disregards not only the radical epistemic turn in Kantian aesthetics but also, and, more prominently, the manner in which culture is shown to be the anti-art in art. As propensity for "free purposiveness," culture sets out to free art for a moment of anti-art in judgment's indelible attribution of the beautiful-in-nature to matters of art.

AN AESTHETICIZATION OF THE INFINITE

In painting Spinoza's nature anew, Adorno makes a disturbance in Kant's later philosophy by twisting the transcendental articulations in the *Critique of Judgment* out of shape. To some extent Kant already pursues this self-deconstruction in his theory of the sublime. Adorno, however, radicalizes Kantian aesthetics by dislodging the concept of the beautiful-in-nature entirely from a transcendental subject.[12] His delimitations of the Kantian project intensify the play of the teleological immanently, freeing judgment and art from transcendental purity. A nonidentical *Naturschöne*, which points to the inexpressive, interlaces aesthetic and teleological concerns. Aesthetics is now desistance of the inhuman beyond pure contemplation. Adorno's secret is open: the beautiful is sublime. Still, it is naturally beautiful and lacking in ground, it is an unavoidable abyss. This aesthetic fall of subject, prompting new mimetic action, breaks with a modernity which grounds the infinite. Adorno renounces the stubborn permanence of representation in subject (Descartes), of substance in nature (Spinoza), of purity in imagination (Kant). Accordingly, he deconstructs several commanding structures in modern philosophy: Descartes' *ego cogito*, Spinoza's *natura naturans*, and Kant's pure aesthetic judging. Adorno's texts interrupt the powerful filiations of nature and reason in this modern genealogy. Beyond subject (consciousness) and substance (nature), the beautiful-in-nature marks a necessary response to the challenge of the end of modernity.[13] What obliges a rewriting of modernity, therefore, is the fear of forgetting the infinite, which for Adorno, is *die Sache der Philosophie*. Here the infinite, however, is not another *absolute itself*. Nor is it hidden *in* nature. Rather, it is spirit, entirely other, appearing radiantly in works of art through the beautiful-in-nature. After Hegel, the task of philosophy is to let spirit be, above all—critique. Yes, a critique of pure reason, practical reason, and transcendental judgment. But more than that: a critique of the inhuman. Desistance, therefore, is not mere indication but ex-position, positioning out the surreptitious mediations, revealing the infinite on another front, perhaps even beyond Kant's *Augenschein*.

Is Adorno's desistance of the inhuman merely an index of utopian surplus as Wellmer suggests?[14] Is desistance of the inhuman merely an aesthetic spinning from within a lavish second reflection? Adorno's investigations, taking off from an *individuum ineffabile*, curiously deframe, play out, indeed picture-out presence in the beautiful-in-nature. Working through Kant's imaginal modernity, second reflection "can no longer be rational in accordance with the norms of discursive thinking" (*AT*, 40). Hence, "the darkness of the absurd"—the inhuman properly other—is not replaced by reason's "artificial brightness"—the inhuman properly its own. The inhuman other than its signified belongs very much to Adorno's unique desistance of truth.

An idiosyncratic moment determines the transition from first to second reflection. Individuation is installed as allegorical desistance, pointing to a mimetic fall of spirit from presence. First reflection anchors self-presence, thereby formulating the need to overcome self-alienation.[15] Second reflection renounces a given (self)presence. Hence, it cannot posit self-alienation as a legitimate category. Properly its own, the inhuman marks the ontotheological unfolding of subjectivity. Here spirit is caught in the web of theoreticist constraints. Other than itself, beyond metaphysical presence, spirit is allowed to be free in art.[16] It permits the circulation of a certain negativity which mirrors social antagonisms. This negativity, which becomes part of the truth content in the work of art, nonetheless, is "part and parcel of their critical content" (*AT*, 52). Alluding to works by Kafka and Beckett, Adorno claims that art must individuate the inhuman in concrete works of art: "True experience of art must include an awareness of the inherent antagonism between the inside and outside of art" (*AT*, 479). Unless the inhuman is reflected in individual works of art, aesthetics cannot overcome the rift between inhumanities and humanity. Indeed, aesthetics marks a desistance of reification in its response to artworks mirroring the inhuman.

Adorno's inscription of the inhuman into aesthetics might seem to bring his thought dangerously close to Heidegger's. Both maintain a philosophy of the modern subject or the inhuman as such. Both renounce a given historical subject and abandon Kant's concept of the person while retaining his sublime imaginal interplay in which the infinite is regarded as art. Thus, Heidegger and Adorno guard the question of how the subject is yet to be. They believe that philosophy's task is to focus on this question by exploring the spirit of truth in art. Adorno, however, ultimately disturbs the dream of *Gelassenheit*. Heidegger's dream is essentially not to rewrite modernity but to let it be (inhuman still). Terrifyingly, even to let it play out its violence while reserving responsibility solely in the poetic terrain of *Denken*. Adorno renounces this strategy. From the very beginning, he is committed to a desistance of the inhuman without pondering it silently or letting it linger in the *Heimat* of language. This means letting the inhuman persist in works of art in order to thwart its power outside of art. "Art is true," says Adorno, "to the extent to which it is discordant and antagonistic in its language and in its whole essence" (*AT*, 241). While Heidegger lets negativity be, lifting *Ge-stell* into his ontology, Adorno believes it must be renounced through the power of art. This renunciation, however, is more of a desistance of the inhuman rather than an outright negation. It allows for an aesthetic manifestation of the inhuman in order to weaken the force of inhumanities. Heidegger, who prefers to think silently, avoids desistance when it comes to the question of art in relation to the social origins of the inhuman.[17] Desistance, on his view, undoubtedly belongs to truth interlaced with the inhuman. Hence, there is not much that can be done about inhumanities. The eleventh thesis on Feuerbach, too, belongs to modernity's truth-making art. We are thrown, therefore, into a "destroyed place," the kind of world in which interpretation is torn from inhumanities. While conceding that works of art may point to social conflict, Heidegger does not accept their participation in critique. Contrarily, for Adorno, truth in art lies not in a letting-be of presence (*Anwesen lassen*) but in desistance of inhumanities. So his idea of art is one of immanent critique. He paints Spinoza's nature as a work culminating in Paul Klee's *Destroyed Place*, pointing to the human yet to be (*TY*, 31). Paradoxically, this advance is made possible by a perpetual *methexis* in the inhuman. As Klee writes: "Art remains loyal to humankind uniquely through its inhumanity in regard to it" (*I*, 2). This "rhythmic desistance," therefore, is not a negation of the inhuman.[18] Instead the inhuman is inscribed into the very circle of desistance in order to show that "thought is no protector of springs whose freshness might deliver us from thinking" (*ND*, 15).

More concretely, then, Adorno's rhythmic desistance ponders art as liberating the human from the inhuman. It involves, first of all, philosophy's withdrawal from totality/identity. This makes it possible for philosophy to go over to works of art and to shed new light on the familiar social antagonisms mirrored in these works. Such aesthetic crossing to second reflection "is older than its significative counterpart" (*AT*, 165). Philosophy takes on the function of identifying art with modernity's departure from first reflection. "This means that art is not to be identified with the subjective mind or with the collective mind of the times" (*AT*, 473). It also means that art accompanies spirit in its fall. Art does not posses spirit securely. Adorno speaks of "the moment of spirit" beyond identity, a crystallization between the human and inhuman. Widely sensuous, "art dreams of being a perfect monad" (*AT*, 481). Yet this monad, paradoxically, is "a syndrome in motion" (ibid., 482), a sublime individuation incompatible with essence. "Art is not what it has always been from time immemorial; it is what it has become" (ibid.). Thus, philosophy respects this open character of art. It grants a *Vergeistigung* of nature in concrete works of art. In effect, works of art exert a certain pressure on philosophy, indeed "a momentary agitation, more precisely a radical trembling (*Erschutterung*)" (*AT*, 346). The inhuman is now linked to an absence of beauty in human nature, no doubt, to "social conflicts and class relations (which) leave an imprint on the structure of works of art" (*AT*, 329). Amplifying the social index of the inhuman, aesthetics undercuts the spell of the principle of exchange. For Adorno, the motif of the beautiful-in-nature, when articulated in spirit crossing over to artworks, reveals that art is quite a bit more for philosophy than an ecstatic-messianic site. With philosophy, art opens itself to desistance, that of the inhuman, first of all.

The question we are posing bears increasingly on the status of desistance. For Adorno, desistance marks the power to think the infinite in the instant of aesthetic trembling. This aestheticization of the infinite, a necessary philosophical gesture, announces a schizophrenic opening to the schemata of works of art. These schemata, which pertain to the truth content in art, are sensible concepts which invariably exceed a conceptual *Auspragung*. They are not brought into any image but signify what Kant speaks of as a "monogram" of imagination's free play.[19] Desistance, then, also marks a *singular writing* whose "art is concealed in the depths of the human soul, (and) whose real modes of activity nature is hardly likely ever to allow us to discover, and to have open to our gaze" (*CPR*, 183). No longer a structural *donne*, Adorno's desistance, advancing toward something yet to be, inverts the Kantian theory of schematism, drawing it into second reflection. He consolidates the monogram into a dimension of hope. Breaking up the theoreticism in schematism, he regards the monogram as the beautiful-in-nature, a nonimaginal inscription in a work of art. A critical reading of the schemata, therefore, focuses primarily on philosophy's desistance of inhumanities. However, the reader who seeks a tangible answer to the question of "what to do" will be disappointed. Maximally, Adorno's gesture of delimiting the Kantian ethics aims "to live so that one may believe himself to have been a good animal" (*ND*, 299). This delimitation does not promote a strong subjectivity. To the contrary, for Adorno: "Men are human only where they do not act, let alone posit themselves as persons. Contemporary art innervates some of this" (*ND*, 277).

The strangest thing about Adorno's desistance is that it strives to induce a standing-still of modernity. It draws on something that is previous to the imaginal. It invariably draws on the infinite which radiates anew in the very absence of its former self. No longer infinitely abstract, the inhuman too belongs to this intriguing aestheticization of the infinite. It is forbidden to be abstract conceptually but not artistically. Artworks themselves may be exchanged but the work without end, imagination's monogram derived from philosophy's response to art, cannot be exchanged. Kant names the unexchangeable a law of reason. Adorno names the infinite a lawless rewriting, the violence of a schizophrenic deframing, the slow erosion of the interior/exterior space of modernity. We encounter fantasy precisely at the margins of imagination. There its destiny is to play with the law of the infinite, at once a monogram of free, subjectless subjectivity. "Properly understood," Adorno writes, "fantasy is the ability to take elements of being and transform them into the opposite of being, simply by bringing them into a new constellation" (*AT*, 248). This new constellation of the beautiful-in-nature interlaces pleasure and displeasure, eros and irony, the infinite and the inhuman. It lets fantasy's entirely other language write in a judging that plays and in a playing that judges. "Fantasy is the unlimited mastery of possible solutions that

crystallize in a work of art" (ibid.). A certain violence determines the interplay of fantasy and work of art. It is the violence of deframing being. The
subject fades. The irony of fantasy sets in motion an aesthetic clearing of
lighting (*Lichtung*)—Adorno's *promesse du bonheur*.[20]

A tactic of fantasy, desistance involves reading art's dream of becoming
a perfect monad.[21] The monadological surfaces in Adorno's transcription of
the Kantian monogram into *das Naturschöne*. The metaphysical matrix of
nature/substance undergoes a monogramic fictioning. Here we encounter a
"spontaneous core of subjectivity," (*K*, 127), the fantasy of a new inscription,
a second reflection, plainly, "the ability deliberately to set in motion the
spontaneous" (*AT*, 249). Accordingly, the beautiful-in-nature reveals a
nonidentitary, nonsubstantive, flowing restless monadic/nomadic "reality."
Individuating itself in art as nomadic/monadic, free and open, sensuous rationality, spirit "protests permanently against a morality which punishes cruelty
with cruelty" (*AT*, 74).

OF EXPRESSION: IMPRESSIONS
OF A PARERGONAL SPIRIT

A radical monadology, Adorno's parergonal aesthetics abandons the
principle of ground. *Natura* is regarded from the perspectives of expression rather than indication. "Expression," Adorno writes, "is the moment
whereby nature seeps most deeply into art" (*AT*, 166). His deconstruction
of nature seeks expression, the language of art. Everything here rests
upon a new itineration of spirit, a second reflection which scans the history of philosophy as first reflection from the standpoint of aesthetic
nonidentity.[21] Expression belongs to this nonidentical operation. "Put more
precisely, through its objectification expression becomes a second nonobjective substance, one that speaks out of the artefact rather than out of the
subject" (*AT*, 163). The word expression arises in connection with mimesis. "Expression in art is mimetic" (*AT*, 162). Its function is to submit the
philosophical concept of nature to the law of the beautiful-in-nature. This
submission, however, does not recast Kant's aesthetic subjectivity. Nor is
it simply an inversion of the latter's theory of the beautiful. *Das
Naturschöne* is only a name for spirit's entirely other painting of *natura*.
"A second nonobjective substance" emerges, one, that loses its ground to
individuation. Freed from the old frame of metaphysical indications, philosophy lets nature be expression. The concept of expression, Adorno
writes, "like so many other concepts which are central to aesthetics, has
never been understood. Never has this recalcitrant concept been domes-
ticated and clarified in the framework of a theory" (*AT*, 163).[22]

Adorno recognizes Husserl's phenomenological explorations of expression in the *Logical Investigations*. He is partially indebted to Husserl's insight regarding the distinction between expression and indication. I can only be very brief about this here. For Husserl, phenomenology highlights the cleavage between indication and expression. Expression marks the language of pure presence. Indication signifies a quantitative presence. Expression, in turn, constitutes a kind of *Geistigkeit*, a distinctive *interieur* that is neither nature nor world nor anything outside consciousness. It is, quite plainly, the pure phenomenological voice of presence. Husserl writes: "All speech (*Rede*) shall count as an expression, whether or not such speech is actually uttered or addressed with communicative intent to any persons."[23] Indicative discourse is not expressive in the sense of signifying an ideal self-presence. This matter deserves a more rigorous reading. In sum, however, it can be said that Husserl reads a distinctive presence into his concept of expression. Expression is therefore prey to a double bind: *epoche* in general and consciousness as pure self-presence in particular.

Contrarily, Adorno subverts this double bind by thinning out the phenomenological texture of expression. Affirming expression beyond presence, he privileges art to the detriment of the Husserlian epoche. His philosophy marks an aesthetic disappearance of presence while reserving "a second nonobjective" operation. The displacement (*Umstellung*) of *natura* to *das Naturschöne* interrupts the conceptual economy of modern philosophy. Moreover, it marks a shift in the history of modern aesthetics, challenging the predominance of conceptual presence over imagination. Under the name of expression Adorno inaugurates the beautiful-in-nature, art's mimesis. Yet, what art imitates does not come to presence. This paradoxical situation has induced certain scholars to regard Adorno's aesthetics as mystical. Reading his aesthetics is rather uncomplicated if one claims, as Wellmer does, that "it is nourished by the yearning for a lost paradise," conceiving "aesthetic experience in ecstatic terms," revealing merely an "utopian-messianic perspective" (*PM*, 12). Surely this Habermasian interpretation offers a trace of truth. Yet Adorno's delimitation of subjectivity is much more complex. Attentive rereadings of *Aesthetic Theory* reveal that expression, reason's other beyond ground, does not lay the foundations for a new *Kunstreligion*, nor the conditions for an inversion of Hegelian aesthetics. Instead, expression permits itself a breaking out of the work of substance and, more importantly, a letting go of the frame that holds together the old picture of nature mirrored by *Geist*. Expression, therefore, appears to be a sublime and uncanny fading away from modern metaphysical theoreticism.

Adorno's concept of expression opens a new problematic of spirit by abandoning both a metaphysics of nature and a metaphysics of pure apperception. Expression now provides a philosophy individuated in art. This means that the power of subject is entirely a function of its participation in the beautiful-in-nature. "By itself the subject is powerless" (*AT*, 288). Vigorously displacing Husserl's epoche, Adorno engages in a rewriting of modernity beyond the measure of consciousness. If rewriting modernity is not to end in ontotheoretic philosophemes, it must open itself to art as expression of the inhuman. At its limits philosophy is entirely preoccupied with an aesthetic transformation of reification. "In art everything passes through spirit, all is humanized in a nonrepressive, nonviolent way" (*AT*, 166). Spirit shines upon artworks which invariably point to the inhuman. In pointing to the inhuman, *Denken* participates in expression as "a phenomenon of interference" (*AT*, 167). Thus spirit does not belong to metaphysics' "good way of forgetting again" (*I*, 29) and Adorno's aesthetics is far from a modernity unaware of expression.

THE SUBJECT IS INHUMAN

Still more precisely, expression invites us to think: "The subject is the lie" (*ND*, 277). The self is yet to be. "Without exception," Adorno writes, "men have yet to become themselves" (*ND*, 278). The possible is *das Naturschöne*, strictly speaking, neither modern nor postmodern. The beautiful-in-nature is nonidentical, a sublime indifference of ends. Art tells of that indifference, of "history standing still and refusing to unfold" (*AT*, 105). It is the narrative of modernity, *another* painting, ever pointing to a concrete work of art, perhaps, Klee's *Destroyed Place*: a de-framed monadology, in his words "visualization of nonvisual impressions and ideas" (*BR*, 112). Klee's work evokes an absence of subject, simultaneously, bringing to light a comforting emptiness, an intriguing anonymity marking the ruin of modernity: "My fervor is more like that of the dead or the as yet unborn . . . I adopt a distant, original standpoint, where I presuppose formulas for man, animals, plants, rocks, and the elements, for all the circulating forces at once. A thousand questions fall silent before they are answered" (ibid.).

The subject is a lie. The ground is demolished. Yet, hope survives. It is vividly revealed in the black windows which, without glass, do not mirror another totality. There is no self in sight. We see uncanny, acinematic instances of identification. There is no single absolute identity. This painting glances at nature without ever seeing her presence. Here individuation precedes subjectivity. "In natural beauty, natural and historical elements form ever-changing constellations. It is this kind of fluctuation, rather than some hard and fast relationship among the elements, which gives life to the beautiful in nature" (*AT*, 105). Concretely sensuous yet undefinable, it is finally a promise of life without fear.

For Adorno, this indeterminate, inexpressive expression remains allegorical "beyond bourgeois work and commodity relations" (*AT*, 102). Its unsayable beauty points to the unthought in philosophical modernity—the inhuman which needs to be rewritten. This rewriting begins with a philosophical turn to works of art. There art becomes a trajectory of human suffering. And the work continues to paint, always imitating the inimitable. The inhuman flickers momentarily. A paradoxical painting expands the power to change the world.

Oddly, "the work is a windowless monad of society" (*AT*, 64). It resists the inhuman/subject and the metaphysical frame imposed on finite/infinite presence. A new law of mimesis, linked to the beautiful-in-nature, lets the work be anamnesis, lest we forget we are not yet. A convergence of *Stimmungen* (attunements) emerges: nature, truth, and spirit lose their *ergon*. Now these fugues become "gifts of mimesis" (*T*, 259) in Adorno's transposition of modernity. Nature and history collapse in a nonidentical grafting, a second reflection, providing a glimpse of hope in the "destroyed place" of a postmodern era in which the subject is human when he is not there.

Individuation at work is not a gesture of radical particularization which "comes dangerously close to being utterly contingent and indifferent" (*AT*, 289). At the simplest level, "individuation refers to the fact that art distances itself from the universal" (ibid.). More precisely, individuation proceeds from spirit's crossing into natural beauty. The individuated in art may, therefore, pass over into the universal. This crossing is parergonal. The particular and universal are twisted out of shape. They have become outlaws of expression. Here metaphysics fades while modernity stands still.

AFTER MODERNITY, A SNAPSHOT OF CAPITAL

Ultimately, Adorno's aesthetic critique does not break the affiliation with modernity. The subject vanishes from individuation yet is always discerned in capital. A particular metanarrative, therefore, burdens expression. Reification is interwoven with a view of capital as a degenerate form of totalization.[24] No doubt, a neo-marxist delusion pervades Adorno's text. A seemingly other absolute named "capital" is held accountable for the inhuman in society. Quite plainly, the inhuman is empirically identifiable. The historical antagonism of subject and object is rigorously repeated, ironically, in the very resistance that calls for a resolution. In his attempt to radicalize Marx's eleventh thesis, Adorno lets *natura* slip out of substance into an unceasing economimesis. Whence the reader is invited to transform proposition fifteen of the first book of Spinoza's *Ethics* to read: "Whatsoever is, is in capital, and without capital nothing can be, or be conceived."[25] This ascription of capital to complete totalization renews the marxist legacy in modernity. A postmodern (i.e., even a newly rational) approach, on the other hand, questions linking the idea of capital solely to the inhuman. Surely, capital can be shown to be just as nonidentical, discontinuous and explosive as Adorno's deconstructive (paradoxically, postmodern) extension of *das Naturschöne*.[26] Adorno, however, fails to grasp the complex relations between capital and power inasmuch as he refuses to interpret capital without its signified and power without representation.[27] Presence is consequently reinscribed into his otherwise intriguing aesthetic critique. Capital's falling from metaphysics eludes him. And so does the idea that capital may affect the *imago* of the new, the not-yet, the possible.

Rewriting modernity may displace capital as a given structure. It may speak of capital (*caput*, head) with regard to a futural flux of reason. Beyond a theory gripped in practical reflections, capital "stands ahead of 'events' only in the sense that it is a 'coming-toward,' a proleptic mode of thought" which can be unfastened from a normative dominance of images.[28] Such a rewriting of modernity may in fact open the way for a constellation of philosophy and art within a new pratique of capital. In the end, however, Adorno does not pursue an entire critique of metaphysics' self-presence. His critique still clings to a mechanism it seeks to desist. Expression now turns to the singular indication of negative totalization. Ironically, totalization lingers by virtue of reading capital solely as totalizing. In Baudrillard's words: "Every critical theory is haunted by this surreptitious religion, this desire bound up with the construction of its object, this negativity subtly haunted by the very form that it negates."[29]

Adorno's spirit of negation, which is purely aesthetic (at times parergonally so), is out of touch with the postmodern. The postmodern which "is always implied in the modern" (*I*, 25), exceeds the gap between art and capital. Spirit's advance toward the beautiful-in-nature does not dispense with this gap. Beyond nature's extension to capital, Adorno transposes, transfers, and deports Spinoza's *natura* into a textuality of art. In turn, nature becomes a spectral silhouette beyond the possibilities of concrete social praxis. What is at stake is precisely the difference between what *natura* has become socially, namely capital and what *natura* signifies aesthetically in the unique word of *das Naturschöne*. The motif, then, on which Adorno's desistance opens is nothing other than that of Apollo.[30] Yet, this god is present merely as shining *principium individuationis*. Lacking a concrete historical negation, Adorno's Apollinian turn is essentially indeterminate, ephemeral, and open.

Desistance of capital, first of all, determines an Apollinian trajectory that is not played out practically. It lets modernity stand still. Nature is captured in an imageless deframing. Klee's *Destroyed Place* dissolves into Cezanne's *Skull and Fruit*. The subject is a mere skeleton head, an afterimage of capital among the fruits or ruins of modernity. A quiet economy of hope unfolds as subjectivity stands still.[31] "Art promises what is not real" (*AT*, 122). And, mirroring the inhuman art becomes part of the Apollinian graft of the beautiful-in-nature. This concept is thus doubly mysterious, at once meaningful and meaningless: "A second nonobjective spirit speaks out of the work of art" (*AT*, 163). The beautiful-in-nature no longer speaks out of a historical subject but rather out of a fleeting stillness which draws spirit into the not yet. "To this day, all happiness is a pledge of what has not yet been" (*AT*, 352). Thus, there is an attempt here to think spirit as first nature, a critique of second nature ending in exchange.

So, is Adorno's desistance merely contemplative, perhaps even a sublime indifference to the inhuman? His painting of Spinoza's *natura*, an intriguing aesthetic antinomy in itself, is, properly speaking, a pointing away from substance as god/nature/capital to something more beautiful, something that "rises above people beyond the reach of their intentions, beyond the reach also of the world of things" (*AT*, 119). The aesthetic dimension, exceeding the world mirrored in artworks, is an index finger striving to show something beyond modernity. We are at a point in Adorno's aesthetics in which theory risks disappearing from view. Indeed, chapters four and five of *Aesthetic Theory* link the central theme of *das Naturschöne* to a possible collapse of theory in philosophy and art. Spirit appears but does not exist. It is the *Angelus Novus* of modernity. The only image Adorno grants is that of the unexchangeable. Notably, the beautiful-in-nature cannot be exchanged. It is the expression of a narrative working itself through (*Durcharbeitung*) modern and postmodern concerns. His gesture of defying the ruling principle of reality is at once dialectical and deconstructive. Haunted by Marx's song of a critique of capital and by Nietzsche's Dionysian formulation of life, Adorno seeks a spectrality which is ultimately impossible to see. Rewriting modernity's *Stimmung*, he interprets society from the perspectives of an entirely other language, the silence of natural beauty. This creative musical gesture provides the reader the privilege of listening. The musical and the social are linked by virtue of art's ability to imitate *das Naturschöne*.[32] Mimesis of freedom (and happiness), the beautiful-in-nature is paradoxically the monadological in the work of art. This aesthetic monadology retains a sense of the inner essence of the Leibnizian concept of the monad while abandoning the metaphysical theme of permanence. In Adorno's transposition, the monad inverts itself, taking on the explosive qualities of the apparitional, the ephemeral, the indefinite so inherent in a work of art. Yet, the language of this aesthetic monad is still windowless. Works of art are allegories of the natural, a "strange fictioning" of the monadic. The word "monad" names something other than "an unquestioned *a priori* of art" (*AT*, 125). There is an immanent history stored up in art works which is not meant to be perpetuated. "What is perpetuated is destroyed by being reduced to an instant" (*AT*, 126). The monadic inversion, then, is an expression of radical individuation, a fashioning of *natura*. Art is no longer the *ergon* of spirit at large but spirit at work individually. The mimetic impulse reveals a framing beyond the Frame. This is possible only because of the alliance of philosophy and art in the unique aesthetic concept of spirit. "Spirit dwells in particular objects, shining forth through appearance. One measure of this objectivity is the irresistible force with which spirit infiltrates appearance" (*AT*, 129).

In sum, Adorno's break with the Kantian matrix provides for a formidable critique of modernity by way of aesthetic desistance. His critique, however, merely commences the necessary rupture with modernity. And even the nomadic/monadic "inner law of motion," the concept of the beautiful-in-nature, which effectively dislodges aesthetics from the metanarrative of substance, is still in part determined by capital, society's negative circle of presence, ever enclosing the art of free subjectivity. Resisting a postmodern reading of capital, Adorno fails to attend to what is hidden in the monadic event of the beautiful-in-nature. The paradoxical expression of that event is yet to be. But what merits attention in Adorno's Kantian snapshot of modernity is the art of a necessary desistance of inhumanities in general.

ABBREVIATIONS

AT	Theodor W. Adorno, *Aesthetic Theory*, trans. Christian Lenhardt (London and New York: Routledge & Kegan Paul, 1984).
BR	Armin Zweite, *The Blue Rider* (Munich: Prestel-Verlag, 1989).
CJ	Immanuel Kant, *The Critique of Judgment*, trans. W. S. Pluhar (Indianapolis: Hackett Publishing Company, 1987).
CPR	Immanuel Kant, *The Critique of Pure Reason*, trans. N. K. Smith (New York: St. Martin's Press, 1965).
I	Jean-Francois Lyotard, *The Inhuman*, trans. G. Bennington and R. Bowlby (Stanford: Stanford University Press, 1991).
K	Theodor W. Adorno, *Kierkegaard: Construction of the Aesthetic*, trans. Robert Hullot-Kentor (Minneapolis: University of Minnesota Press, 1989).
ND	Theodor W. Adorno, *Negative Dialectics*, trans. E. B. Ashton (New York: Continuum, 1973).
PM	Albrecht Wellmer, *The Persistence of Modernity*, trans. David Midgley (Cambridge: MIT Press, 1991).
T	Phillipe Lacoue-Labarthe, *Typography—Mimesis, Philosophy, Politics*, ed. Christopher Fynsk (Cambridge: Harvard University Press, 1989).

NOTES

1. While Albrecht Wellmer underscores this constellation of art and philosophy in Adorno's thought, he does this at the expense of breaking it up again into "two

halves of a negative theology." See his *The Persistence of Modernity* (Cambridge: MIT Press, 1991), 7.

2. Of the *intérieur* Adorno writes: "Inwardness presents itself as the restriction of human existence to a private sphere free from the power of reification" (*K*, 47).

3. A distinction of first and second nature is made by Nietzsche in *On the Advantage and Disadvantage of History for Life*, trans. Peter Preuss (Indianapolis: Hackett, 1980). First nature marks the unhistorical and superhistorical while second nature indicates an excess of history. Nietzsche also speaks of "*die erhöhte Praxis*," the elevated praxis of a new "historical" (Dionysian) creativity.

4. "The philosophers have only interpreted the world, in various ways; the point is to change it." *Karl Marx Selected Writings*, ed. David McLellan (Oxford: Oxford University Press, 1977), 158.

5. See chapter 2, "Rewriting Modernity," of Lyotard's *The Inhuman: Reflections on Time* (Stanford: Stanford University Press, 1991). Henceforth, *I*.

6. Desistance (in French, *désistement*) by Lacoue-Labarthe in *Typography— Mimesis, Philosophy, Politics*, ed. Christopher Fynsk (Cambridge: Harvard University Press, 1989). In the introduction to this text, Derrida writes: "Desistance perhaps brings into the light of day, gives birth to, the insanity or unreason, the *anoia* against which Platonic onto-ideology, or even Heidegger's interpretation of it, is established, installed, stabilized" (24).

7. A detailed exploration of a Kantian rewriting of aesthetic modernity can be found in my *Filming and Judgment: Between Heidegger and Adorno* (Atlantic Highlands, NJ: Humanities Press International Inc., 1990).

8. "Eine Naturschönheit ist ein *schönes Ding:*" Immanuel Kant, *Kritik der Urteilskraft*, ed. W. Weischedel (Frankfurt: Suhrkamp Verlag, 1974), 246. Henceforth *KU*.

9. "Art is no longer art when anti-art is completely weeded out" (*AT*, 120).

10. *Apparatio—ap-pareo-pareo*: "appearance—to appear—show—to appear upon demand."

11. Following Kant, Adorno later writes: "From now on no art will be conceivable without the moment of anti-art" (*AT*, 43).

12. It is not accidental that Jean-Francois Lyotard, too, discovers this possibility in his own philosophy. He writes, "I shall simply point out how close the description of rewriting is to Kant's analysis of the work of imagination in taste, in the pleasure of the beautiful" (*I*, 32).

13. See Gianni Vattimo, *La fine della modernita* (Italy: Garzanti, 1985), particularly chap. 3, "Morte o tramonto dell'arte."

14. Wellmer speaks of the "immeasurability of the gap between reality and utopia" (*PM*, 12).

15. Kant's aesthetic denegation of the infinite still belongs to the margins of first reflection. While expressing resistance toward closure, Kant's widening of imagination still happens in an economy of the subject.

16. "der Geist, der in der Kunst frei sein muß" (*KU,* 238).

17. He is fascinated by Spinoza, no doubt. Yet, he appears to give him little thought. Also, more attentiveness is shown toward Hölderlin than to Goethe, a fervent reader and student of Spinoza.

18. Derrida's idiom in "Introduction: Desistence," in Lacoue-Labarthe's *Typography.*

19. "The image is a product of the empirical faculty of reproductive imagination; the schema of sensible concepts is a product and, as it were, a monogram, of pure *a priori* imagination, through which, and in accordance with which, images themseves first become possible" (*CPR,* 183). ("und gleichsam ein Monogramm der reinen Einbildungskraft," KU, 200.)

20. Essential to Adorno's desistance is the Kantian theme of imagination elevated (*erhaben*) above nature. Imagination is now regraded as judging nature aesthetically, thus, drawing nature, as something unrepresentable, into the subject. Indeed, for Kant, nature is aesthetically transformed from a presentable power into an unrepresentable feeling within the mind (*Gemüth*). This Kantian transformation introduces modernity as a philosophy of "nature in the subject," beyond nature itself. Nature, absent from itself, yet ever so present to reason in the form of aesthetic judging, is sublimely at play in *nova imaginatio*. For Adorno, however, this new imagination still indicates a relapse into subjectivity, which, while partially free from logocentric design, is nonetheless the very expression of a moral philosopheme. What is social about art is not the moral echoing of a substantive identity. The aesthetic dimension is henceforth always other than moral *Vorhandenheit*. Surprisingly, with regard to the question of morality, Adorno is closer to Spinoza than to Kant without, of course, the former's grounding gesture. Spinoza's other than natural understanding of ethics envelops the human imagination interlaced with fantasy. Spinoza's critique of morality is confined to substance ideology. This critique must be freed by art. But not by art itself for art relies on philosophy to interpret what works of art cannot say. "While art dreams of being a perfect monad unto itself, it is for better or worse suffused with universality" (*AT,* 481).

21. "Expression is diametrically opposed to conceptualization" (*AT,* 163). " 'Second reflection' here denotes the opposite of what the term reflection means in usual philosophical parlance, where the concept might for example be applied to Schiller's theory of the sentimental, which boils down to an attempt at imbuing art works with intention. In the present context, second reflection is something else. It seeks to grasp the method and language, in the broadest sense, of the work of art, but in doing so it aims at blindness" (*AT,* 40).

22. Indeed, Adorno believes that expressionism was not successful in articulating the relevance of expression with regard to an aesthetic concept of spirit. "Kandinsky," he writes, "is a case in point. In his well-intentioned revolt against the predominance of sensualist elements in movements like *art nouveau*, he abstractly isolated and reified the antitheses to sensualism, the result being that it becomes difficult to distinguish artististic enthusiasm for something higher" (*AT*, 129).

23. *Logical Investigations*, trans. J. N. Findlay (New York: Humanities Press, 1977), *I*, 5:275.

24. See chapter 5, "The Aesthetic Fall of Modernity," in my *Filming and Judgment*.

25. "Whatever is, is in God, and nothing can be or be conceived without God." *Ethics*, trans. S. Shirley (Indianapolis: Hackett, 1992), 40.

26. I have shown the possibilities of capital's independence from a positive and negative construction in chapters 7 and 8 of *Filming and Judgment*.

27. "Capital is not an economic and social phenomenon. It is the shadow cast by the principle of reason on human relations" (*I*, 69).

28. See pp. 82-91 in *Filming and Judgment*.

29. *Mirror of Production*, trans. Mark Poster (St. Louis: Telos, 1975), 116.

30. See also F. Nietzsche, *Die Geburt der Tragödie, Nachgelassene Schriften KSA I–IV*, 1870–73, ed G. Colli and M. Montinari (Berlin/New York: de Gruyter, 1988).

31. "For here it is not the law of the world which applies, but the law of art. In the picture, crooked houses do not fall down, trees no longer need to blossom, people do not need to breathe. Pictures are not living images." Paul Klee, from Armin Zweite's *The Blue Rider* (Munich: Prestel-Verlag, 1989), 110.

32. "Art negates the literal reality of its material content" (*AT*, 123).

Chapter 7

Fragment, Fascination, Damaged Life: "The Truth about Hedda Gabler"

J. M. Bernstein

NONIDENTITY AND THE NIGHT

Philosophical modernism is premised on an observation and a risk. The observation is that ethical experience, the exigency of ethical life, the experience of the ethical as exigent, is no longer available as a routine accompaniment of everyday life, but appears, if at all, fleetingly or obliquely; and even those appearances are equivocal, as if issuing from the sanctuary of a conscience that has been rendered private and solitary, the last velleity of a subjectivity whose substantiality has become as idle and empty as the objects of religious belief and the words that carried that belief: law, commandment, promise, salvation, prayer, neighbor, love, sacrifice. Empty words, empty rituals. All that is left is the velleity of conscience no longer believed in but acted on anyway.

This ethical desert is crammed with the assertive and mocking pleasures of twentieth century life: the bazaar of the shopping mall, the department store, the mail order catalogue, the ethical situation become a situation comedy, violence become statistics and spectacle, and fulfillment now the quick fix of a casual sexual encounter (what illusion is more insistent and dangerous than that of flesh upon flesh, the spirallings of tongues and limbs, the assertions and surrenders of orgasm?). Philosophical modernism inhabits the ethical desert critically, finding the new idols of the tribe as illusory as the old ones. As a consequence, it comes to risk itself on the achievements of artistic modernism: illusions divorced from pleasure and satisfaction, illusions that declare themselves as illusions, semblances without objects offering nothing except the exigency of their presence, as if just that, the reiterated experience of objects whose meaning is exhausted in the necessity that attaches our gaze to them, were a reminder of what was left behind or glimpsed from afar in the course of our nomadic wanderings. How could this philosophical practice be more risky, aligning itself with and subtending its cognitive claiming to a historically specific practice of art, one posing only illusions against the reign of illusion, posing only a violent art without beauty or seduction as a stand-in for human mattering, philosophy binding itself to an art that seeks to deprive us of even the last derisory comforts a worn-out culture can offer?

Philosophical modernism begins with Kant's third *Critique* and becomes self-conscious in the writings of the Jena romantics, who displace the transcendental ambitions of the critical philosophy into the contingency of the accomplishments of the reflective judgment that announces itself as art, as the judgment of taste and the production of genius. The paradigm of the work of art is generalized in the romantic fragment (as well as in the aphorism, the essay and the constellation—a system of fragments), which is neither art nor philosophy but both at once, complete in itself through its incompletion. What the fragment and the modernist work reveal is the possibility of what was the exigency of the ethical being found in the utterly contingent, the transient, and the ephemeral. Thus the philosophical gamble: so long as art exists, so long as as there remains an objectivity and necessity transcending mere liking, taste, want, and desire, so long as passion is possible, there is no postmodernism. While postmodernism is equivalent to difference without hierarchy, judgment, or necessity, parodically reviewing forms in which those distinctions were still prized, philosophical modernism looks for affirmation in "the work's power to be and no longer to represent: to be everything, but without content or with content that is almost indifferent, and thus at the same time affirming the absolute and the fragmentary; affirming totality, but in a form that, being all forms—that is, at the limit, being none at all—does not realize the whole, but signifies it by suspending it, even breaking it" (*IC*, 353).[1]

These last words are from Maurice Blanchot's "The Athenaeum," an essay (arguably the source of Lacoue-Labarthe and Nancy's *The Literary Absolute*) in which he attaches his project of modernist writing to the philosophy of the fragment pursued by German Romanticism. "The Athenaeum" follows immediately upon "Ars Nova," an essay on the new music of the Schönberg school in which Adorno's *The Philosophy of Modern Music* is enlisted by Blanchot to defend the new music in a form which is presumed to be explicitly continuous with writing, as, for example, exemplified in the previous essay "A rose is a rose . . ." and the workless work of the fragment. For present purposes I want to employ the crossing of Blanchot and Adorno as an emblem for a more complicated set of engagements. This seems legitimate to the extent, first, we recognize in Blanchot's appropriation of Heidegger a refusal to hand literature over to philosophy, revealing against Heidegger that it is in the experience of modernist writing that fear, dread, death, nothingness, and existence are encountered in a manner which does not portend the meaning of Being generally, but some other relation. And secondly, we recognize in Blanchot's writing a crossroad in which German romantics, Nietzsche, Levinas, and Derrida (say, in *Parages*) are equally discovered to be fellow travellers, self-conscious nomads in the pursuit of what will infringe upon death-dealing repetition without affirming or repeating.

What all these philosophies share is an analogous negative structure wherein the totalizing force of modernity, socially and in the order of reason, is construed as a negative closure. This negative closure is identified under a host of different titles: metaphysics, presence, identity thinking, the same, the Book, the symbolic, beauty, exchange, the Said. Modernist art, for at least some of these writers, functions as the dissonant conscience of this totalization, its other which in turn signifies another other: absence, nonidentity, the Other, the work, the semiotic, the sublime, the (pure) gift, the Saying. This simple negative structure (the Same and the Other) tends toward equivocality because the terms designating what eludes identifying thought and practice are posed as themselves being the other of reason and as referring to or standing-in for what it is that identifying thought dominates, represses and denies. Thus the equivocality in the others of identifying reason is itself equivocal in that each refusal of the logic of the Same inevitably reconfigures its philosophical and historic meaning. In this respect, the different titles for the Same also become different despite the fact that diagnostically none would depart far from the structures and strictures of my opening two paragraphs. The desert grows.

Within this desert the modernist work is neither quite oasis nor mirage, but both object and semblance at once. However the modernist work is interpreted, its grammar remains bound to that of the Kantian aesthetic, that is a grammar in which necessity and objectivity are elicited in manner homologous with that of scientific cognition and moral reason, but where precedence is accorded to the object. Blanchot figures the syncopation of necessity (and so objectivity) with the precedence of the object in terms of fascination. Fascination, as an account of aesthetic perception, combines cognition's perceptual orientation with the exigency of the ethical, implicitly thereby dissolving the categorial distinction between the epistemic and the moral.

> Seeing implies distance, the decision that causes separation, the power not to be in contact and to avoid the confusion of contact. Seeing means that this separation has nevertheless become an encounter. But what happens when what you see, even though from a distance, seems to touch

you with a grasping contact, when the manner of seeing is a sort of touch, when seeing is a *contact* at a distance? What happens when what is seen imposes itself on your gaze, as though the gaze had been seized, touched, put in contact with appearance? . . . What fascinates us, takes away our power to give it meaning, abandons its "perceptible" nature, abandons the world, withdraws to the near side of the world and attracts us there, no longer reveals itself to us and yet asserts itself in a presence alien to the present time and to presence in space . . . Fascination is . . . vision that is no longer the possibility of seeing, but the impossibility of not seeing. (*GO*, 75)

Blanchot's strategy here, as throughout "Literature and the Right to Death," seems to be to provide a phenomenology of aesthetic perception on the general model of our encounters with the literature of the modern gothic and horror story from Poe and Maupassant to Kafka. This literature models, as we shall see, the aesthetically sublime. Nonetheless, what gives Blanchot's elegant phenomenology of aesthetic perception, which has writing as its means (*GO*, 76–77), a claim to generality is that it encapsulates and reinscribes all the basic elements of Kant's grammar of the aesthetic.

Fascination is a form of reflective judgment in which the dominating categories of determinate, subsumptive judgment (viz., space and time) are suspended. As a consequence, the object takes away our power to give meaning, to subsume and comprehend, and in this sense it becomes "imperceptible." Despite that suspension, what is issue here is still judgment and cognition ("seeing"), a putting oneself or being put into relation to the object, a mental *response* to what is there. In this situation, action and instrumentality ("the confusion of contact") are also displaced. It is because action and instrumentality are displaced that Blanchot assimilates fascination to the order of "the image" (the title of the section in which the analysis of fascination occurs)—the modernist, sublime work of art. The fascinating is the sublime, what dislocates constitutive subjectivity; so "the gaze finds the power that neutralizes it" (*GO*, 75), what renders it neutral, disinterested, and thus no longer the gaze of a subject. Throughout Blanchot, aesthetic experience is characterized in terms—"neutrality," "the outside," "the neuter," "the impersonal," and so forth—that imply its being objective in a mode beyond the objectivity available through subjective practices; aesthetic disinterest is the suspension of the interests of knowing and morality for the sake of a more originary interest in existence.

The fascinating is the successor of the auratic, and the experience (*Erfahrung*) of fascination is the experience of the aura, of what possesses strangeness and distance, holding our gaze, demanding it, without relinquishing itself to it. Again, as in reflective judgment, the moment of intuition and sensuality, the feeling aroused by the object, what Kant figured in terms of the discriminating but non-subsumptive activity of reflective judgment, is aligned with perception of it: the "contact" and "touch" of the other. Logically, the fascinating attains to its objectivity or neutrality through an intensification of subjectivity (touch and contact). Hence the near perfection of the formula that states that fascination occurs "when seeing is a contact at a distance." The modal articulation of fascination is derived directly from the entwinement of contact and distance: "the *impossibility* of not seeing." The removal of possibility by what is fascinating, as if the gaze of the subject is in its turn gazed upon, making the subject also an object, sets up an affinity between subject and object that belongs to both registers, subject and object, simultaneously. The impossibility of not seeing is the impossibility of turning way, of relegating what is seen to one's own possibilities and desires, of being free to choose or not choose the object. Isn't this enough to suggest that modally fascination approximates to the exigency of the ethical, what is obligatory, but as semblance rather than fact?

Evidence for this claim is provided when we discover that Blanchot discovers the paradigm for aesthetic impossibility in the experience of suffering: "The present of suffering is the abyss of the present, indefinitely hollowed out and in this hollowing indefinitely distended, radically alien to the possibility that one might be present to it through the mastery of presence" (*IC,* 44). Suffering cannot be turned away from or grasped; it imposes itself as an immediacy opposed to the very subjectivity it violates. Suffering, its timeless incessance, is impossibility without distance; hence, fascination is the addition of distance through image to the experience of suffering. Once fascination is recognized as an aestheticization of a suffering that is both subjective and objective, then not only does the ethical character of fascination become perspicuous, but we can more clearly recognize how Blanchot's whole analysis of aesthetic perception is an elaboration of the modernist sublime. The pain of the sublime can be recorded as a grammatical memory of suffering, the semblance of an unforgettable, albeit always forgotten, empathy.

"Empathy," to be sure, is not a Blanchotian word. Yet in his grammatical tracing of the impossible Blanchot approximates just such an originary empathy. Grammatically, the necessity entailed by aesthetic impossibility, the inability to not see, contains three moments (*IC,* 45–46): incessance; a presence which cannot be made present, hence, inversely, "the ungraspable that one cannot let go of" (ibid., 45); and, finally, the fact that such features belong not to an immoveable in itself, the perception of a contingent perfection, but rather are components of a movement containing an address to the subject, an approach, whose very immediacy is what withdraws it from comprehension and control. In specifying the movement of aesthetic impossibility, Blanchot is adding to the distance that separates it from suffering the requisite dimension of an affirmation: "we perceive that in impossibility it is not only the negative character of the experience that would make it perilous, but also 'the excess of its affirmation' (what in this excess is irreducible to the power to affirmation)" (*IC*, 46). The suffering and affirmation that are directly implied by the grammar of aesthetic impossibility, and indeed may be considered components of it, naturally enough refer us to the traditional pain/pleasure structure of the sublime without Kant's temporal ordering of that structure (first the pain of what refuses comprehension, then the pleasure of our ultimate moral triumph through our awaking to the measurelessness of the moral law within us).

If a memory of ethical necessity is enjoined by aesthetic impossibility, does not Blanchot also require some account of the universality implied by this experience if it is truly going to attain to a categorial reinscription of ethicality? He will not disappoint us here. Having elaborated the traits of impossibility, Blanchot contends that impossibility is nothing other than the mark of "experience," "for there is experience in the strict sense only where something radically other is in play" (ibid.). Fascination can attain to this exemplarity in virtue of its previous categorial articulation: as the appearance form of an objectivity that is antecedent to the activities through which states of affairs become cognitively or morally objective through the projection of a transcendental affinity between subject and object, fascination must claim for itself a generality, namely, our relation to exteriority as such. Hence aesthetic perception, as categorially constituted by impossibility, becomes exemplary for what it is to have a relation *überhaupt* to exteriority, to what is other than self, with the obvious implication that this experience, the experience of experience, has been grammatically withdrawn from everyday practice and migrated into the aesthetic. Blanchot offers no explanation of this fact.

Because the pain of this relation, its negativity, is always subtended by an affirmation, Blanchot considers it to have the logical structure of *passion:* "impossibility is relation with the Outside; and since this relation without relation is the passion that does not allow itself to be mastered through patience, impossibility is the passion of the Outside itself" (ibid.). Passion as a desire that is suffered explicitly links the moments of pain and pleasure. Passion, however, is always equivocal in that in it the desire for the object is so overwhelming that the subject becomes the Object of what it would grasp. Thus our relation to exteriority belongs as much to the order of affection and desire as it does to the order of perception and cognition.

Nonetheless, to speak about the "passion of the Outside itself" is dangerous and awkward since part of Blanchot's point in aligning impossibility and experience is to vanquish the idea that the notion of exteriority, as revealed in the nonempirical experience of the aesthetic, refers to a transcendent being, that is, to what can never belong to the order of empiricity. Yet in shifting passion from us to the "Outside itself" he appears to be ontologizing the grammatical meaning of aesthetic experience in a manner that solicits just such a transcendent/transcendental interpretation of exteriority, as if, we might say, empirical relations between persons and world were grounded in an agapic gift, with each and every object bearing a trace of that agapic giving in a manner never coequal with the experience of the object itself. We are familiar enough with this idea from Derrida, when for example, he states: "It is this exteriority [of the pure gift] which sets the cycle [of exchange] going, it is this exteriority that puts the economy in motion."[2] Or, analogously, in *Glas*: "the gift, the giving of the gift, the pure *cadeau,* does not let itself be thought by dialectics to which, however, it gives rise."[3] In speaking of the Outside itself, does not Blanchot approximate this transcendental interpretation of exteriority by making literature the site of a "faith" beyond knowing and ethical life, making literary modernism a procedure for limiting knowledge in order to make room for faith?

Until this final interpretation of what is revealed by aesthetic experience, there was nothing in Blanchot's grammatical analysis which Adorno would need or want to deny. Yet, what are we to make of a passage like the following?

> When, for example, Simone Weil says simply, "Human life is *impossible*. But misfortune alone makes this felt," we understand very well that it is not a question of denouncing the unbearable or absurd character of life—negative determinations that belong to the realm of possibility—but of recognizing in impossibility our most human belonging to immediate human life, the life that it falls to us to sustain each time that, stripped through misfortune of the clothed forms of power, we reach the nakedness of every relation, that is to say: the relation of naked presence, the presence of the other, and the infinite passion that comes from it. (*IC,* 47)

The nakedness of every relation? Naked presence? Relations without power bound together through an infinite passion? Where have we heard these words before? Why should we not interpret Blanchot's essential night as the noumenal substrate of the phenomenal appearances revealed by language? How can we make sense of the idea of relations without power (synthesis, language, or affinity) except as referring us to a perspective in which truth would be possible without the negativity which belongs to denomination, the name which gives the object by murdering its unmediated presence? Why should we think there is an origin of meaning prior to negativity? How could it be the case that the possibility of meaning belongs both to the negativity of language in relation to exteriority, and exteriority as such be an origin of meaning prior to language?

We can hear Blanchot's anxiety about language as such in his comments on Gertrude Stein's line "a rose is a rose is a rose is a rose" (*IC*, 343). On the one hand, the line intrigues the rose itself, beautiful beyond what language can say; on the other hand, the reiterative saying reveals how language in the very act of attempting to name the rose in its integrity suddenly dissolves it, loosens the tie between word and thing until the rose becomes merely a counter, an exchangeable commodity, the chatter of a Valentine's Day card. Blanchot raises this ambiguity in the heart of language, its dynamic logic of disclosure and disintegration, expression and communication, to a second-order function, as if antecedent to its pungent smell, its dark red, darker than blood but blood-like, its skin-like petals, its evanesence and fragility, its seductive look and tearing thorns, as if without any of this affinity with the human form there could be even the potentiality for meaning, an integrity to be squandered or liquidated. Yet it is just this that Blanchot's notion of exteriority implies and which thus governs what he construes as the project of modernist writing.

Blanchot's hyperbole is based on a false inference. The specific ways in which regimes of identity, particular practices of language, refuse nonidentity do entail the existence of an original aporia at the heart of language, viz., the unavoidability of death and so identity within every disclosure. Even if language intends to name and reveal, because it operates through a process of reflection and negation, all linguistic practice contains a negativity which potentiates the loss of the object. Adorno considers this aporetic structure to be a consequence of language having a dual structure: an orientation toward expression (revealing the object) and an orientation toward communication (making the meaning of the object an exchangeable item); this latter ideal is realized in deductive demonstrations. From this double orientation, however, it does not follow that the aporia of language itself is considerable, that it can reverberate as a project within social practice, apart from the particularities of specific identitarian regimes, particular ways in which objects are covered over, experience repressed, the claims of the world denied. Which is to say that we cannot intelligibly pursue nonidentity or exteriority except as the nonconceptual moment of this or that conceptuality. That language and meaning are locked within an aporetic structure which explicates both the possibility of nonidentity (the beautiful rose) and the unavoidability of identity thinking (the Valentine's Day card) does not entail that there is a question concerning an exteriority that is as such the opaque condition for every identification. On the contrary, to accept that thesis would involve making the uncovering of particular cases of identity thinking irrelevant since they would imply a deeper stratum of identification that could never be removed and hence one which we could never put ourselves in relation to. But if no relation to this second-order exteriority is possible, then how could it matter to actual practice? If only the transcendental is truly exterior, and if experience is truly only of this exteriority, then all empirical experience belongs to the order of the Same and no significant differences within the Same (between the dominated and the free, the repressed and the not repressed, the dirempted and the whole) can be meaningfully drawn. To inhabit the aporia of language is not to search for an exteriority prior to all negation, but to acknowledge an open-ended and unsatisfiable responsibility toward the world implicit in each and every act and utterance.

Adorno and modernists like Blanchot take the side of things against language, hence both intrigue a pre-reflective encounter with the world that language cannot get on level terms with, to which language can never be equal. Fascination and aesthetic experience are exemplars of such experiential access. Meaning cannot be reduced to language and what is conveyed strictly through it: the smell of the rose is neither a pure intuition, meaningless, nor is it the equal of the words "sweet and pungent"; nor is it the passion of the outside as such, an ontological solicitation and potentiality for meaning (its contingent connection with our capacity for smelling voids that hypothesis). For Adorno the idea of an original passivity, of a passivity more basic than the coordination of passivity and activity in everyday experience, can only be a grammatical and critical reminder of the limits of the communicative axis of linguistic practice, and hence a reminder of the ineliminable dependence of language on its objects. Meaningful discourse will forever include a moment of contingent responsiveness, what I am calling the affinity of subject and object, beyond subjective control and desire, conditioning subjectivity and making it possible. Since, however, this responsiveness is relational, the smell of the rose for me, a touch and a contact that draws language to it while remaining forever at a distance, then exteriority too must be relational and empirical. For Adorno nonidentity gestures toward what *this* regime of practice and language represses and fails to acknowledge, not a primal signification or potentiality for signification permanently lost to human experience while being a trace within every experience. Because the subject cannot be an origin or a first, the dream of idealism, it does not follow that object is. The preponderance of the object is a feature of meaningful discourse, not beyond it.

Blanchot's phenomenology of aesthetic experience is prescient and compelling. The suspicion that it, like the analogous theories of his companions, ontologizes a particular configuration of art and society might be vindicated if we could bind the traits of fascination and impossibility to a precise social content. Yet, it is just this which modernism's excision of content and representation would seem to make impossible. Do not the new music or abstract expressionism or modernist literature attain their power by removing themselves from representational sense? Does not the elimination of ordinary representational sense suggest an outside to language beyond the relational and the representational? Does not the performative self-reflexivity of "exteriorized" writing, like that of Blanchot, Derrida and Levinas, seek an equivalent de-representationalisation of meaning for the sake of an outside prior to representation?

Aphorism 58 of *Minima Moralia,* "The truth about Hedda Gabler," considers just one fragmentary moment of that play, the scene concerning Aunt Julle's hat, as an emblem for the whole; with the play itself coming to have the same fragmentary status in relation to its social world as the hat does to the play. Aphorism 58, of course, belongs to a system of fragments whose purpose is to reveal "damaged life," a negative image of the ethical totality, while the aphorism is offered as complete within itself "like a porcupine." Hence this aphorism entwines all the difficulties with and claims about fragment, totality and negativity—together with the connection between the philosophical and the aesthetic they imply—that are essential to the logic of philosophical modernism. The possibility of such a modernism can thus be interrogated through a reading of it, while simultaneously permitting us to place Adorno's construction in relation to the adjoining position of Blanchot. Could *Hedda Gabler,* a play whose social content is unmistakeable, be fascinating and impossible in Blanchot's sense? In Adorno's fragmentary reading of the play might we locate the specific social forms that are the suppressed content of Blanchot's categories? Before engaging with this reading, for the single purpose of measuring it, a slight detour will prove useful.

NEGATIVE CLOSURE, NEGATIVE TOTALITY

Near the center of Adorno's thought, one consistently finds two hyperbolic expressions, each reenforcing and defining the other: "The whole is the false" and "Not a word in it [contemporary literature] has any value now if it does not say the unsayable, the fact that it cannot be said."[4] The first expression ironically vents Adorno's belief that society, the whole and "universal," is becoming increasingly reified, "a charnel-house of long-dead interiorities,"[5] in virtue of its becoming more and more a closed functional system in which the rule of the whole, for Adorno the rationalized principle of exchange, dominates all of the parts. To *say* the whole is false is, of course, impossible since the saying itself performatively proves the claim untrue: society does not yet have the power to silence a judgement upon it. Yet noting the hyperbole and irony of Adorno's discourse does nothing toward compensating for what makes his rhetoric necessary, namely, the difficulty of making objective truth count and matter subjectively. It is all but anthropologically necessary for each of us to consider our sayings and doings as our "own," as things said and done by us because we believe the saying true and the action a product of individual desire and choice. To believe otherwise would involve collapsing the distinction between saying and repeating, speaking for oneself and being spoken for, acting freely and being coerced. To have a conception of oneself is to be able distinguish oneself *from* society, to consider oneself a locus of speech and action rather than a mere conduit through which societal demands are channeled. Hence, objective claims about unfreedom or meaninglessness are bound to be met with subjective resistance; such claims are, in a sense, incommensurable with subjectivity.

The performative contradiction involved in saying "The whole is the false" brings in its train a further epistemological difficulty: from what point of view or perspective, if not the one inhabited by me here, is such a judgement lodged? How could a particular form of human life, which as such provides the means through which its inhabitants judge all else, be deemed false as a whole? Is there not an epistemological impertinence in making such a judgement? The second of Adorno's central formulations that contemporary literature must attempt to say the unsayable, saying that it cannot be said— should be considered as growing out of these performative and epistemological difficulties with his claim about the "false" totality of modern society. At one level, the demand to say the unsayable is another way of stating the requirement to perform what would be empirically contradictory. But fictional discourse possesses potentialities for suspending conditions for the formation of statements that empirical discourse does not. Proleptically, for example, fictional characters can inhabit objective despair or meaninglessness either by the suspension of the requirement of sustaining the worth of their subjectivities or through the narrational technique of dialectically fusing first and third person points of view. By identifying with such characters, we inhabit a perspective on ourselves not commonly vouchsafed to us. Further, literature's constitution by rules of formation other than those required of rational statements, which provide its "illusory" distance from empirical reality, entail conceptions of "rightness" or "correctness" that are an alternative to criteria for judging the truth of statements. Of course, we must have reasons for valuing this alternative standard of correctness, typically a judgement of beauty, as trumping empirical truth if the sort of judgement of society Adorno is concerned to make is to succeed.

To say the unsayable is to give voice to meaninglessness or to the wrong of society as a whole; to say that this is unsayable is to acknowledge that the conditions for so speaking are not themselves properly empirical conditions, not conditions that belong to the routine practices of society. The practices of formation for literary works are nonetheless social practices, practices for the making of "meaningful" wholes. Works accomplished through literary practices "mean" in ways other than ordinary empirical meaning. To philosophically underwrite the worth of such modernist literary practices, the task of philosophical aesthetics according to Adorno, would thus be to point to a potentiality for meaning that is not fully commensurable with what ruins empirical speech and action. However, in making his focus the rules governing literary production, Adorno emphatically privileges form over content, making the central dialectic of works the relation between their form and their content. This distinctly modernist aspect of Adorno's aesthetic does not obviously fit the dramaturgy of a writer like Ibsen.

Yet, there can be little doubt that the significance of his discovery or turn to the problem of the position of women in society is that it permitted Ibsen to write works that are judgements against society as whole. Ibsen's female characters, in becoming conscious of themselves within the morally repressive social whole, become points of resistance to the blind or unconscious perpetuation of society. They are, to use Adorno's terms of art, the nonidentical within the identitarian whole. The relentless negativity of Ibsen's dramaturgy is in evidence even in the final, chilling conversation between Torvald Helmer and Nora in *A Doll's House*.[6] In it Nora does not seek equal rights or equal respect with those already possessed by Helmer; if that were the case she might have stayed with him and fought for equal treatment and opportunity. She regards the wrong of the injury done to her as having deeper sources than that, as providing no concrete possibility for a future life with Helmer. Each such possibility, monetary assistance, communication in writing, is rejected by Nora as links to a world in which she could never be a self for herself. That world must be rejected in its entirety. Her only conceivable response to the kind of wrong done to her is to leave. In leaving her home and marriage she is, for all intents and purposes, really and metaphorically taking leave of society. What Nora comes to find intolerable in herself, namely, the self she has been given by society via her father and Helmer, must also count against Helmer, canceling him as she has been cancelled, left without voice or individual agency. It is society itself, its laws, the roles assigned to her of being a wife and mother, that Nora condemns; but this is just to say, she condemns society of no specific wrong—no specific principle or moral norm or "law" has been infringed. The injury done to her and so the wrong of the society is just its being "this" society; in judging it, Nora is already outside it: "I must try to satisfy myself which is right, society or I." The presumption here, that whole could be the false, is not properly inhabitable; which is what gives point to Helmer's response to Nora that to say such things she must be ill or mad. Only by being mad or deranged or, to remind ourselves of how literature has given itself space for critique, a child or an adolescent or a dung beetle or a head in a mound of sand can one speak about society as whole. The position of women is like this, already outside society because submerged within it too emphatically.

Nora's counter to the charge of madness, "I have never felt so sane and sure in my life," does not token the possession of a secure place of judgement, an intact subjectivity with which to judge. Only *against* society, negatively, does Nora possess an individuality and subjectivity; for herself she is nothing. If we take "honor" as Ibsen's term for the self-valuing constitutive of subjectivity, the value we are required to possess for ourselves as having standing for ourselves in the eyes of others, what we now might call self-respect, then Helmer is not wrong in saying that "no man can be expected to sacrifice his honour, even for the person he loves," since to sacrifice one's honor would be to sacrifice oneself. Nora's flat reply, "Millions of women have done it," is not a statement of moral superiority but an acknowledgement that "millions of women" have been deprived of the conditions of selfhood, what would make them persons in their own right. Hence, the intense self-loathing and self-laceration that concludes Nora's next speech: "Torvald, in that moment I realized that for eight years I had been living here with a complete stranger, and had borne him three children—! Oh, I can't bear to think of it! I could tear myself to pieces." In leaving Helmer, Nora is tearing to pieces herself as wife, mother, daughter—the "dolls" or roles allotted to her by society. A comment of Adorno's on the very idea of social roles is appropriate here: "This notion is derived from the pure being-for-others of individual men, from that which binds them together with one another in social constraint, unreconciled, each unidentical with himself. Human beings find their 'roles' in that structural mechanism of society which trains them to pure self-preservation at the same time that it denies them preservation of their Selves."[7] If we reduce Nora's complaint that she has been treated as a doll by her father and husband as only a statement of domination, which it is also, then we miss her larger complaint, that society as a whole is only a doll's house without room for true selves of any sort. If Nora cannot be a daughter, wife, or mother since as roles these deprive her of the possibility of being a self for herself, then *a fortiori* Helmer cannot be a husband or father and a self. The difference in power and privilege between men and women gives a firmer basis to the self-deception that men suffer as opposed to women. But both are deceived if they believe that, say, what passes for marriage is truly a relation between two autonomous selves. There are no such selves in this society. Thus Helmer is a "complete stranger" to Nora in two senses: morally, he has proved himself not to be the man she thought and hoped he was because, secondly, he has acted only as his roles required and hence shown that he is not, in a sense, a self at all.

For Nora and Helmer to have a marriage, for there to be any hope for them—"the miracle of miracles"—they "would both have to change so much that . . ." Nora's silence here, the impossibility of her completing her statement, saying exactly in what ways they would have to change is the unsayability of all she has been saying. When Nora answers Helmer's request to complete her description of the change required with "That life together between us two could become a marriage," the term marriage designates nothing positive; "marriage," as used by Ibsen, is an empty name for a possibility opened up only by the reiterative preceding negations. Marriage names utopia, by not naming it.

Despite Ibsen's sustaining of a negative procedure throughout this closing scene, *A Doll's House* remains aesthetically unsatisfactory. Firstly, the strength of character Nora demonstrates in the final scene is implausible against the background of her previous doll-like performances with Helmer and her frenetic activity with respect to the loan. The objection here is not that it is implausible that Nora should have the strength to leave Helmer—it is a wonder that she should have stayed with him so long. Rather it is the degree of her self-possession, her utter sanity, her unclouded perception of herself, of him and of the possibilities that society provides for them both that is incompatible with her sense of herself as not knowing her own mind, of being torn and without resource. Secondly, it is difficult to fathom why the "final" Nora believes her children would be "in better hands" with others if her critique of Helmer and society in general is true. This lapse, justified by the desire to demonstrate that for herself Nora is nothing and so, as she is, can be "nothing" to her children, hence completing the tearing of herself to pieces, signals a third fault, namely, the unresolved or indeterminate tension between Nora's critique of the position of women in society and the critique of society as a whole. The events concerning the loan and the IOU, and the "doll" theme connect most easily through the question of the position of women, hence making the more radical gesture of the final conversation exorbitant with respect to the events precipitating it. At the same time, it is clear that for Ibsen the issues of money and bourgeois respectability are central to his general critique of society. To say that the narrative of the play justifies Nora as a woman against society but not the more general critique misses the point. No plot, no straightfoward narrative could be the bearer of the more general critique. What I am claiming are the aesthetic faults of the play are just consequences of Ibsen not paying sufficient attention to the performative and epistemological difficulties of totalizing critique. Nora's strength and clarity of vision at the end of the play embody the very individuality and sense of self she claims neither she nor anyone else in society can possess. Although the plot of the play justifies Nora's judgement on Helmer as the representative of society, unless we could trust her final judgements on their situation we would not find her final departure, the final slamming of the door, compelling. Ibsen registers Nora as *both* "sane and sure" of herself and as nothing for herself, but at this juncture his dramaturgy cannot reconcile those conflicting yet necessary perspectives. Nora says the unsayable, but does not convincingly say that it cannot be said; she says it, but we cannot perceive from where. Or rather, it looks too much as if Nora's protest against society presupposes the transfigured one she is about to quest after. It is this that transforms the chill of the play's negativity into the warmth of affirmation, making Nora after all a beautiful heroine, an heroic beauty to be emulated and admired. Since beauty and admiration, which is equally the play's beauty, its allusive harmony and affirmation, are co-extensive with the play's aesthetic collapse, then Ibsen will have to depart from the order of the aesthetics of the beautiful if his critical stance is going to be sustainable. Only in the the fascination of the hateful and horrible can we recognize ourselves without illusion or self-deception.

At this juncture, Ibsen's dramaturgy has no choice but to present the self of nonidentity as both fully self-possessed and as fully dispossessed. Nora's self-possession is a representationally affirmative moment that cancels the play's critical integrity. If so, then Ibsen requires a more austere modernism to accomplish his ends.

NEGATIVITY: LIFE WITHOUT DEATH

In Aphorism 58 of *Minima Moralia* Adorno very briefly suggests a modernist reading of *Hedda Gabler,* which I shall elaborate and expand in what follows.[8] By "modernist" I mean a self-conscious dramaturgy which formally embodies the negativity of meaning that is equally the thematic core of the play. The play *Hedda Gabler* is thus as much a focus of attention as the character of Hedda herself. The context of Adorno's few remarks on the play is nineteenth century aestheticism, the "uprising of beauty against bourgeois good." I hinted at the significance of this uprising earlier when I noted that literary discourse's challenge to the reign of empirical discourse, which in Ibsen is always the discourse of bourgeois morality and its codes of respectability, needed vindication if it were to be something more than the presentation of another perspective—the idea of literature as an imaginative variation on the possibilities of human life. If beauty is linked to appearance and illusion in this way, then the aesthetic critique of modernity becomes a feeble idealism. But the Platonic conception of beauty that permits this negative judgment misconstrues its inner logic which, according to Adorno, involves an impulse in all art to end art, an "innermost striving towards an image of beauty free of appearance."[9] In saying this Adorno does not imagine that beauty is ever free of appearance; rather, he is pointing to the fact that modernist works of art do not seek to "participate" in the beautiful, as a Platonist would have it, nor do they seek an aesthetic meaningfulness forever divorced from empirical life; rather, they immanently strive to throw off their appearance character, to be more (or less) than works of art, to be mere things. What speaks most forcefully for this view is the claim to uniqueness by specifically modern works, seeking their worth in opposition to other works and the tradition, not in exemplifying something called "art" or "beauty" that exists independently of them, but by being worthy of attention, our attention, irrespective of anything else.

Modernist works of art, according to Adorno's line, seek like Nora to have their own voice, an independent claim to worth and integrity; and like Nora, they attempt to attain this independence critically and negatively, opposing in their dynamic unfolding the existing laws and norms of artistic respectability and acceptability.

In making Nora a doll, society gave her a self that was for others; dolls and roles imply a certain theatricality in the constitution of the self, which is the precise equivalent to what Adorno means by the "appearance character" of works. Hence, for a dramatic work to throw off its appearance character it must contain a moment of anti-theatricality, anti-drama, anti-art. Such a moment would not and could not utterly remove a work's appearance character since that character is just a work's being for others, as there for others. And so equally, our being for ourselves must equally have an appearance character, a being there for others. Adorno's and Ibsen's concern is that the demands for appearing, our social roles and our notion of aesthetic acceptability, being beautiful, have driven out autonomy, personal and aesthetic, and that the social spaces available for appearing rule out the possibility of combining being for ourselves while being for others, being beautiful, a harmonious aesthetic object, and being aesthetically authentic (not kitsch or resigned or melodramatic, etc.). Only this connection between the impossibility of aesthetic appearing and the impossibility of authentic existence can begin explicating Blanchot's discernment of a connection between Simone Weil's "impossibility of human life" and the modalization of aesthetic perception; a point I shall return to. Hence, being for self can only appear as dissonance, unbeautiful, workless, as taking one's leave of society altogether. Ibsen certainly meant Nora's departure, the slightly distant sound of the slamming door, to carry this kind of weight, to be morally and aesthetically dissonant. It fails to be so for the reasons already cited, which is underlined by the fact that the trope of the heroine taking leave of her repressive past and going off into the sunset to discover herself as a independent woman has become a staple of a familiar sort of neo-romantic feminist fiction.

What Ibsen discovered, and what remains a central ingredient in Adorno's aesthetics, is the isomorphism or homology between the position of women in society and the position of art and art works in society. If what I have said about dolls, roles and theatricality is correct, then the question of the emancipation of women or the transfiguration of society is not simply a moral or political question but essentially involves "aesthetic" categories: beauty, illusion, appearance, uniqueness, theatricality, and so on. Adorno does not seek to aestheticize the social and political, as he is often accused of doing; rather, he perceives aesthetic categories as already implicated in the forms of repression and domination to which modern societies are subject, and perceives in modernist art a self-conscious engagement with those categories. Although I am aware of descriptions of *A Doll's House* as a dramatic equivalent of cubism, I find the analogy unconvincing; in that play, Ibsen leaves the connections between societal theatricality and his dramaturgy unreflected. The same cannot be said about *Hedda Gabler*.

Adorno situates the arrival of nineteenth century aestheticism within an account of a rupturing and deformation of moral experience.

> The uprising of beauty against bourgeois good was an uprising against 'goodness'. Goodness is itself a deformation of good. By severing the moral principle from the social and displacing it into the realm of private conscience, goodness limits it in two senses. It dispenses with the realization of a condition worthy of men that is implicit in the principle of morality. Each of its actions has inscribed in it a certain resignation and solace: it aims at alleviation, not cure, and consciousness of incurability finally sides with the latter. In this way goodness becomes limited within itself as well. Its guilt is intimacy. It creates the mirage of direct relations between people and ignores the distance that is the individual's only protection against the infringements of the universal.

There is much in this that needs unpacking. Although not altogether apt, it is heuristically useful to consider Adorno's critique here as directed at Kant's moral theory. On Adorno's reading, "goodness" is equivalent to Kantian worthiness to be happy, hence the moral worthiness of the individual apart from what that worthiness brings about either for the moral subject herself or for the objects of her actions. Goodness is doing the right thing for its own sake and not for what it brings about. Adorno construes such goodness as a severing of "the moral principle" and its migration inward. Goodness, as essentially norms and principles prescriptive for individual conduct, severs private from public morality; in so doing, because private morality perceives itself as acting on norms that require equal treatment for all, hence as privately and reflectively taking everyone into account, it displaces justice, insinuating morality in the place of justice. Because doing the morally correct thing is now self-sufficient, an end in itself, indeed for Kant our overriding end, the *actual* realization "of a condition worthy of men," which Adorno regards as implicit in the moral principle, has been dispensed with. The consequence of this is that morality, goodness, tacitly invokes a stocial acceptance of the wrongness of the world. Hence, moral action, good and worthy action, involves a certain "resignation and solace" about the world: our condition is incurable. The best that can be achieved is reform, amelioration. If our overriding and unconditional obligation is to become *worthy* of being happy, becoming good and virtuous in ourselves, then surreptiously bringing about true justice is neither necessary nor obligatory. Such a morality leaves the injustice of the world untouched. It is in this sense that goodness is "limited within itself."

The second sense in which goodness limits the good is a direct consequence of the first. Nothing in morally worthy or virtuous action bespeaks its stoical acceptance of injury, injustice, and wrong. On the contrary, if acting in a morally worthy manner is unconditional, then the recipients of moral action must perceive it as providing all they can reasonably want or deserve. If in being treated in a morally proper manner an individual is receiving all she can rationally expect, then her sense that she is suffering unjust harm cannot be given voice: no moral principle or law is being infringed upon, hence no injustice is being done to her. It is this that Adorno has in mind when he continues the above: "Retention of strangeness is the only antidote to estrangement. The ephemeral image of harmony in which goodness basks only emphasizes more cruelly the pain of irreconcilability that it foolishly denies." Nothing in actual moral action express the gap between its doings and "the good," a condition truly worthy of persons. Exisitng morality, the reign of goodness, fails to accomodate the unreconciled condition of present action, and thereby suffuses a harmony between individuals that can only be felt by the recipients of such morality as a transgression against their awareness that life is unreconciled, broken. Hence, for the sake of justice, they refuse morality. It is this refusal that Adorno is referring to when he speaks of retaining "distance" and "strangeness." The manner of this refusal is aestheticism, the "uprising of beauty against bourgeois good." As will become evident this "beauty," Hedda Gabler's object of devotion, is only possible if rendered unbeautiful; strangeness is preserved only in the horror and the pain of the sublime.

In focusing on Hedda, Adorno is holding onto the thought that it is only micrologically that we can grasp the logic of identity and nonidentity, general and particular, justice and morality—their diremption from one another. Hedda's "doll house" is the petty bourgeois respectability of Tesman and his

Aunt Juliana, and the cynical bourgeois morality of Judge Brack; for them, however differently, morality and appearance are one. The repressive constraints of that morality and its defiant refusal, the overthrow of appearance and the assertion of distance and strangeness, are represented for Adorno by Aunt Julle's "abominable hat," the hat she bought in order to be able to be seen walking with Hedda, and Hedda's malicious pretence of taking it as belonging to the maid Bertha. Adorno's fragment mentions no other detail from the play. Aunt Julle's hat represents propriety, fittingness, normal generality, how society counts, it rules; Hedda's sadistic snub critically begins by recounting, identifying by misidentifying, those rules, their harmonic projection into the future, revealing them as without point or value—mere appearance. Everything that occurs in the play, its suppressed sexuality and passions, the hope and the future that are sequestered in Eilert Loevborg's manuscript (an allegorical figure of the play itself: a history of the future in flames), its shabby deaths, are all figured in Aunt Julle's hat and Hedda's snub. The hat, Adorno implies, is the emblem of the whole, the false totality lodged in a hopeless and absurd particular. The hat is, micrologically and monadologically, the false totality.

It is difficult to imagine a less propitious heroine than Hedda; she is not only extravagant and "absurd," but sadistic, vindictive, and manipulative. She is an ugly heroine, a horror and a grotesque, full of ennui and spleen. The goodness in her life, the love of her husband and his adoring Aunt Julle, her role as mother, are denied, mocked, desecrated, and destroyed, as she destroys the future, real and written, as represented by Eilert Loevborg. In destroying Eilert's book, the "child" of him and Mrs. Elvsted, Hedda commits infanticide and simultaneously consummates her rejection of her pregnancy and so of motherhood as a state or role in which she could fulfil and realize herself, a role worthy of a self. Everything is brought to ruin because anything that would come of any of the characters' best efforts, above all Eilert's book and his becoming a "new man," would be mere reformation, more of the same. For women society is explicitly a "second nature," a world without room for them as selves. As Ibsen has it in the notes he wrote in preparation for *A Doll's House:* "A mother in modern society, like certain insects, retires and dies once she has done her duty by propogating the race."[10] It is this fate that society has planned for Hedda, as it had planned for Nora, justifying thereby their different but analogous rejections of motherhood. Aunt Juliana's cloying welcome of Hedda's pregnancy reveals how society inscribes itself on her body as implacably as the writing machine of Kafka's penal colony does its inhabitants. Even Hedda's body is not her own: propriety and fittingness reach into her womb, claim it and grasp it until it belongs to them.

What Hedda truly desires is a moment of difference, of otherness, something good, beautiful in and of itself. The image of this beautiful life, of life transfigured, is Eilert crowned with vine leaves, which Hedda conceives of occurring through her individual agency. At the end of act three, Hedda renounces the image of transfigured life in words—"I don't believe in that crown any longer"—that precisely echo Nora's renunciation of the miracle of miracles—"I don't believe in miracles any longer." In Hedda's world, the "dung hill," there is no possibility for transfigured life; only a certain kind of death, a death whose very enactment would negate as meaningless the life departed from and in so doing individuate Hedda, could make what was her life meaningful—as, by the manner—of her death, being revealed as unworthy. Ideally for Hedda a "beautiful" death would substitute for the impossible good life, her death the image of what her life could not be. Beauty substitutes for the good here because the death Hedda seeks for Eilert and herself is not conformable to a full life, not the completion or consummation of such a life, but the negative image of life's emptiness. In being a rejection of the life society offers, the individuation and particularity achieved through a beautiful death would be only a semblance of individuation and particularity, fleeting and evanescent. To be sure, the idea of a beautiful death, of a death opposed to the life on offer, involves an incoherence, as if death could be beautiful without being connected to a meaningful life, as if the notion of beauty, which involves harmony, coherence, individuation, and self sufficiency, could adhere to a wholly negative act, as if negativity on its own could be sufficient for the possibility of individuation—which is what, after all, Hedda is seeking. Her desire for a beautiful moment is a desire for experience, for otherness, which can now be recognized as a condition of possibility of her having a nonempty self-relation. The incoherence of the idea of a beautiful death is precisely the incoherence of the conclusion to *A Doll's House*: Nora's departure is both wholly negative and wholly self-affirming, hence a beautiful death. However, if the negativity is total, then it excludes heroic self-affirmation; if the self-affirmation is real, then the negativity is only partial and the whole is not false; if she truly can go in quest of herself, then that is a possibility which society offers her. If the whole is not false, then it would be reformation and not transfiguration that was required. If that was the case, then the presumption of a holistic critique of society must itself have been false. The fact that Nora cannot depart absolutely and beautifully nullifies the play while informing us about how closed and negative her doll's house of a society is.

What we learn from *Hedda Gabler* is that neither a beautiful death nor a beautiful play are possible. Eilert's death is tawdry and demeaning: it happens in a brothel and probably by accident; the gunshot wound that kills him destroying his sexual organs. Death is death, and not the inverted symbol of absent life. Hedda's suicide, despite everything, is only an offense against good taste: "But, good God! People don't do such things!" the final lines of the play, which are equally the very words that Hedda uses hypocritically about Aunt Julle leaving her hat in the drawing-room (in fact placed on a chair by Tesman), and ironically when Mrs. Elvsted describes Hedda's own original threat to shoot Eilert. Her mocking use of convention hence comes to mock her attempt at heroically denying it. Convention and society make her the same in the very act through which she removes herself from them. There can be nothing beautiful in this society, even a death. If a beautiful death were possible, or a beautiful play, then it would be a possibility that society itself provided. If the whole is the false, then there is no such possibility. The deaths of Eilert and Hedda are prefigured by the long invalidated Aunt Rena's ugly and meaningless death; "ugly" because in truth she had been "dead" for years. Aunt Rena's invalid life is the image of nonlife, her dreary passing indistinguishable from her life. What dies in Aunt Rena's bed, dully and peacably, is a bourgeois and so fully proper "specimen," a doll. Aunt Julle will find, she is sure, another invalid to care for, another nonlife whose pains might be "alleviated" not "cured," another nonlife for which she can sacrifice her own.

Hedda then "sins against what is best in her own life [its goodness], because she sees the best as a desecration of the good." Hedda reacts against the transgressive intimacy of goodness as represented by, for example, George Tesman's calling his Aunt Juliana by the childish "Julle," a form of address that Hedda cannot bring herself to employ. Ibsen honours this rejection by entitling the play *Hedda Gabler;* in a sense, Hedda is never married. The goodness of love, marriage, motherhood, worldly success are for Hedda nothing but smothering propriety, correctness, whose hidden violence is captured in Judge Brack's overt attempt to blackmail Hedda into an affair—a "sophisticated" imitation of the life that public morality prohibits. Adorno does not have to mention any of this; it is all there in the scene with the hat. It is thus that despite her sadism, vindictiveness, jealousy and desire to manipulate and control, that it is Hedda who "is the victim," a victim of Aunt Julle's morality, society's morality, which is but society itself. "Unconsciously and absurdly," Adorno claims, Hedda represents, against the old woman, "the absolute." Adorno does not mean this last term lightly. Hedda represents, absurdly, which is to say negatively, the good, the harmonization of virtue and happiness, justice satisfied. It is at this juncture that Adorno returns to the "uprising of the beauty" against morality. The beauty that is Hedda's *idée fixe* is also, for Adorno, her dissonant beauty. The trope of "beauty as a symbol of the morally good" is indeed at issue here but not quite in in Kant's sense since Adorno is after the "truth about Hedda Gabler," which is to say, he wants to raise the claim that beauty of a certain sort, negative beauty, anti-art, can contest the claims of morality and empirical truth. Negative beauty, the sublime, is more "true" than what empirical truth states about how things are. If Hedda is the "absurd" absolute, then she is also the truth about truth now.

Beauty is not a symbol of the morally good in Kant's sense because beauty "opposes morality before mocking it." Beauty opposes morality, in every destructive and self-destructive act of Hedda's, by "balking at anything general [i.e., social propriety and form], and posits as absolute differences determined by mere existence, the accident that has favoured one thing and not another. In beauty, opaque particularity asserts itself as the norm, as alone general, normal generality having become too transparent." The flickering appearance of that beauty in the play is Mrs. Elvsted's hair, which even as a girl Hedda pulled at and threatened to burn, a burning which is metonymically achieved when she burns Eilert's manuscript. Mrs. Elvsted's hair is, I think, for Hedda the counter-image of Aunt Julle's hat, for only on that assumption can we explain the depth of Hedda's jealousy. Mrs. Elvsted's "beautiful, wavy hair" is, as image and so logically akin to a work of art, a promise of happiness, a promise that nothing in Hedda's life can match: "Oh, why does everything I touch become mean and ludicrous? It is like a curse!" In fact, there is a "curse" on Hedda, the curse of society; it is that which deforms her: do we not see in her jealousy a desire for beauty? In her manipulativeness a desire for agency? In her sadism a hatred of a state unworthy of any human being? In her ennui a true registering of the spiritual emptiness of her world? Hedda is indeed cursed.

Beauty is found nowhere in the play, nowhere in the world it depicts. There is no such beauty; it is, finally, only beauty for which Hedda hopes and intrigues, but by intriguing, manipulating others through pretence and deceit, which are the only avenues of agency available to a woman of Hedda's position, destroys its possibility. But we must be careful in how we judge Hedda; on the reading of the play that Adorno obliquely suggests, Hedda's actions are each meant to undo the presumptive forms and claims of goodness that constitute her existence. She is an anti-hero in the quite precise sense that her actions are meant to reduce to nought the morality of her society; but this path of destruction cannot be innocent, which is to say that the beauty Hedda longs for cannot be innocent since it is not a path toward anywhere, not even, unequivocally, the promise of a life. Beauty without negativity is a lie, as the promise of happiness in the beauty of Mrs. Elvsted's hair is a lie, and as Nora's beautiful departure is a lie. All these items, like Hedda's original perception of Eilert's suicide, are, in Judge Brack's words, "charming illusions," illusions that Ibsen will destroy for us as Judge Brack "robs" Hedda of her's about Eilert. Hedda herself is the antidote to such beauty: only as an anti-hero can there be a hero. Hedda is to the idea of the tragic hero what Beckett's plays are to traditional dramaturgy generally. Ibsen's anti-hero is the precursor of Beckett's anti-art. In Hedda's relentless negativity, in her grostesque liquidation of heroic action, *we* discover the otherness and experience for which *she* longs. Hence, all the beauty of *Hedda Gabler* derives from its renunciation of the semblance of beauty, all its affirmation from a recognition of misery.

If Hedda cannot have a beautiful death, the failure of her death becomes the play's meaning, its moment of dissonance whereby it transcends both the morality Hedda opposes and the illusory unity and wholeness of the beautiful aesthetic object. The awkward and abrupt ending to the play reveals Ibsen's dramaturgy as participating in the same destructive activity as Hedda's actions, sinning against dramaturgical propriety, artistic goodness, as she sins against moral goodness. The play must leave us dissatisfied, both aesthetically assenting to (with pleasure) and being appalled by (with pain) Hedda's suicide and Judge Brack's response. The "opaque particular" of which Adorno speaks is the play itself, meaning through its negation of what has been moral and artistic meaning.

> So [beauty] challenges [normal generality], the equality of everything unfree. But in so doing it becomes guilty itself, by cutting off, with the general, all possibility of transcending mere existence whose opacity only reflects the untruth of bad generality. So beauty finds itself in the wrong against right, while yet being right against it. In beauty the frail future offers its sacrifice to the Moloch of the present: because, in the latter's realm, there can be no good, it makes itself bad, in order in its defeat to convict the judge.

In *Hedda Gabler* reality is neither reformed nor transfigured. Nor are we offered an image of transfigured reality. But even if the latter were to arise, the object of Hedda's desire, because it would be only a moment of beauty, it still would not be the highest good realized but only a semblance of it. This is the guilt that anything beautiful must bear in a world in which the good, goodness and happiness, is broken. If beauty is necessary against goodness, its withdrawal from generality, its status as mere semblance, is an indictment of it. Hedda's offense is the necessary condition of beauty; and if that offense indicts bourgeois morality, it is itself condemned with it. The futility and pointlessness of Hedda's death is also that of the play—it changes nothing in the world it is in.

Both Hedda and the play as a whole are objects of neither love nor admiration; Hedda's quest for experience and identity unfold only in order to empty her narrative of everything narrativity promises; what was to be meaning dissolves at the last moment, leaving no trace but its stuttering failure. We watch with fascination, unable to love but equally unable to turn away. Blanchot consistently associates aesthetic impossibility not with death but with being unable to die. Death, for him, is not the worst thing imaginable since in death, in suicides, there is an affirmation: "He who kills himself is the great affirmer of the *present*. I want to kill myself in an absolute instant, the one which will not pass and will not be surpassed" (*SL,* 103). This is Hedda's idea of a beautiful death. The lesson of her suicide agrees with Blanchot—such a death is impossible (ibid.). The horror of Hedda's death, of Judge Brack's appropriation of it, is that Hedda cannot die, and it is this impossibility, this fixation of life into an image without substance, that transfixes us. Hedda cannot die because she cannot live; this is why it is suffering, the feeling of life as pain without possibility, that forms the appropriate image of the impossibility of life. The overt object of our fascination, Hedda's self consumed yet casual malignancy, compels because it is a deformed affirmation, a monstrous passion; but if her malevolence is so constituted, then we can only see her life as, finally, pure suffering—cursed. But if Hedda's suffering is exemplary, it becomes a world suffering, a world-passion (the "passion of the Outside"), and thus a disclosure of an ethical exigency beyond the morality of principles and goodness.

Hedda's life is not ontologically impossible; only the very precise social forms of her society, as emblemized by Aunt Julle's hat, deprive her of a life. The curse upon Hedda is that of an abstract morality and of abstract social forms of interaction denying individuality, keeping each individual within a set of habits and routines that make society "safe." That safety is secured not by brute power or an illusory authority beyond the self (God or King or aristocracy), but by the predominance of social forms, institutions, and practices, whose character demands utter compliance, conformity, repetition, the Same for their reproduction. Our evidence that this is how our society is, that such a predominance exists despite our necessary subjective belief to the contrary, is provided by the justness of Hedda's action, the perverted probity of her character, our capacity, despite everything, to perceive her as society's victim. As *pure* victim, unable to die because unable to live, deprived of any agency appropriate to an individuated self, Hedda is a "pure gift." Thus the workless work of the play presupposes the desire for meaning, Hedda's and Ibsen's, which its logic defeats. Aesthetic negativity, carried through to its completion, presupposes an impossible affirmation. That affirmation, the quest for meaning, is thus realized through relentless negativity. Victim, gift, negativity and affirmation all belong in this scenario to the empirical world, to its possibilities and impossibilities, even if the realization of those possibilities, say the idea of being an individual or a mother or having a marriage, would require the transfiguration of society. There is nothing transcendental about these categories, nor about Hedda's want of experience. That the realization of certain possibilities is only possible on the basis of a transfiguration of self or world does not entail that this futural object is in any sense beyond the world. The play's workless work itself is the signing of the transfigurability of the world, without illusion or semblance, beyond its present configuration.

Hedda can be faithful to the good only by offending and destroying goodness for the sake of beauty. Her fidelity to the good in her destructive behavior is the necessity by which beauty supplements morality. But that necessity, Hedda's fidelity to the good, survives, if it survives at all, in the *aesthetic necessity* which is the play's "truth," its truth against the counting of bourgeois morality: "Beauty's protestation against the good is the bourgeois, secularized form of the delusion of the tragic hero. In the immanence of society, consciousness of its negative essence is blocked, and only *abstract negation acts as a substitute for truth*"[11] (emphasis mine). *Hedda Gabler,* the play, is that abstract negation. It is abstract because nothing is transformed or transfigured in it. Nonetheless, its compulsion, both the "rightness" in Hedda's rejections of society and the necessity by which each intrigue that would let beauty arise is undermined including her suicide, the necessity which leads us to acknowledge Hedda's fidelity to the good and its impossibility, the impossibility of a beautiful moment, a beautiful death, is a "substitute for truth," a cognition of our moral counting. The play hence provides a "hypnotic suggestion of meaning amid the general loss of meaning."[12] Aesthetic necessity, the necessity by which the aesthetic object works, is not another truth, but a critique of truth as it now is and a substitute for another concept of truth, another way of human counting.

Our belief in the truth of Ibsen's totalizing critique and our somewhat slimmer belief that a transfigured reality is both morally necessary and humanly possible derives from our aesthetic judgement of Ibsen's play. My evidence for the first belief resulted from the contrast between the aesthetic falsity of the conclusion of A *Doll's House,* Nora's beautiful departure, in comparison with the aesthetic rightness of Hedda being an anti-hero and her stupid, pointless, and yet, at one remove, tragic death. This same result could have been achieved through a contrast of Helmer with Tesman. Helmer is both a repressive and insensitive patriarch, and morally deficient. Against him Nora can legitimately make *specific* complaints: he fails to fulfil demands for equality and reciprocity, as signalled by the fact that he and Nora did not have a "serious" conversation, "exchange a serious word on a serious subject," in their eight years of marriage, and he fails morally in choosing to uphold his honor in opposition to loyalty to Nora. Nora has reason to believe that Helmer has never loved her. In contrast, however bumbling, Tesman is morally decent, well-meaning, and loving. If there are deficiencies in his character, they are not moral deficiencies; on the contrary, his spiritual deficiencies are a consequence of his moral probity, his goodness. It is this that makes an innocent or internally legitimate moral complaint against him and Aunt Julle impossible. If he and Aunt Julle wrong Hedda, and we believe they do, it is not because they do anything wrong, but because in a difficult sense their life, and so the kind of life of the society to which they belong, is wrong. Their goodness thus requires that in criticizing them, in repulsing their propriety, Hedda must morally wrong them. In Hedda's evil is her fidelity to the good beyond goodness; in her meaningless but nonetheless tragic death lies Ibsen's aesthetically wrought fidelity to the good beyond aesthetic beauty. His sacrifice of beauty for the sake of the good, however, is something that could only be accomplished aesthetically.

From the fact that Ibsen's sacrifice of beauty and meaning is accomplished only aesthetically, it does not follow that his accomplishment is restrictedly aesthetic. On the contrary, it is essential to our aesthetic judgements about *A Doll's House* and *Hedda Gabler* that we measure them both in relation to the moral possibilities and characters of their personae and through an aesthetic deployment of cognitive categories: consistency, unity, necessity. More precisely, a working assumption of my argument to here has been that the possibility of aesthetic beauty—the unity, coherence, and density—of a literary text depends upon access to positive moral meaning. Only on this assumption can we make sense of the fact that when moral meaning, here being construed as co-extensive with the possibility of a life to be meaningful, itself becomes repressive, then a work cannot be beautiful. This implies literature's *wholly nonaesthetic* investment in the categories of moral meaning. It is because the conditions of possibility for narrativity are parasitic on modes of empirical meaningfulness that when narrative fails internally, that is, when it fails through obedience to the injunctions concerning social meaning at work in it, that we can pose the failed narrative, the workless work of the modernist sublime, against society's claim to provide forms adequate to a meaningful life. Because works involve closure, they can become laboratories for the testing of social forms.

Nonetheless, this non-aesthetic investment in the social forms of meaningfulness is played out in aesthetic terms, in the language of literature. *Hedda Gabler*'s dissonance, its refusal of positive affirmation, must possesses an aesthetic rightness if it is to be compelling, even if that compulsion migrates from a judgment of taste voicing the beautiful to a fascination at a sublime monstrosity. But this entails, as Adorno suggests, that an art that rigorously negates meaning must nonetheless live up to the "postulate of meaning": "That is why the best absurdist works of today are more than just plain meaningless. By negating meaning, they attain a semblance of substantiality. The rigorously meaning-negating works are faithful to the same ideal of density and unity as the old meaning-constitutive ones. Works of art willy-nilly become complexes of meaning, even if they negate meaning."[13] That a work can be a complex of meaning through its negation of meaning entails that meaningfulness is not exhausted by the positive meanings negated. It is this fact, in conjunction with the precise character of the meanings that are negated, that permits works to make both cognitive claims and moral demands. This is only a semblance of meaning because true meaning requires generality, the possibility of "going on." Since aesthetic individuation is achieved negatively, this notion of projection into the future is significantly under-determined by modernist works. Yet, that there are such works is our form of hope.

The necessity that binds us to such a form of hope cannot be derived from exteriority itself, the Outside itself. This is because the work of self-dispossession that is Hedda's evil and Ibsen's negative dramaturgy derive the whole of their force from the promises of meaning made by extant moral and literary forms. There is horror only because beauty and meaning are absent. Modernist writing does procede through authorial self-dispossession, a giving up on the idea of works being meaning-constitutive. But this self-dispossession is preceded by the self-dispossession of the tragic hero, by Hedda, whose cruelty anticipates and locates the cruelty of modernist art. Blanchot's literary and philosophical modernism forgets Hedda, forgets the specific suffering and the precise evils (against goodness) that are the substance of modernism's cruel formality.

Adorno's identification of his practice in the "Dedication" to *Minima Moralia* points emphatically to Ibsen's play: "If today the subject is vanishing, aphorisms take upon themselves the duty 'to consider the evanescent itself as essential.' They insist, in opposition to Hegel's logic and yet in accordance with his thought, on negativity." If, under conditions of the vanishing of the subject, say Nora's or Hedda's life, negativity has become the source of affirmation, then only as art is affirmation possible since in empirical practice such negativity would be simply destructive, no work would eventuate, no postulate of meaning announced and satisfied. That works are still possible entails that the social forms of meaning negated in them do not exhaust the possibility of meaning. Such items are fragments because they are vehicles of experience without a world in which the experience they report and provide could be located; still such fragments project a world. The work of art is privileged here because the diremption of art from practice, art's becoming autonomous, makes works evanescent, hence capable of affirming their status as appearances without delusion if not without regret. In circumstances where the possibility of a meaningful life is not socially structured or underwritten, if philosophy is not to pretend to an ordination it cannot sustain, it must place itself in relation to what of experience remains. At the level of social grammar, modernist art is, and was until recently, the repository of that possibility.

ABBREVIATIONS

IC   *The Infinite Conversation,* trans. Susan Hanson (Minneapolis: University of Minnesota Press, 1993).

GO: *The Gaze of Orpheus,* trans. Lydia Davis (Barrytown, New York: Station Hill, 1981).

SL: *The Space of Literature,* trans. Ann Smock (Lincoln: University of Nebraska Press, 1982).

NOTES

1. My reading of Blanchot presupposes the invaluable introduction to his thought provided by Simon Critchley's *"Il y a -*A Dying Stronger than Death (Blanchot with Levinas)," *The Oxford Literary Review* 15:1–2 (1993), 81–131.

2. *Given Time: I. Counterfeit Money,* trans. Peggy Kamuf (Chicago: University of Chicago Press, 1992), 30.

3. *Glas,* trans. John Leavey and Richard Rand (Lincoln: University of Nebraska Press, 1986), 243. For more general comments on this see my *The Fate of Art: Aesthetic Illusion from Kant to Derrida and Adorno* (State College: Penn State University Press, 1992), chap. 3, especially sec. 6 and 7; and Simon Jarvis, "Soteriology and Reciprocity," *Parataxis* 5, (Autumn 1993), 30–39.

4. The first quote is from *Minima Moralia: Reflections from Damaged Life,* trans. E. F. N. Jephcott (London: New Left Books, 1974), no. 29; the second quote is from *Notes to Literature* vol. 2, trans. Shierry Weber Nicholson (New York: Columbia Unversity Press, 1992), 4.

5. Georg Lukács, *The Theory of the Novel,* trans. Anna Bostock (London: Merlin Press, 1971), 64.

6. All quotes from Ibsen are from Michael Meyer's translations, to be found in Henrik Ibsen, *Plays: Two* (London: Methuen, 1980). My reading of *A Doll's House* initially follows and then implicitly criticizes the reading to be found in Stanley Cavell's *Conditions Handsome and Unhandsome* (London: University of Chicago Press, 1990), 108–115.

7. "Society," trans. F. R. Jameson, to be found in Stephen Eric Bronner and Douglas Mackay Kellner, *Critical Theory and Society: A Reader* (London: Routledge, 1989), 270.

8. All further quotes from Adorno, unless otherwise noted, are to no. 58 of *Minima Moralia.*

9. Ibid., no. 47; the corollary of this moment in Blanchot is the worklessness that is the horizon of the modernist work; see *GO,* 99–104.

10. Quoted in Meyer's introduction in *Plays: Two*, op. cit., 13.

11. For more on this see Adorno's "Trying to Understand *Endgame*," in *Notes to Literature* vol. 1, trans. Shierry Weber Nicholsen (New York: Columbia University Press, 1991), 241–275.

12. T. W. Adorno, *Aesthetic Theory*, trans. Christian Lenhardt (London: Routledge and Kegan Paul, 1984), 222.

13. Ibid., 221.

Chapter 8

Theodor Adorno on Tradition

Eva Geulen

In their introduction to a representative collection of essays on the postmodern, Andreas Huyssen and Klaus Scherpe point their German readership to the "*gravierenden Unterschiede*" between the structure of German and American debates on this subject.[1] German critics, they observe, tend to discuss the question of postmodernity in terms of the familiar paradigm of modern vs. anti-modern (where the "postmodern" is one version of the latter), while American critics have generally overcome such fruitless oppositions by deliberately employing postmodern as a "*Relationsbegriff.*" Whether or not this distinction is valid, it still reveals an interesting topographical dimension directly pertinent to the debate in question: If the United States, justifiably considered by Huyssen and Scherpe the "*Exportland des neuen Superlativs*" (p. 10) is more postmodern in its response to the postmodern, then Germany's resistance is to be attributed to its "modernism"—which is to say that the old opposition is reintroduced along geographical lines. This symmetry is, of course, complicated when German philosophers come to figure prominently in the American scenario. A particularly striking case of the return of modern Germans in postmodern America is the recent interest in selected works by Theodor W. Adorno.[2] Besides *Minima Moralia*, whose format and style are admired for their postmodern features—in apparent ignorance of the long tradition Adorno's book partakes in—the *Dialectic of Enlightenment* enjoys remarkable popularity. Its critique of instrumental reason is frequently considered a direct forerunner of the critique of rationality ascribed to the postmodern agenda. The curious fact that both of these texts originated at the crossroads of the United States and Europe hardly ever enters the discussion; the specific context of exile is commonly overlooked. Indeed, the eclectic nature of this new reception might be judged by some as the typical instance of a uniquely postmodern form of reception. However, a hasty rejection of new approaches to reading Adorno seems as inappropriate as the appeal to a "traditional," canonical Adorno, particularly in light of the fact that Adorno would have been the first to acknowledge the dialectic which binds the two positions together: "*Man muß die Kraft der Tradition in sich haben, um diese recht zu hassen.*"[3]

That Adorno's ouevre offers itself to a (re)discovery by postmodernists is in part conditioned by the largely self-reflective nature of postmodern theories. They constitute and understand themselves vis-à-vis (a theory of) modernity as the predecessor, counterpart, or dialectical opposite of postmodernity. Since Adorno has provided one of the most rigorous and challenging constructions of modernity, they are bound to engage him in a discussion.[4] Adorno's role seems all the more decisive since his conceptualization of modernity is rooted in the complicated dialectic between the forces of tradition and those opposed to it; an issue which postmodern theories cannot afford to neglect since it concerns their own status. Insofar as the problems of continuity and discontinuity in cultural, social, political, and historical contexts are crucial to the self-definition of postmodern theories, Adorno is indeed a very well chosen subject. The following notes attempt a rereading with regard to Adorno's own theory, or theories, of tradition. Instead of casting Adorno as the last hero of modernity or the first hero of postmodernity, these remarks turn or rather return to Adorno in light of the very questions raised by his status in recent debates.

I.

"There is no such thing as the postmodern." If modernity has defined and reasserted itself as critique and denial, this negation of postmodernity's existence is a truly modern statement. But if a broad notion of pluralism is the index of the postmodern, what could be more postmodern than claiming it does not exist? An attempt to think through the consequences of these possibilities would have to lead to a reformulation of the question of the postmodern itself. Perhaps its existence or essence are not at all the issue. Perhaps the postmodern is not a new answer to old questions but indicates new questions for old answers, or perhaps what is old and what is new is itself the very question in question.

Still, many debates on the postmodern are dominated by different concerns. Undisturbed traditions of thinking and questioning remain firmly in place precisely in those discourses which tend to hail the event of the postmodern as a rupture, as a radical and dramatic change. Criteria and stylistic features are enumerated in the name of the postmodern while those very (frequently not so new) criteria would in fact require a rethinking of the very categories to which they appeal: style, criteria, and epoques.[5] On the other hand, those who choose not to reduce the postmodern to a bundle of stylistic features also often operate within a rather limited and restricted discursive sphere. The governing paradigms of legitimacy and legality force any participant in this debate to assume a position either as defendant or as critic of whatever happens to be on trial: enlightenment, modernity, postmodernity, rationality, and the like.[6] Such metaphors and their accompanying strategies serve to ensure that the form, content, and outcome of most discussions are predetermined by the alternatives of yes and no, for or against. This intolerance is frequently quasi-legitimized by the prevailing atmosphere of urgency and the rhetoric of crisis, which expresses itself primarily in the production of histories, those of modernity in particular. And while each side assumes that there is only one history to be written, the most important result of all debates is perhaps the fact that together they shatter the myth that there ever was *one* enlightenment, one modernity or one history. In an essay entitled "*Aufklärung, was sonst? Eine dreifache Polemik gegen ihre Verteidiger*" Dietmar Kamper has presented a provocative theory of this phenomenon.[7] Arguing for a positive understanding of the postmodern as our last chance to end all those discourses of "The End" which have fascinated modernity to the extent that it is capable of bringing about its own end, he proposes to value the postmodern as a timesaving mechanism: Let's *write* histories, so that we do not end up *being* history. This thought recalls the oldest of old narratives. That we tell stories to survive is indeed a modern feature which Kamper, however, employs in support of the postmodern. As a result of this discrepancy, Kamper stages an apology for a "postmodernism" whose very project would repeat the central gesture of all modernisms. As a modern, in other words, Kamper evidently cannot afford to reject the postmodern. On the other side of the spectrum is Odo Marquard, an undeniable master in the rhetoric of legality, who presents himself as the advocate of modernism.[8] Indeed, he calls for a return to the premodern times of the enlightenment philosophy of the eighteenth century. Marquard's implicit philosophy of history is what grants such direct recourse to past times and past thought, a philosophy of history which resembles the pluralism presumably characteristic of a postmodern conception of history. Accordingly, Marquard chooses to speak of "Neohistorismus." Thus, his eloquent defense of modernity effectively turns into a document of (postmodern) historicism which, incidentally, serves a politically conservative purpose, while Kamper's leftist appproach has the opposite effect: His postmodernity looks suspiciously modern. One might indeed ask: What is old and what is new?

Since the *Dialectic of Enlightenment,* Adorno has been increasingly concerned with the contamination of old and new. The *Aesthetic Theory* repeatedly focuses on that moment in works of art where their advanced tendencies can no longer be distinguished from the regressive or conservative aspects. This potential indifference between conservative and progressive tendencies is grounded in a telos; a telos, however, which is paradoxically projected into the past. In Adorno's view, the fundamental experience of an "end" gives rise to the possiblity of convergences between progressive and regressive, continuities and discontinuities. This end takes a variety of forms in Adorno's work and its analysis would require a separate investigation of Adorno's relation to Hegel, since the fact that Hegel's philosophy was, in a certain way, philosophy's end is the crux of Adorno's post-hegelian dialectic. In non-philosophical terms, fascism represents such an intrinsically ambivalent end. Indeed, it is not fascism as such but rather 1945 that marks the end and the break that changed everything, precisely because not enough changed: "*Der Nationalsozialismus lebt noch, und bis heute wissen wir nicht, ob bloß als Gespenst dessen, was so monströs war, daß es am eigenen Tode nicht starb, oder ob es gar nicht erst zu Tode kam ("Was bedeutet Aufarbeitung der Vergangenheit?," GS, 10, 2:555*). In other words, the truly disruptive effect of this break consists in the ensuing continuity.

With surprising consistency all of Adorno's major texts therefore begin by articulating their position beyond and yet not beyond an end. The first sentece of *Negative Dialektik* reads: "Philosophy, which once seemed obsolete, lives on because the moment to realize it was missed." (*ND*, 15:3) Philosophy's afterlife is not a life after the end nor is it the uninterrupted resumption of a previous life. Since philosophy survived its own apocalypse it has become untimely—it comes, from now on, always too late, it will always be a philosophy *post festum*, a postmodern philosophy, as it were. However, only because philosophy paradoxically survived the experience of outliving itself, is there yet a faint chance of one day arriving in time. The "no longer," so to speak, holds open the possiblity of the "not yet;" the negative telos sustains the positive. *Negative Dialectics* draws the consequences of this reversed eschatological model with respect to philosophy's attitude towards tradition: "Yet philosophy's methexis in tradition would only be a definite denial of tradition. Philosophy rests on the texts it criticizes." (*ND*, 64:55). The determinate negation of tradition asserts and performs the end of tradition in the hope that uncompromised, rigorous negation will once reveal itself as the "*Spiegelschrift*" of the positive.[9] This strictly negative dialectic has been rightly criticized by Michael Theunissen and Herbert Schnädelbach, among others. Both claim that the *Negative Dialektik* is ultimately philosophically untenable and has to fall back into metaphysics which, according to Theunissen's convincing arguments, is eventually sublated into theology.[10] Schnädelbach, however, is willing to entertain the possiblity that the philosophical failure of negative dialectics does not preclude another kind of consistency, vaguely termed *"diskursive Stringenz."*[11] This suggests the rereading of Adorno according to other than strictly philosophical, namely hermeneutic and narrative criteria. Adorno's marginal essay entitled *"Über Tradition"*[12] lends itself to such an experiment. It remains a question, however, if the so-called hermeneutic and narrative aspects can or should be severed from the conceptual arguments, as Schnädelbach seems to suggest.

II.

Despite the negative dialectic unfolded in the larger works, Adorno's essay on tradition provides one solid reason why tradition can never be subject to determinate negation: There is no such thing as tradition.

The latinzing title *"Über* Tradition"* (that is, the Latin *de* or English *of*) recalls the tradition of the philosophical treatise, imitated as well by the eight numbered thesis of the text. Yet the format of a *"Thesenpapier"* also alludes to the opposite of this weighty tradition, for it implies that the theses are preliminary and incomplete. Thus, the title and format already point to the ambivalence of gestures of quoting, an ambivalence that turns out to be essential to this text, whose first two sentences read: *"Tradition kommt von tradere, weitergeben. Gedacht ist an den Generationszusammenhang, an das, was von Glied zu Glied sich vererbt"* (*GS*, 10, 1:310). The philosophical gesture of the title is followed by a philological account of the word's etymology. Thus Adorno chooses a genealogical approach to his subject: Defining tradition means to inquire into the history, the tradition of tradition. And it is decisive that the history of the *word* tradition has the first word in this text. The fusing of philological history with natural history ("was sich vererbt") points to the janus-face of tradition. The apodictic, definitory character of the first lines, which only *quote* a philosophical tradition which has been lost, is relativized by the invisible quotation marks surrounding the title and opening of the text. The coexistence of a straightforward definition of tradition with the implied invalidity of any attempt to define lies at the core of Adorno's arguments. If tradition is indeed the permanent passing on from generation to generation, then tradition's effects can be registered but tradition itself remains forever absent. And yet: *"Im Bild des Weitergebens wird leibhafte Nähe, Unmittelbarkeit ausgedrückt, eine Hand soll es von der anderen empfangen"* (ibid.). But what is handed down and received is not tradition as such, for tradition is the always already pre-given in which we find ourselves and which we find in ourselves. As this naturally pre-given, tradition is nothing but sheer form and thus the opposite of the natural: true and natural tradition, Adorno suggests, exists only as an unconscious formality: *"Nicht Bewußtsein ist ihr Medium, sondern vorgegebene, unreflektierte Verbindlichkeit* *sozialer Formen . . ."* (ibid.). Accordingly it thrives in the most formal of societies: *"Die Kategorie Tradition ist wesentlich feudal"* (ibid.). Tradition lives in the formal ceremony of the aristocratic etiquette. Its emblem might be the *"leibhafte Nähe"* of a handkiss, performed in pure and unknowing obedience to ritualistic and formal requirements without any thought of whose hand is kissed and what significance this might have. Tradition exerts its influence where the traditions are insignificant, where the hand that hands down tradition—and Adorno makes excessive use of the word "hand" in the opening section—is empty, devoid of meaning and content. Traditions, then, pass through hands but tradition can never be had because it refuses the grip of the hand through which it passes, *"ein Unwillkürliches, (das) dem Zugriff sich entizeht"* (*GS*, 10, 2:312).

If tradition is this withdrawal then, clearly, it cannot be negated: For if tradition were ever *posited* it would have already ceased to be tradition. Tradition "which comes from tradere" and never arrives, gives itself but it cannot be received or posessed but only passed on. Tradition is permanently on the way.

Tradition becomes historically manifest in the feudal system, but as the philosophical term *"Kategorie"* and the epitaph *"wesentlich"* imply, tradition seems to remain untouched by and immune to historical movements. Indeed, tradition did not die along with the feudal aristocracy. *"Offenbar zerfällt für die Menschen der Zusammenhang der Zeit"* (*GS*, 10, 1:311), but in the present time the fetishized gestures of the completely reified subjects and their equally reified discourses are of the same order as the feudal ceremony. This is not a tragic relapse but a perversion that has always been constitutive of tradition. If tradition *is* not but instead gives and is given only where it is passed on, then the law of exchange governing the subjects of the post-bourgeois era functions exactly like the law of tradition. Indeed, the English word "trade" also comes from tradere, and it is, if not quoted, yet overtly present in this section: The truly traditional country, Adorno remarks, is the United States— from which Europe could learn tradition (ibid.). Perceived by Adorno as the radically antibourgeois country, the United States has no relation to tradition, and nothing could be more natural and thus more naturally traditional than the lack of a conscious relationship to tradition.

The feudal tradition which derives from "tradere" and the American tradition which derives from "trade" have a common denominator in the concept of *translation*, itself related to "tradere" and thus to "trade" and "tradition": Tradition appears to be a problem of linguistic exchange and economy, as Adorno's shifts between Latin, German, and English indicate. Later on he confirms on a conceptual level what his rhetoric and style already suggest at the beginning: We are always already in tradition, *"vorab durch die Sprache"* (*GS*, 10, 1:314). Traditions speak in us, they speak in the words we choose—like trade or tradition or translation—but we cannot speak of (*über*) tradition, except in translation (*Übersetzung*). This is why there can be no lasting definition of tradition: Tradition remains untranslatable because it is itself the very movement that allows for and necessitates translations. What is said of tradition stands permanently in quotation marks. Insofar as Adorno's own text plays with translations and quotations, it opens up the possibility of a linguistic theory of tradition which is not linked to the model of a reversed telos but suggests instead an "*Ungleichzeitigkeit*" belonging to language. This becomes evident in translations and quotations, both of which are in the untimely and untenable position between an act or gesture on the one hand and a description, or a statement on the other. In terms of contemporary speech act theory, they occupy the space between a constative and a performative function. This would mean that the assumed identity of assertion and performance characteristic of the movement of tradition's negation in the *Negative Dialektik* falls apart and reveals an unbridgeable gap. A linguistic theory of tradition, if it is possible, would allow us to think the intertwinement of old and new without taking recourse either to beginnings or to ends. It would have to be a philosophical theory on the relationship between words and acts, something like a speech act theory for quotations and translations. Some aspects of such a theory already appear in an earlier review essay by Adorno, but their radicality is still compromised by the ever effective mechanism of dialectics. According to Adorno, the heroine of Aldous Huxley's *Brave New World* is a model of utter traditionality: "*Aber indem sie bis zum Kern mit der Tradition eins ist, zergeht die Spannung des Konventionellen und der Natur und damit die Gewalt, welche das Unrecht der Tradition ausmacht*" (*GS*, 10, 1:108). This interpretation still takes nature and convention to be dialectical opposites, whereas the essay on tradition suspends both of them in the act of quoting. The hope that utter traditionality would lead directly to its opposite—that is, to liberation—is legitimate within negative dialectics but it cannot be sustained in light of Adorno's essay on tradition.

Nevertheless, if this earlier remark on tradition fails the test of the later theses, then this might be due to systematic reasons. For is it not the case that Adorno's reflections attribute to tradition trans-historical qualities that preclude their application to concrete historical cases? In other words, what option remains if tradition is not? And more specifically, what can the essay "Über Tradition" still have to say after, in the first section, having removed its object so far from analysis that one must fear for the remainder of the text? Subsequently, Adorno's strategy is to subject all possible attitudes and theories of tradition to a radical critique in order to find all of them flawed.

At the end of section 4, in the exact middle of his essay, Adorno summarizes the aporetic situation with regard to tradition as follows: "*Wie die in sich verbissene Tradition ist das absolut Traditionslose naiv. Inhuman aber ist das Vergessen, weil das akkumulierte Leiden vergessen wird. Darum stellt Tradition heute vor einen unauflöslichen Widerspruch. Keine ist gegenwärtig und zu beschwören; ist aber eine jegliche ausgelöscht, so beginnt der Einmarsch in die Unmenschlichkeit"* (*GS,* 10, 1:315). As so frequently in Adorno's essays, the total aporia is the turning point. But his turn here is not motivated by reading the negative as the symmetrical *"Spiegelschrift"* of the positive. Instead, the turning point is a return. In the middle of his essay, Adorno begins all over again, and at the turning point he *quotes* another turning point: *"Kants Satz, der kritische Weg sei allein noch offen ist einer von jenen verbürgtesten, deren Wahrheitsgehalt unendlich viel größer ist, als das an Ort und Stelle Gemeinte"* (ibid.). This quotation does nothing to revive the transcendental tradition nor can it be considered the inauguration of a new tradition; but as a quotation at this point of the essay, it puts the categories of old and new, beginnings and ends into question. Once more, it stages rather than prescribes a relationship to tradition from within tradition that pivots around the problematic nature of quotations. After Kant, Adorno gives other, literary, examples: George, Hofmannsthal, and Borchardt, the poets of quotation and the poets of the gesture. They, he claims, *"haben den Übergang der Tradition ans Unscheinbare, nicht sich selbst Setzende registriert"* (*GS,* 10, 1:316). They have realized—in the ambivalent sense of registering and making real—the doubleness of tradition's linguistic dimension. They realized the permanent passing, and by quoting this passing tradition of passing-on, they continued and broke with it at the same time, in the act of staging a tradition with which they are no longer in harmony.

This notion of staging is perhaps the theoretical background of Adorno's well-documented interest in gestures such as the handkiss. That he, having devoted so much thought to gestures should, at the end of his life, forget about the gesture's double nature and interpret it onesidedly—I refer to the famous scene in Frankfurt in 1969—is not an argument against their theoretical relevance in his work.[13] *Minima Moralia* in particular, is full of remarks on gestures, for example, the pieces entitled *"Zur Dialektik des Takts"* (4:38ff.) and *"Bitte nicht anklopfen"* (*GS,* 4:43ff). In the latter, Adorno appears to be lamenting the lack of manners because it eradicates the very ambivalence of gesture that first allows for the space in which experience can take place. Without manners, the individual is exposed to the *"gleichsam geschichtslosen Anforderungen der Dinge. So wird etwa verlernt, leise, behutsam und doch fest eine Tür zu schließen"* (*GS,* 4:44). In almost all of these instances, the physical gesture is supposed to mediate the immediacy of sensation with its opposite. By virtue of this mediation the gesture is indeed elevated to a medium of experience and historicity.

Adorno's biographer Hartmut Scheible interprets his interest in gestures as a sign of Adorno's secretly harbored desire to belong to the aristocracy.[14]

But this psychologizing misses the point. Adorno's occupation with gestures gains philosophical and theoretical significance if viewed in the context of his emphasis on quotations. The thematization of gestures in his work should perhaps be read *as* a gesture towards a philosophy of quotation; and it can be read as such because of the affinity between the formal gesture and the quotation, an affinity which resides in their shared ambivalence and ultimately in their sign character. The first place to look for a theory of tradition informed by a theory of language is Adorno's own writing, with its complicated and often deliberately antiquated prose. In the case of the essay on tradition, these "mannerisms" are the basis for the argument. Another indication that Adorno's thinking of traditions and gestures might mark the entry point for a reconstruction of his philosophy of language are the names of the authors whom he praises, none of them a hero of modernity: not Baudelaire but Hofmannsthal, not Beckett but George. Indeed, Adorno's essays on authors whose language is marked by quotations, (on Heine, Eichendorff, and Borchardt in particular),[15] reveal more detailed reflexions on language than any of the larger works. If the thematics of quotation and gesture were allowed to enter the rigorous thought of dialectic, this might provide a way, not to escape negative dialectic, but to locate that which takes leave from dialectic within dialectic.

Among the many gestures Adorno has considered, there is one that fully corresponds to the double understanding of passing that he finds in Hofmannsthal or Borchardt. In *Minima Moralia* under the title "Les Adieux" (*GS*, 4:288) Adorno firmly states the impossiblity of any longer taking leave, taking "*Abschied*." The title—in French and in the plural, thus betraying the uniqueness of "*Abschied*"—is a sign of this impossiblity. *Abschied*, Adorno suggests, implies a certain tradition which can no longer be conjured up nor appealed to in the world of estranged subjects. But even as they are deployed to confirm this impossiblity, Adorno's very words continue—as translation and quotation—the process of *Abschied* in the movement of taking *Abschied* from *Abschied*. *Abschied*—and one must insist here in the context of translation and tradition on the word's untranslatability—is *the* gesture of tradition because it is the gesture in and of all gestures. Every gesture and every quotation, suspended in the undecidability of performative and constative aspects, is a staging, a performance of *Abschied*, of giving up claims for reference in favor of reverence, of parting with the quest for identity and continuity in the very repetition of seemingly identical gestures. No *Abschied* ever leaves intact what it takes leave from, it precisely does not preserve the past nor does it prevent its destruction. Exactly the opposite is the case: *Abschied* produces "*Abgeschiedenes*." *Abschied* performs, it is the critical act, critical in the philosophical sense of "*scheiden*," that produces useless particles, broken remnants that cannot be restored to the order of the whole because, strictly speaking, they were never part of it. While they cannot be re-discovered they can, however, be discovered in the first place; that is if one understands this finding as a mode of production which can reassure the finder neither of eternal values nor of eternal transitoriness. If the postmodern is the continuing *Abschied* from the modern tradition, then its relation to that tradition cannot be one of overcoming or preserving, liquidating or reinterpreting. All of these depend upon a stable distinction between old and new, and that is the first thing that *Abschied*—and tradition—take leave of.

ABBREVIATIONS

GS: Theodor W. Adorno, *Gesammelte Schriften,* edited by Rolf Tiedemann (Frankfurt: Suhrkamp Verlag, 1972–).

ND: Theodor W. Adorno, *Negative Dialektik* (Frankfurt: Suhrkamp Verlag, 1975), English *Negative Dialectics,* translated by E. B. Ashton (New York: Continuum, 1973). Page references are to the German followed by the English edition.

NOTES

1. Andreas Huyssen, Klaus R. Scherpe, eds., *Postmoderne, Zeichen eines kulturellen Wandels* (Hamburg: Rowohlt, 1986), 9.

2. For example Andrew Benjamin, ed., *The Problems of Modernity: Adorno and Benjamin* (London: Routledge, 1989).

3. Theodor W. Adorno: *Minima Moralia*, in *Gesammelte Schriften* (Frankfurt: Suhrkamp, 1977), vol. 4:58. All quotations from Adorno's texts are from this edition. Further references will be given in the text by volume and page number.

4. See Albrecht Wellmer, *Zur Dialektik von Moderne und Postmoderne. Vernunftkritik nach Adorno* (Frankfurt: Suhrkamp, 1985).

5. For a still valid account of various definitions and histories of the term see Ihab Hassan: "Pluralismus in der Postmoderne" in *Die unvollendete Vernunft. Moderne vs. Postmoderne*, ed. Dietmar Kamper and Wilhelm Reijen (Frankfurt: Suhrkamp, 1987), 157-184. An overview of more recent publications is given in a review article by Ingeborg Hoesterey, in *German Quarterly* (Fall 1989), 505–509.

6. For example Manfred Frank, "Zweihundert Jahre Rationalitätskritik und ihre postmoderne Überbietung," in *Die unvollendete Vernunft. Moderne vs. Postmoderne*, 99-122. Jürgen Habermas, *Der philosophische Diskurs der Moderne* (Frankfurt: Suhrkamp, 1985). The Adorno chapter of Habermas's influential book is perhaps partially responsible for Adorno's emergence in postmodern discourses.

7. Dietmar Kamper, "Aufklärung: was sonst? Eine dreifache Polemik gegen ihre Verteidiger" in *Die unvollendete Vernunft. Moderne vs. Postmoderne*, 37–45.

8. Odo Marquard, "Nach der Postmoderne. Bemerkungen über die Futurisierung des Antimodernismus und die Usance Modernität," in *Moderne oder Postmoderne. Zur Signatur des gegenwärtigen Zeitalters*, ed. Peter Koslowski, Robert Spaemann, and Reinhard Löw (Weinheim: VCH Verlagsgesellschaft, 1986), 45–59.

9. At the end of *Minima Moralia*, Adorno writes: "weil die vollendete Negativität, einmal ganz ins Auge gefaßt, zur Spiegelschrift ihres Gegenteils zusammenschießt" (4:281).

10. Michael Theunissen, "Negativität bei Adorno" in *Adorno-Konferenz 1983* (Frankfurt: Suhrkamp, 1983), 41–65.

11. Herbert Schnädelbach, "Dialektik als Vernunftkritik." Zur Konstruktion des Rationalen bei Adorno," in *Adorno-Konferenz 1983*, 66–94.

12. Originally published in *Inselalmanach auf das Jahr 1966*.

13. In a text entitled "Adornos Erschauern. Variationen über den Händedruck," Gunzelin Schmid Noerr interprets Adorno's hasty flight from the three bare-breasted students as a scenic image of Adorno's "*leibgewordene Angst vor der Leiblichkeit.*" The formal gesture, the handkiss, the handshake, are designed to protect the individual from this "*Leiblichkeit.*" Noerr interprets the scene as the symbolic failure of theory confronted with a practical form of protest: "*Die theoretische Rede aber konnte die Hoffnungen und Sehnsüchte des leibgewordenen Protests nicht mehr aufnehmen.*" Wilhelm van Reijen and Gunzelin Schmid Noerr, ed., *Vierzig Jahre Flaschenpost. "Dialektik der Aufklärung" 1947 bis 1987* (Frankfurt: Fischer, 1987), 233–241, here 239–240.

14. *Theodor W. Adorno in Selbstzeugnissen und Bilddokumenten* (Hamburg: Rowohlt, 1989), 39ff.

15. Collected in *Noten zur Literatur*, vol. 11 of the *Gesammelte Schriften*.

Contributors

J. M. Bernstein is Reader in Philosophy at the University of Essex. His books include *The Philosophy of the Novel: Lukács, Marxism, and the Dialectics of Form* (Minnesota, 1984) and *The Fate of Art: Aesthetic Alienation from Kant to Derrida and Adorno* (Pennsylvania State University Press, 1992). His newest book is *Recovering Ethical Life: Jürgen Habermas and the Future of Critical Theory* (Routledge, 1995).

Hauke Brunkhorst has been Professor of Social Philosophy and Political Science at the universities of Frankfurt, Berlin and Duisburg. He is currently Fellow at the Kulturwissenschalftlichen Institut des Wissenschaftszentrums Nordrhein-Westfalen in Essen. His books include *Der Intellektuelle im Land der Mandarine* (Suhrkamp, 1987), *Theodor W. Adorno, Dialektik der Moderne* (Piper Verlag, 1990), *Der entzauberte Intellektuelle* (Junius Verlag, 1990), and *Demokratie und Differenz* (Suhrkamp, 1994).

Eva Geulen teaches in the German department at New York University. She has published articles on critical and contemporary theory and Nineteenth century literature and is currently completing a book on "the End of Art from Hölderlin to the Present."

Ute Guzzoni is Professor of Philosophy at the University of Freiburg. Her works include *Identität oder nicht. Zur Kritischen Theorie der Ontologie* (1981), *Wendungen, Versuche zu einem nicht identifizierenden Denken* (1982), *Veränderndes Denken, Kritisch-ontologische Stücke zum Verhältnis von Denken und Wirklichkeit (1985)*, and *Über Natur, Aufzeichnungen unterwegs: Zu einem anderen Naturverhältnis* (1995).

Miriam Bratu Hansen is Ferdinand Schevill Distinguished Professor in the Humanities and Director of the Film Studies Center at the University of Chicago. Her most recent book is *Babel and Babylon: Spectatorship in*

American Silent Film (Harvard, 1991; 1994). She is a co-editor of *New German Critique* and has published widely on American and German cinema, feminist film theory, and concepts of the public sphere. She is currently completing a study of the Frankfurt School's debates on film and mass culture.

Peter Uwe Hohendahl is Jacob Gould Schurman Professor of German and Comparative Literature at Cornell University. His books include *The Institution of Criticism* (Cornell, 1982), *Building a National Literature: The Case of Germany, 1830–1870,* and *Reappraisals: Shifting Alignments in Postwar Critical Theory* (Cornell, 1991). His most recent work is *Prismatic Thought: Theodor W. Adorno* (Nebraska, 1995).

Max Pensky is Associate Professor of Philosophy at Binghamton University. He has published articles on Critical Theory, poststructuralist theory and the contemporary German political public sphere, and is the author of *Melancholy Dialectics: Walter Benjamin and the Play of Mourning* (Massachusetts, 1993), and the editor and translator of Jürgen Habermas's *The Past as Future* (Nebraska, 1994). He is currently completing a book on ethics and remembrance in Critical Theory.

Albrecht Wellmer has taught at the University of Konstanz, the University of Ontario, and the New School for Social Research. He is Professor of Philosophy at the Free University of Berlin. His works in English translation include *Critical Theory of Society* (Herder and Herder, 1971) and *The Persistence of Modernity: Essays on Aesthetics, Ethics, and Postmodernism* (MIT, 1991). An English translation of his latest collection, *Endspiele, Die unversöhnliche Moderne* (Suhrkamp, 1994) will soon appear with MIT Press.

Wilhelm S. Wurzer is Professor of Philosophy at Duquesne University. He is the author of *Nietzsche and Spinoza* and *Filming and Judgment: Between Heidegger and Adorno* (Humanities Press, 1990), and has written numerous articles on the relation between deconstruction, postmodernism, and Critical Theory.

Index